Lecture Notes in Computer Science   7365

Commenced Publication in 1973
Founding and Former Series Editors:
Gerhard Goos, Juris Hartmanis, and Jan van Leeuwen

T0213189

Services Science

Subline of Lectures Notes in Computer Science

Subline Editors-in-Chief

Subline Editorial Board

Maritta Heisel (Ed.)

Software Service and Application Engineering

Essays Dedicated to Bernd Krämer on the Occasion of His 65th Birthday

Springer

Volume Editor

Maritta Heisel
Universität Duisburg-Essen
Fakultät für Ing.-wissenschaften
Abteilung INKO
Fachgebiet Software Engineering
47057 Duisburg, Germany
E-mail: maritta.heisel@uni-duisburg-essen.de

ISSN 0302-9743   e-ISSN 1611-3349
ISBN 978-3-642-30834-5   e-ISBN 978-3-642-30835-2
DOI 10.1007/978-3-642-30835-2
Springer Heidelberg Dordrecht London New York

Library of Congress Control Number: 2012938718

CR Subject Classification (1998): F.3, D.2, F.1, H.3, H.4, C.2

LNCS Sublibrary: SL 2 – Programming and Software Engineering

Typesetting: Camera-ready by author, data conversion by Scientific Publishing Services, Chennai, India

Printed on acid-free paper

Springer is part of Springer Science+Business Media (www.springer.com)

Bernd J. Krämer
ⓒVeit Mette, Bielefeld

Preface

This volume appears on the occasion of Prof. Dr. Bernd Krämer's 65th birthday. Close scientific companions, who have worked with Bernd for many years, contributed to this volume. The papers reflect the remarkable span of Bernd's own research. Bernd's career started with research in formal languages to enable parser generation for programming language definitions with van Wijngaarden grammars, which became popular with Algol 68. Working in the Institute for Software Technology at GMD (Gesellschaft für Mathematik und Datenverarbeitung mbH Bonn) in the direct neighborhood of the Institute for Information Systems Research led by Carl Adam Petri, he soon became interested in Petri nets as adequate means to model distributed software systems. Together with his colleague Heinz Schmidt he developed a specification and modeling language, SEGRAS, combining high-level Petri nets and algebraic specifications. These works led to a large ESPRIT project (1983-1988) aiming at the development of a software engineering environment for non-sequential software systems. With this project he widened his research activities to software engineering, in general, taking into account distributed and safety-critical systems, in particular. This was the context in which I met Bernd, who has been an important mentor for me since then. He not only served as a reviewer for my habilitation thesis, but was always there to support me in my academic career and encouraged me during the long road to becoming a professor for software engineering myself. His experience of teaching at a distance learning university inspired Bernd's later work on e-learning. Following the evolution of the field, he also turned his attention to such important and highly promising research fields as middleware, component-based software engineering, service-oriented computing, and, more recently, social computing.

The articles contained in this volume reflect most of Bernd's research themes. They cover Petri nets and theoretical computer science, software and service engineering, cloud computing, and e-learning.

Wolfgang Reisig discusses various extensions of Petri nets, concerning, for example, fairness, hot and cold transitions, and distributed runs. Such extensions aim at not only extending the expressive power of Petri nets, but at the same time retaining the well-established analysis techniques coming with Petri nets.

Karsten Gabriel and Hartmut Ehrig use algebraic high-level (AHL) nets and their processes to model communication platforms and evolutions of such platforms. Algebraic high-level nets combine Petri nets and algebraic specifications. The corresponding processes model concurrent firing behavior of AHL nets. Gabriel and Ehrig use the example of the Apache Wave communication platform – together with a possible evolution – to demonstrate the power of AHL nets and processes and to illustrate their formal properties.

Herbert Weber discusses the role of modeling in engineering. He proposes *profiling* as a methodology to describe computing artifacts and their application environment along different axes, namely, abstraction, granularity, and virtualization. The methodology consists of three stages, where the expressiveness of the notation is increased gradually.

Marco Konersmann and Michael Goedicke present a conceptual framework that serves to link software architectures and their implementation. They define an intermediate language to which different architectural description languages can be mapped. The resulting architecture descriptions are then embedded into the component model used to implement the architecture by means of code patterns. Since bi-directional mappings are defined between the intermediate language on the one hand and architectural description languages or component models on the other hand, changes in one description can be propagated into the other description. Thus, architectural descriptions can be kept consistent with their implementation.

Djamshid Tavangarian gives an overview of virtualization techniques and shows how virtualization can be used to optimize power consumption of computing centers and to enhance security in cloud computing.

Frank Leymann's contribution builds on the concepts of compute units and social compute units. Compute units specify the structure of an application as well as plans needed to manage it. Social compute units consist of a compute unit, augmented with people who have some relation to the software, for example, they created it. Leymann proposes to enhance (social) compute units with data sets serving as input or output of the compute unit, which results in *linked (social) compute units*. Such linked compute units support scientific work based on computer simulation or software-based data analysis.

Kristian Beckers, Stephan Faßbender, Maritta Heisel, and Rene Meis propose patterns for establishing the context of SOA (service-oriented architecture) systems. These patterns represent the different layers making up such an architecture as well as the relations between those layers. They also structure the environment of SOA systems and identify relevant classes of stakeholders that are described using specific templates. The authors also present a method to instantiate the patterns, which can be embedded, for example, in secure software development life-cycles.

Michael Papazoglou addresses the problem of cloud federations. He proposes the concept of cloud blueprinting to make cloud computing more flexible and give cloud developers more influence on cloud-based applications. Cloud blueprinting makes it possible to combine different cloud services offered by different providers. Cloud developers can orchestrate and configure their applications using a *blueprint framework* that offers a variety of languages to support the approach.

Ingolf Krüger, Barry Demchak, and Massimiliano Menarini present the architectural definition language OpenRichServices (ORS). ORS allows one to define services as functions. It distinguishes application and infrastructure concerns and comes with a deployment sub-language. Moreover, it allows for dynamic changes of the structure and behavior of the system.

Kirill Mechitov and Gul Agha show how cyber-physical systems (i.e., systems comprising networked physical devices) can be engineered. They propose a service composition-based software architecture that supports a network-wide programming model, sharing and re-use of resources, and late binding of services and resources. The architecture consists of two layers. On the knowledge layer, meta-actors and meta-objects control the execution process. On the operational layer, dynamically composed and deployed services are executed.

Christoph Rensing, Stephan Tittel, and Ralf Steinmetz present novel approaches to support authors and learners in location-based learning scenarios. In the first scenario, authors can generate location-based content with the help of their smartphone. In the second scenario, learners are provided with a semantic media wiki, which allows them to enter their notes on the spot.

Thus, the interested reader can find in this volume a rich fund of novel approaches and interesting discussions of various important research topics that have been inspired by Bernd Krämer's diverse research activities and contributions.

April 2012   Maritta Heisel

SDPS Conference 2001 in Pasadena, California

First Dagstuhl Seminar on Service-Oriented Computing (SOC), May 2005
©Leibniz-Zentrum für Informatik Schloss Dagstuhl

The organizers of the symposium, R. Valk, B.J. Krämer, and W. Reisig (from left), with T. Petri holding the IEEE Computer Pioneer Award Carl Adam Petri received in 2009

Introductory Address

I am deeply honored and pleased to be able to write a short foreword – or "Grußwort" in German – to this very special volume – or "Festschrift" – that constitutes contributions written as a token of appreciation of the scientific community to one of its prominent members, Professor Bernd Krämer from FernUniversität in Hagen in North Rhein-Westphalia, Germany. The idea of a Festschrift, though primarily being characteristic of the German academic system, has also become popular in many other countries as people realize that such a book can play an important role as a sign of a natural need to appreciate a long service, and as a sign of continuity of the school founded by the person to whom the volume in question has been devoted.

This Festschrift is very important to all of us in the academic community. First of all, it honors a prominent scholar and scientist, one of those who have recognized early that issues related to broadly perceived information technology, software engineering, etc. will become key fields due to theoretically interesting and challenging problems to pose and solve, and to their vital practical importance. Professor Krämer has been one of the most active members of the academic communities in these fields, both as a teacher, researcher and mentor to his numerous students, a founder of new research groups that have quickly become leaders in their respective fields, editor of many journals, member of international program committees and invited speaker at numerous highly respected conferences, member of advisory boards of various bodies, etc. Second, the collection of contributors to this Festschrift indicates that he has really founded and established over the years a school in the best scholarly tradition that goes back to ancient times. Third, on a personal basis, I am happy to write these few words to honor a great human being and friend with whom I not only share a very similar type of engineering education and academic career but also research interests and views.

To summarize, I wish to express my deep appreciation for all that Professor Krämer has done for his university and his group and – more generally – for science and the entire research community. However, since looking into the future is always more interesting and fruitful, I think that his future works will continue to shape research both at his university and all over the world. His scholarly and research stature, vision and passion will continue to inspire all of us.

April 2012   Janusz Kacprzyk

A Professional Passion for Software Engineering

It is indeed a great pleasure to write a foreword for this book dedicated to Bernd Krämers on the occasion of his 65th birthday. Bernd Krämer has been a full professor of software engineering for many years and has made significant contributions to service-oriented computing such as Web-based hypermedia systems, component-based software engineering, technology for e-learning, distributed systems management and engineering, safety-related software, and formal methods. His dedication to software engineering research and practice significantly impacted the fundamental underpinnings of the field.

The term "software engineering" (SE) was first coined at a NATO conference in 1968. It was gradually accepted as an academic discipline after the establishment of *IEEE Transactions on Software Engineering,* and the International Conference on Software Engineering (ICSE) in 1975. Much, of course, has happened during the past 37 years as the field exploded in all directions. As we enter the age of ubiquitous computing, computing systems networked together constitute a tremendous amplifier of the human mind with the amplification factor growing at an ever-increasing pace. Software will be a core part of this formidable power that is destined to alter our world in a most fundamental way.

What SE is up against is keenly in line with how the human race will be addressing our coming grand challenges including poverty, health and health management, security, energy, transportation, sustainability, etc. The systems needed to tackle these problems are unprecedented in scale, with billions of lines of code, and of a mind-boggling complexity as far as the amount of data, number of routines, number of connections and interdependencies, and emergent behaviors, etc., are concerned. While SE alone cannot solve these major issues, software will definitely play a key role in finding the solutions to these problems not only as key components of the overall solution, but also in the form of basic infrastructure which supports the collaboration of various communities of different disciplines working together.

Most of these mega-problems are inherently "wicked" as we are dealing with complex systems of systems which undergo continuous evolution while being used; systems built from heterogeneous elements that are constructed for different purposes at different times; decentralized systems with no clear ownership, etc. The wickedness of these problems includes, for example, "problem formulation and its solution cannot be separated," "symptoms and causes cannot be distinguished," and "there are usually no rules to determine when a solution is complete," etc. Given the scale and complexity of these potential systems, it is essential to understand what the key underpinnings of SE are, as many of the users/developers will not be software professionals.

Historically, SE began as a computational approach to problem solving. The thinking process behind such an approach is usually referred to as "computational thinking," or how people formulate problems and solutions so that the solutions can effectively be carried out by one or more computing devices.

But good software should also have logical beauty by reducing the detailed reasoning needed to a doable amount by utilizing principles such as "separation of concerns," etc. Over time, software professionals learned that they must develop systems which are not only logically elegant, functional and within budget, but also emotionally appealing in terms of user experience. As such, "design thinking," or how people utilize their intuitive ability to recognize patterns and to construct ideas that have emotional meaning as well as functionality, has been an integral part of the SE consciousness.

As SE is required to tackle complex problems which are systems of systems, the boundary between SE and that of system engineering begins to blur. SE must deal with not only systems of ultra-large scale, but also emergent systems, such as Wikipedia, which are developed by groups of people collaborating together, each contributing to different aspects of the system with an evolving infrastructure, over time. As a consequence of this system-oriented evolution, SE must include "system thinking," or how to negotiate complex interrelationships and processes of change, as part of its core make-ups as well.

If we accept that these three kinds of thinking, namely, computational, design, and system, form the core of SE's approach to problem solving, we must agree that SE is transdisciplinary in nature. It seems that the next evolution of SE could be the harmonious merging of these three kinds of mental disciplines into the SE consciousness in order to take up the many great challenges facing the SE community in the years to come. In this regard, Prof. Krämer has been a major contributor via his involvement in transdisciplinary research and education. He is the editor-in-chief of the *Journal of Integrated Design & Process Science*, and has been the longest serving President of the Society for Design and Process Science (SDPS). It is through his efforts that I see SE in a much larger context.

I would like to conclude with a personal note, as I have known Prof. Krämer for nearly two decades. He is one of the nicest gentlemen I have had the pleasure of meeting. He is always on the lookout to help a colleague, and he provides a calm presence, with a shy smile, even in the context of a heated debate. He has gained a great deal of respect not only for his intellectual prowess being a great teacher, but also for his leadership in service. I sincerely congratulate Prof. Krämer on the publication of this commemorative volume.

March 2012   Raymond T. Yeh

The University Teacher and Researcher

Computer science is a relatively young specialist discipline as many people who have witnessed the rapid growth of this discipline will remember. Nowadays it is an integral part of the curricula framework of many universities. It has produced results, without which our information technology-driven world would not work.

Prof. Dr.-Ing. Bernd Krämer is one of the pioneers of this discipline. He has shaped and enriched it by his research. In 1992 he became a full professor and the head of the Chair of Data Processing Technology of FernUniversität in Hagen. A media-based university like the FernUniversität, naturally profits to a high degree and valuable way from the experience of such a national and international well-known and respected expert.

In the development of data management solutions there are two inseparable questions: Will the system be developed in the right way? And: Will the right system be developed? The first question is related to the technical functionality. The second question is focused toward usability and user requirements. Otherwise the program will not be used and is therefore without any value.

Bernd Krämer always has both questions on his mind. This can be shown clearly by "edu-sharing" as one of his key projects.

In 2002, the Deutsche Forschungsgemeinschaft (German Research Council) announced a nationwide call for the development of centers of excellence in two fields. In each field, only four projects from universities were funded. Edu-sharing was one of the winners in the field "Digital Text and Data Centre for Collecting, Securing and Providing of Digital Sources in Research and Education." In March 2012, the four project teams presented their results in a final workshop, which was organized by Prof. Krämer at the FernUniversität. It was a great success.

Edu-sharing is an open educational resources (OER) program for a networked administration of e-learning and e-knowledge content. Via open archives initiative interfaces, different knowledge archives can communicate with each other and exchange metadata. "Find what will help you," with these words Bernd Krämer himself once described the benefit of edu-sharing for an effective learning and working process. The benefit for our university is obvious. It is a major step forward that the large amount of e-learning and e-knowledge content can now be administrated in a systematic way and can be made re-usable for scientists and students.

As an open educational resource, edu-sharing can be used by all schools and universities interested as well as by enterprises. Via this system, for example, teachers can exchange, add on, improve, adapt and evaluate content. Or to bring it to a point: to learn from and with each other. The results can be made directly available to teachers and students. In North Rhine-Westphalia (NRW) this system is run on some of the public computer centers, which support all schools in the country with IT-services and learning content. In the long term, 6,800 schools in NRW will be connected to the edu-sharing platform.

This is only one of many shining examples of the innovative power of Bernd Krämer.

Furthermore, a special commitment was made by him to young scientists. As one activity among many others, he is busy in the "International Cooperation in Ambient Computing Education (ICACE)," a program for a transatlantic exchange of students.

He is editor-in-chief and member of several editorial boards of high ranked international scientific journals. At FernUniversität, he is the editor of our ejournal *eleed*. Prof. Krämer chaired several international congresses and program committees and has often been invited as keynote speaker.

Besides this, his engagement for our university goes far beyond the scientific part. He has supported and is supporting the development of FernUniversität as a member on several boards, in the Senate, and presently on the Supervisory Board of our university appointed by the minister of science.

I appreciate Bernd Krämer as a scientist, as a colleague for many years and especially as a person. It is a great honor and pleasure for me to make a contribution to this commemorative publication for his 65th birthday.

April 2012   Helmut Hoyer

Table of Contents

A Fresh Look at Petri Net Extensions

Wolfgang Reisig

Humboldt-Universität zu Berlin, Institut für Informatik,
Unter den Linden 6, 10099 Berlin, Germany
reisig@informatik.hu-berlin.de

Abstract. Extensions for Petri nets have been suggested since the 1970s. In this contribution, we look at some of them and discuss less known, but quite useful extensions.

Keywords: Petri nets, fundamentals, teaching, faithful models, expressive power, properties.

1 Introduction

Since the very beginning, the basic Petri net formalism has been subject to extensions and generalizations. In the 1970s, when classes of formal languages provided the benchmark for the expressive power of formal modeling techniques, the Chomsky hierarchy with its classes of regular, context free, linear bounded and recursive languages has been the most prominent scale. Petri nets have been ranked into this scale with the idea to assign each transition of a net N a label and, consequently, to assign each finite occurrence sequences of N a sequence of such labels, viz. a word over the set of labels. This way, the set of all finite occurrence sequences of N characterizes a formal language.

In this framework, Petri nets appeared to be "weak", as there exist recursive languages that cannot be generated by Petri nets. This observation frequently motivated generalizations of Petri nets that cover all recursive languages. Inhibitor arcs, which test the emptiness of places, are the best-known such extensions. Carl Adam Petri always insisted that the formal language hierarchy provides no adequate benchmark for the expressive power of formal modeling techniques, in particular for nets. He rather pointed at the *faithfulness* of models, insisting that systems are in general *distributed* and that corresponding models should respect and represent this aspect.

In this paper we discuss extensions of Petri nets that are intended to model discrete systems faithfully.

2 Variants of the Occurrence Rule

A Petri net model N of a dynamic system is a finite representation of an infinite set of runs (executions, behaviors). A run may be finite or infinite. The *occurrence rule* of Petri nets is a decisive aspect of the definition of the runs of N.

M. Heisel (Ed.): Krämer Festschrift, LNCS 7365, pp. 1–9, 2012.

The literature suggests many different variants of this rule. Some of them can be "simulated" (a notion to be made more precise) in some way; others extend substantially the expressive power of the formalism. A typical example is the assumption of capacities (upper bounds) for the number of tokens in a place p: This feature can be simulated by an additional place $\bar{p}$, the *complement* place of p. In contrast, the test of a place being empty or the assumption of priorities among concurrently enabled transitions extend the expressive power of the formalism: Conceived as a means to generate formal languages, Petri nets become Turing powerful this way. Temporal constraints likewise increase the expressive power nets. Place capacities, inhibitor arcs, priorities and temporal constraints affect single transition occurrences, i.e. prevent single transitions to occur that otherwise would be enabled. Other generalizations affect *sets* of runs or challenge the notion of runs of a Petri net.

3   Stochastic Choice

The elementary Petri net formalism includes nondeterminism whenever two enabled transitions t_1 and t_2 share a pre-place that contains only one token. This situation may be reached many times. In this case it is useful to regulate the nondeterministic choice between t_1 and t_2 by stochastic assumptions about the frequency of deciding the choice in favor of t_1 or of t_2, respectively.

A typical example is the system of mutual exclusion, where two agents l and r complete for a scarce resource.

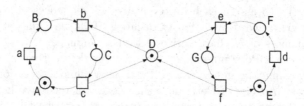

Fig. 1. The MUTEX system of mutual exclusion

Figure 1 shows a Petri net model of this system. One may assume an average frequency of obtaining the scarce resource key is 30% for the left agent, l and 70% for the right agent, r. Similar assumptions on the relative frequency of the transitions a and d would be weird, as they never compete for a token.

In contrast to the above-mentioned variants of the occurrence rule, stochastic decisions of alternatives affect the set of runs of a Petri net N: Each run is assigned a relative occurrence frequency in the context of the other runs.

Many applications of Petri nets and particularly models for performance evaluation and models of theoretical biology frequently apply this version of Petri nets.

4   Fairness

The issue of fairness is best explained by means of an example. We consider again the model of the mutual exclusion system as in Fig. 1. This net fulfills the *mutex* property, i.e. no reachable marking has tokens in both places critical$_l$ and critical$_r$. However, this net does not guarantee each waiting agent to eventually become critical. It is well-known that no elementary Petri net would cover *each* run where each waiting agent eventually turns critical, and at the same time would exclude each run where a waiting agent never turns critical [1]. Therefore, the assumption of fairness for the transitions b or e is inevitable. Intuitively formulated, this requirement rules out each run that enables b or e only finitely often. Hence, fairness assumptions substantially increase the expressive power of Petri nets.

5   Hot and Cold Transitions

So far, we have tacitly assumed that an enabled transition is actually going to occur. For the transitions a and f in Fig. 1 this is reasonable: Obviously, no agent should eventually remain critical forever. For the transitions b and e, progress must be guaranteed by means of fairness assumptions, as discussed above. For the transitions a and d, however, it was far too strong to demand each agent to infinitely often strive at the shared resource. Furthermore, the environment of the system may specify further requirements for a and d to occur. This would imply further places in the pre-set of a and d. These places may eventually remain empty. Consequently, two kinds of transitions must be distinguished, denoted as *hot* and *cold*. A finite sequence $M_0 \xrightarrow{t_1} M_1 \xrightarrow{t_2} \ldots \xrightarrow{t_n} M_n$ of transition occurrences is a run of a net only if M_n does not enable a hot transition. For the mutual exclusion net in Fig. 1 we require a and d to be cold transitions, and the other transitions remaining hot. Consequently, each finite run of the net in Fig. 1 terminates in the initial state.

Experience shows that usually most transitions are hot. So it is convenient to graphically highlight cold transitions, e.g. by the inscription "c". Furthermore, fair transitions may be inscribed by "φ". This results in the full-fledged version of the mutual exclusion system shown in Fig. 2.

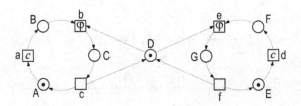

Fig. 2. Fair and cold transitions

6   Distributed Runs

With its explicit representation of locally and causally distributed (detached) transitions not only on the level of systems, but also on the level of occurrences in each single run, Petri nets provide a most adequate starting point to model systems in a faithful manner. The idea of distributed runs may be conceived as an extension of the sequential runs semantics of Petri nets. A sequential run can be conceived as a totally ordered set of transition occurrences. In contrast, a distributed run is only partially ordered: Detached transition occurrences remain unordered. Distributed runs did not gain much attendance since they have been established in the 1960s. The reason for this is that, so far, not too many interesting consequences have been drawn from this notion. This may, however, be subject to change: New variants of notions such as scenarios, sequential consistency, refinement and equivalence may be based on distributed runs to provide an extension of the usual sequential run semantics of Petri nets.

As an example, we consider the distributed runs of the MUTEX-system in Fig. 2. This system exhibits two scenarios L and R, i.e. behavioral snippets, shown in Fig. 3. Each scenario starts and ends in the initial state of the system.

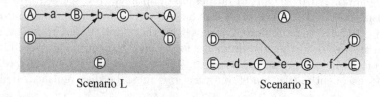

Scenario L   Scenario R

Fig. 3. The two scenarios of MUTEX

Instances of L and R can be composed in an obvious manner, as Fig. 4 shows. Each finite as well as each infinite distributed run of MUTEX is composed from instances of L and R, and each such composition is a distributed run of MUTEX. For example, Fig. 5 shows the finite distributed run $L \cdot L \cdot R$. Hence, the set of finite runs of MUTEX can be written as

$$\{L, R\}^*$$

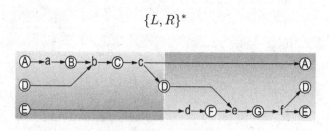

Fig. 4. Composition $L \cdot R$

where, as usual, A^* denotes the set of finite sequences over an alphabet A. Consequently, the set of infinite runs is

$$\{L, R\}^\infty$$

with A^∞ denoting the set of infinite sequences over an alphabet A.

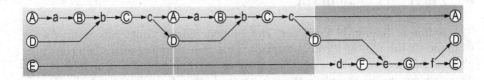

Fig. 5. Run $L \cdot L \cdot R$

This example shows that the composition of fairness assumptions, the distinction of hot and cold transitions, and the semantics of distributed runs together yield the technically simple and intuitively most adequate characterization of the semantics of MUTEX as in Fig. 2.

7 The New Operator

The generalizations of this and the next section apply to high-level nets only. High-level nets are a decisive extension of elementary Petri nets.

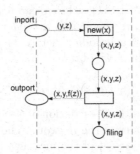

Fig. 6. Workflow with unique identifier generation

Tokens are no longer uniform, undistinguishable entities. In contrast they are "colored", i.e. distinguishable. A place in general then contains a multiset of colored tokens. (A multiset contains for each color c a number of tokens of color c.) Occurrence of a transition t updates the multiset of tokens on the places in its environment $\cdot t \cup t \cdot$. As an example we consider a typical workflow of a company that receives orders from its clients. An order (c, t) consists of the client's address c and the ordered task t, which the company has to perform. The company assigns each order (c, t) a unique identifier i. Then it performs the task t, resulting in the outcome $f(t)$. The company sends the triple $(i, c, f(t))$ to the client and files the order together with the identifier i in its stocks.

Figure 6 shows a high-level Petri net that models this workflow. The essential aspect here is that for each incoming order (c, t), the operator new $(\times)$ generates a new, unique identifier.

8 Petri Net Schemata

The notion of high-level Petri nets can be generalized to net *schemata*. As an example we discuss the *Echo Algorithm*. This algorithm organizes behavior of a given network of computing agents, called *nodes*, represented as a high-level net. Then we generalize the algorithm to be applicable to *any* connected network and represent this generalization as a net *schemata*.

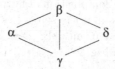

Fig. 7. The network A

Figure 7 shows an example of a connected network A of nodes $\alpha, \beta, \gamma, \delta$. Two nodes may be neighbored, represented by an *arc* in Fig. 7. In A, all pairs of nodes are *neighbored* except α and δ. In technical terms, A is an undirected, connected graph. In the network A, neighbors can exchange *messages*. Ignoring its contents, a message has a *recipient* and a *sender* and is represented as the tuple (*recipient, sender*). For each node x, let $\overline{N}(x)$ denote the set of messages received by x. For example, in A we obtain

$$N(\alpha) = \{(\beta, \alpha)(\gamma, \alpha)\} \text{ and } \overline{N}(\alpha) = \{(\alpha, \beta)(\alpha, \gamma)\}.$$

The Echo Algorithm organizes the distribution of a message from a distinguished *initiator* node to all other nodes of the network. The initiator terminates when all nodes have confirmed the receipt of the message.

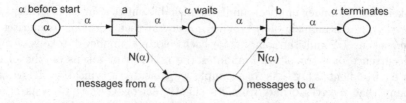

Fig. 8. The behavior of the initiator α

We choose the node α of the network A as the initiator. Figure 8 shows the behavior of α, sending messages to its neighbors β and γ and receiving messages from them.

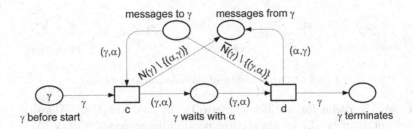

Fig. 9. Node γ, receiving a message from α

Figure 9 shows the behavior of γ upon receiving the message (γ, α): Transition c sends the set $(\beta, \gamma)(\delta, \gamma)\}$ of messages. The strange representation of this set as $N(\gamma)\backslash\{(\alpha, \gamma)\}$ will be motivated later. Along transition d, the node γ then expects the message set $\overline{N}(\gamma)\backslash\{(\gamma, \alpha)\} = \{(\gamma, \beta), (\gamma, \delta)\}$ and returns the message (α, γ) to α.

We will see later on that γ may also receive the message (γ, β) or (γ, δ) from β or δ, respectively. In any case, γ may process these messages analogously. The Echo Algorithm leaves unspecified which neighbor's message γ would start with. Figure 10 specifies this behavior with the variable y, to be interpreted as *any* neighbor of γ.

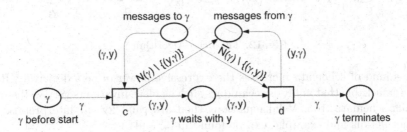

Fig. 10. Node γ, receiving a message

The behavior of γ as shown in Fig. 8 follows a pattern for all nodes except the initiator node α.

Figure 11 shows this pattern, with U denoting the set $\{\beta, \gamma, \delta\}$ of non-initiator nodes, and the variable x to be interpreted as any node in U. For the final model of the Echo Algorithm, the four places for sent, but not yet received messages in Fig. ?? and Fig. ?? are combined into a single place D in Fig. 12. This net shows the Echo Algorithm running on the network of Fig. 7, provided the symbols N, $\overline{N}$ and U are interpreted as described above. There is however no need to interpret N, $\overline{N}$ and U in this way. A different interpretation of those symbols would show

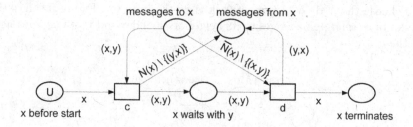

Fig. 11. The behavior of the non-initiator nodes

the Echo Algorithm for a different network. In fact, the Echo Algorithm for *any* network can be gained via a corresponding interpretation of N, $\overline{N}$ and U! Conceived this way, Fig. 12 shows a *schema* for infinitely may different Petri nets!

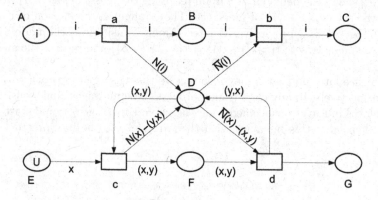

Fig. 12. The Echo Algorithm

This kind of schemata increases the expressive power of nets decisively. It is most remarkable that analysis techniques such as place invariants very well apply to such schemata, too. Valid equations then are valid for *all* interpretations. Further details and examples can be found in [3] and [4].

9   Conclusion

The expressive power of the elementary Petri net formalism can be increased in different ways. Early proposals of the 1970s suggested additional versions of arcs and variants of the occurrence rule for transitions. This comes with the disadvantage that fundamental analysis techniques get lost, in particular place invariants.

Smarter extensions try to retain analysis techniques and to extend the expressive power together with corresponding analysis techniques. Analysis techniques for stochastic nets have been designed and implemented for decades [2]. Analysis techniques that exploit fairness, hot and cold transitions, distributed runs and the schema aspect, have been described and exploited in [3] and [4].

References

1. Kindler, E., Walter, R.: Mutex needs fairness. Information Processing Letters 62(1), 31–39 (1997), http://dx.doi.org/10.1016/S0020-01909700033-1
2. Marsan, M.A., Balbo, G., Chiola, G., Donatelli, S., Franceschinis, G.: Modeling with Generalized Stochastic Petri Nets. John Wiley & Sons (1995)
3. Reisig, W.: Elements of Petri nets. Springer (1998)
4. Reisig, W.: The Book on Petri Nets. Springer (to appear, 2012)

Modelling of Communication Platforms Using Algebraic High-Level Nets and Their Processes

Karsten Gabriel* and Hartmut Ehrig

Technische Universtät Berlin, Germany
{kgabriel,ehrig}@cs.tu-berlin.de

Abstract. Algebraic high-level (AHL) nets are a well-known modelling technique based on Petri nets with algebraic data types, which allows to model the communication structure and the data flow within one modelling framework. In this paper we give an overview how to model the system behaviour of communication platforms and scenarios based on algebraic high-level nets and their processes. For modelling the evolution of communication platforms we show by example how to use transformations of AHL-nets inspired by the theory of graph transformation. As running example we show the modelling and evolution of Apache Wave platforms and Waves.

1 Introduction

Algebraic specifications for data types have been proposed about 35 years ago in the US [1,2,3] and studied in more detail in Europe since 1980 [4,5,6]. The theory of concurrency, on the other hand, has its roots in Petri nets advocated in the PhD thesis of Petri [7] already in 1962, but a break through from an algebraic point of view was the development of CCS by Milner [8] and the concept of Petri nets as monoids by Meseguer and Montanari [9]. High-level nets based on low-level Petri nets [7,10,11] and data types in ML have been studied as coloured Petri nets by Jensen [12]. The combination of Petri nets and algebraic specifications was mainly initiated by Krämer [13,14] and extended in [15,16,17,18,19] leading to the notion of algebraic high-level (AHL) nets.

The concept of processes in Petri nets is essential to model not only sequential, but especially concurrent firing behaviour. A process of a low-level Petri net N is given by an occurrence net K together with a net morphism $p : K \to N$. Processes of high-level nets AN are often defined as processes $p : K \to Flat(AN)$ of the corresponding low-level net $Flat(AN)$, called flattening of AN. However, this is not really adequate, because the flattening is in general an infinite net and the data type structure is lost. For this reason high-level processes for algebraic high-level nets have been introduced in [20,21], which are high-level

---

* Supported by the Integrated Graduate Program on Human-Centric Communication at Technische Universität Berlin.

M. Heisel (Ed.): Krämer Festschrift, LNCS 7365, pp. 10–25, 2012.

net morphisms $p : K \to AN$ based on a suitable concept of high-level occurrence nets K. In fact, high-level processes can be considered to have a set of initial markings for the input places of the corresponding occurrence net, whereas there is only one implicit initial marking of the input places for low-level occurrence nets. Furthermore, due to so-called assignment conflicts even for a fixed initial marking there may be different firing sequences depending on data values used at the transitions. A way to fix the data and thus obtain (up to concurrency) a concrete firing sequence are instantiations of AHL-processes [21].

Inspired by the theory of graph transformations [22,23] transformations of AHL-nets were first studied in [18] which – in addition to the token game – also allow to modify the AHL-net structure by rule based transformations. Moreover, in [24,25,26,27,28] also the rule-based transformation of AHL-processes is studied.

The main aim of this paper is to give a comprehensive introduction to the framework of algebraic high-level nets and processes and to show how they can be used to model modern communication platforms. In [29] it has already been shown how the framework of AHL-nets can be used to model Skype. The modelling of Google Wave and Apache Wave with AHL-processes was shown in [25,27]. In this paper we give an overview how AHL-processes can be used to model basic aspects of Apache Wave. In addition to [25,27] we consider also instantiations of AHL-processes [21] in more detail.

In Sect. 2 we introduce our case study Apache Wave. In Sect. 3 we show how the platforms can be modelled using AHL-nets, and in Sect. 4 we show how different scenarios in a platform can be modelled using AHL-processes and instantiations. The conclusion in Sect. 5 includes a summary and future work.

Acknowledgements from Hartmut Ehrig for Bernd Krämer

Bernd Krämer is one of the pioneers working on high-level Petri nets, especially on the combination of algebraic specifications and Petri nets. He has strongly influenced our TFS group in Berlin, especially myself, to extend our research approach of algebraic specification techniques to modelling and transformation of algebraic high-level nets. While we have focused on the theoretical foundations his main aim has been to show how to use the approach in software engineering.

Moreover I am in good personal contact with Bernd Krämer since about 25 years by now and I wish him all the best for the future. I am very glad to have the opportunity to contribute to his Festschrift according to his 65th birthday with this article.

2 Case Study Apache Wave

In this section we introduce our main case study Apache Wave which is a communication platform that was originally developed by the company Google [30] as Google Wave. Google itself has stopped the development of Google Wave, but the development is continued by the Apache Software Foundation [31] as Apache Wave [32].

One of the most interesting aspects of Apache Wave is the possibility to make changes on previous contributions. Therefore, in contrast to email, text chat or forums, due to possible changes the resulting data of the communication does not necessarily give a comprehensive overview on all interactions of the communication. For this reason, in Apache Wave for every communication there is a history allowing the users to replay interactions of the communication step by step. So for the modelling of Apache Wave it is necessary that we do not only model the systems and the communication but also the history of the communication.

We have chosen Apache Wave as running example for this paper because it includes typical modern features of many other communication systems, such as near-real-time communication. This means that different users can simultaneously edit the same document, and changes of one user can be seen almost immediately by the other users. Note that we do not focus on the communication between servers and clients in this contribution but on the communication between users.

In Apache Wave users can communicate and collaborate via so-called waves. A wave is like a document which can contain diverse types of data that can be edited by different invited users. The changes that are made to a wave can be simultaneously recognized by the other participating users. In order to keep track of the changes that have been made, every wave contains also a history of all the actions in that wave.

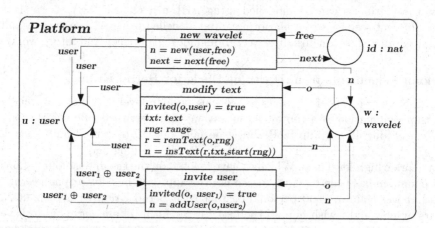

Fig. 1. AHL-net *Platform* for an Apache Wave platform

Apache Wave supports different types of extensions which are divided into gadgets and robots. The extensions are programs that can be used inside of a wave. The difference between gadgets and robots is that gadgets are not able to interact with their environment while robots can be seen as automated users that can independently create, read or change waves, invite users or other robots, and so on. This allows robots for example to do real-time translation or highlighting of texts that are written by different users of a wave. Clearly, it is intended to use different robots for different tasks and it is desired that multiple robots interact without conflicts. This makes the modelling and analysis of Apache Wave very important in order to predict possible conflicts or other undesired behaviour of robots.

In [25,27] we have already shown that Google Wave and Apache Wave can be adequately modelled using algebraic high-level (AHL) nets, which is an integration of the modelling technique of low-level Petri nets [10,11] and algebraic data types [33].

Figure 1 shows a small example of the structure of an AHL-net *Platform* which has 3 places and 3 transitions with firing conditions, where the pre and post arcs are labelled with variables of an algebraic signature. The AHL-net *Platform* models an Apache Wave platform with some basic features like the creation of new waves, modifications to existing waves, and the invitation of users to a wave which are modelled by the transitions *new wavelet*, *modify text* and *invite user*, respectively.

A wavelet is a part of a wave that contains a user ID, a list of XML documents and a set of users which are invited to modify the wavelet. For simplicity we model in our example only the simple case that every wavelet contains only one single document and the documents contain only plain text. In order to obtain a more realistic model one has to extend the used algebraic data part of the model given by the signature $\Sigma\text{-}Wave$ shown in Table 2 and the $\Sigma\text{-}Wave$-algebra A in Table 3 of Sect. 3.

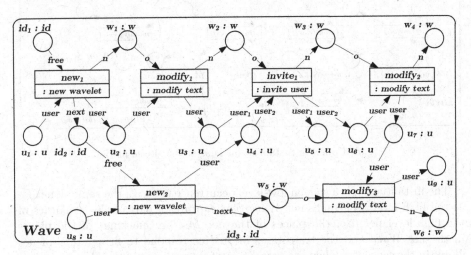

Fig. 2. AHL-process $Wave$ of a wave

The transitions of the net contain firing conditions in the form of equations over the signature $\Sigma\text{-}Wave$. In order to fire a transition there has to be an assignment v of the variables in the environment of the transition such that the firing conditions are satisfied in the algebra A. The pair (t, v) is then called a consistent transition assignment. Moreover, there have to be suitable data elements in the pre domain of the transition. For example, in order to fire the transition *modify text* in Fig. 1 we need a wavelet on the place w which can be assigned by the variable o and a user on the place u that can be assigned by the variable *user* such that the user is invited to the selected wavelet. Further, we need a text *txt*, a pair of natural numbers *rng* and a new wavelet n such that n is the wavelet which is obtained by replacing the text in the wavelet o at range *rng* with the text *txt*.

The assignment v then determines a follower marking which is computed by removing the assigned data tokens in the pre domain of the transition and adding the assigned data tokens in the post domain. In the case of the transition *modify text* this means that we remove the old wavelet from the place w and replace it by a new wavelet n which contains the modified text at the specified range. For more details on the operational semantics of AHL-nets we refer to [21].

Due to the parallel semantics of the real-time communication in Apache Wave a suitable modelling technique to capture the waves with their history, i.e. all states outgoing from their creation, are AHL-processes with instantiations. Fig. 2 shows an example of an AHL-process *Wave* which abstractly models a wave that contains two wavelets created by possibly different users. A concrete instantiation *Inst* of the wave is shown in Fig. 3.

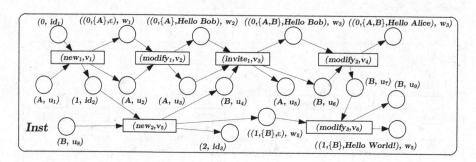

Fig. 3. Concrete Instantiation *Inst* of the *Wave* model

The instantiation is a special low-level occurrence net with the same structure as the high-level occurrence net *Wave* that captures a part of the semantics of the high-level net, i.e. the places of the net *Inst* are markings of the places in the net *Wave* and the transitions of *Inst* correspond to firing steps of net *Wave* in the sense that they are pairs (t, v) of transitions t of the *Wave* together with an assignments v (see Table 1) such that (t, v) is a consistent transition assignment and the pre respectively post domain of (t, v) in *Inst* is the assigned pre respectively post domain of t under v in the net *Wave*. In fact, there can be different instantiations of one AHL-occurrence net, each one capturing one concurrent firing sequence in the platform *Platform*.

Table 1. Assignments of the Instantiation *Inst*

$v_1 : free \mapsto 0, user \mapsto A, next \mapsto 1, n \mapsto (0, \{A\}, \epsilon)$
$v_2 : o \mapsto (0, \{A\}, \epsilon), user \mapsto A, pos \mapsto 0, txt \mapsto Hello, n \mapsto (0, \{A\}, Hello)$
$v_3 : user_1 \mapsto A, user_2 \mapsto B, o \mapsto (0, \{A\}, Hello), n \mapsto (0, \{A, B\}, Hello)$
$v_4 : o \mapsto (0, \{A, B\}, Hello), user \mapsto B, pos \mapsto 5, txt \mapsto !, n \mapsto (0, \{A, B\}, Hello!)$
$v_5 : free \mapsto 1, user \mapsto B, next \mapsto 2, n \mapsto (1, \{B\}, \epsilon)$
$v_6 : o \mapsto (1, \{B\}, \epsilon), user \mapsto B, pos \mapsto 0, txt \mapsto Hello\ World!, n \mapsto (1, \{B\}, Hello\ World!)$

Of course, our modelling approach can also be used to model other types of communication systems like wiki-based systems. A wiki is a website that manages information and data which can be easily created and edited by different users. Today wikis are used in many systems for communication, documentation, planning or other types of activities that involve the sharing of information. The most famous example of a wiki is the on-line encyclopaedia Wikipedia. The collaboration via wikis is very similar to the one via Apache Wave except for the near-real-time aspect. Due to the possibility to change contributions of other participants also the history of a wiki page is of importance and it is also usual to use automated scripts ("bots") for minor changes like the correction of common spelling mistakes. So also in the case of wiki-based systems it is relevant to have a process model of the system in order to analyse possible conflicts.

The example of an Apache Wave platform given above can be modified to model a wiki-based system. This can be done by changing the transition *new wavelet* into a transition *new wiki page* with corresponding changes to the signature, algebra and the firing conditions of the transitions in order to model wiki pages instead of wavelets (e. g. with an URL instead of an ID).

3   Modelling of Apache Wave Platforms Using AHL-Nets

In the following we review the definition of AHL-nets and their processes from [21,20] based on low-level nets in the sense of [9], where $X^\oplus$ is the free commutative monoid over the set X. Note that $s \in X^\oplus$ is a formal sum $s = \sum_{i=1}^{n} \lambda_i x_i$ with $\lambda_i \in \mathbb{N}$ and $x_i \in X$ meaning that we have λ_i copies of x_i in s and for $s' = \sum_{i=1}^{n} \lambda_i' x_i$ we have $s \oplus s' = \sum_{i=1}^{n} (\lambda_i + \lambda_i') x_i$.

An algebraic high-level (AHL-) net $AN = (\Sigma, P, T, pre, post, cond, type, A)$ consists of a signature $\Sigma = (S, OP; X)$ with additional variables X; a set of places P and a set of transitions T; pre- and post domain functions $pre, post :$ $T \to (T_\Sigma(X) \otimes P)^\oplus$; firing conditions $cond : T \to \mathcal{P}_{fin}(Eqns(\Sigma; X))$; a type of places $type : P \to S$ and a Σ-algebra A.

The signature $\Sigma = (S, OP)$ consists of sorts S and operation symbols OP, $T_\Sigma(X)$ is the set of terms with variables over X, the restricted product $\otimes$ is defined by

$$(T_\Sigma(X) \otimes P) = \{(term, p) \mid term \in T_\Sigma(X)_{type(p)}, p \in P\}$$

and $Eqns(\Sigma; X)$ are all equations over the signature Σ with variables X.

An AHL-net morphism $f : AN_1 \to AN_2$ is given by $f = (f_P, f_T)$ with functions $f_P : P_1 \to P_2$ and $f_T : T_1 \to T_2$ satisfying

(1) $(id \otimes f_P)^{\oplus} \circ pre_1 = pre_2 \circ f_T$ and $(id \otimes f_P)^{\oplus} \circ post_1 = post_2 \circ f_T$,
(2) $cond_2 \circ f_T = cond_1$ and
(3) $type_2 \circ f_P = type_1$.

The category defined by AHL-nets (with signature Σ and algebra A) and AHL-net morphisms is denoted by **AHLNets** where the composition of AHL-net morphisms is defined component-wise for places and transitions.

Note that it is also possible to define a category of AHL-nets with different signatures and algebras which requires that the morphisms not only contain functions for places and transitions but also a signature morphism together with a generalized algebra morphism (for details see [18]).

The firing behaviour of AHL-nets is defined analogously to the firing behaviour of low-level nets. The difference is that in the high-level case all tokens are equipped with data values. So, a marking

$$M = \sum_{i=1}^{n} \lambda_i(a_i, p_i) \in (A \otimes P)^{\oplus}$$

of an AHL-net AN means that place p_i contains $\lambda_i \in \mathbb{N}$ data tokens $a_i \in A_{type(p_i)}$.

Moreover, for the activation of a transition t, we additionally need an assignment asg of the variables in the environment of the transition, such that the assigned pre domain is part of the given marking and the firing conditions of the transition are satisfied.

Given an AHL-net AN with marking M a transition $t \in T$ is enabled under M and an assignment $asg : Var(t) \to A$, if all firing conditions $cond(t)$ are satisfied in A for asg and we have enough token in the pre domain of t, i.e. $pre_A(t, asg) \leq M$, where

$$pre_A(t, asg) = \sum_{i=1}^{n} (\overline{asg}(term_i), p_i) \text{ for } pre(t) = \sum_{i=1}^{n} (term_i, p_i)$$

with $term_i \in T_{OP}(X)$ and $\overline{asg}(term_i)$ is the evaluation of $term_i$ under asg. In this case the follower marking M' is given by

$$M' = M \ominus pre_A(t, asg) \oplus post_A(t, asg)$$

where the sub expression $M \ominus pre_A(t, asg)$ is well-defined because of $pre_A(t, asg) \leq M$.

Given an AHL-net morphism $f : AN_1 \to AN_2$ the firing behaviour is preserved, i.e. for $M_1' = M_1 \ominus pre_{1,A}(t, asg) \oplus post_{1,A}(t, asg)$ obtained by firing of a transition t with assignment asg in AN_1 we also have that $(f_T(t), asg)$ is activated in AN_2, leading to a follower marking $M_2' = M_2 \ominus pre_{2,A}(f_T(t), asg) \oplus post_{2,A}(f_T(t), asg)$ in AN_2 with $M_2 = (id \otimes f_P)^{\oplus}(M_1) = \sum_{i=1}^{n}(a_i, f_P(p_i))$ for $M_1 = \sum_{i=1}^{n}(a_i, p_i)$. Moreover, M_2' can be constructed directly as $M_2' = (id \otimes f_P)^{\oplus}(M_1')$.

Example 1 (Apache Wave Platform). The model of an Apache Wave platform in Fig. 1 is an AHL-net $Platform = (\Sigma\text{-}Wave, P, T, pre, post, cond, type, A)$ where the signature $\Sigma\text{-}Wave$ is shown in Table 2 and a part of the $\Sigma\text{-}Wave$-algebra A is shown in Table 3 (for more details see [28]). This signature and algebra are also used for all the following examples. Let us consider the marking

$$M = (Alice, u) \oplus (Bob, u) \oplus (1, id) \oplus ((0, \{Alice, Bob\}, \epsilon), w)$$

of the AHL-net *platform* in Fig. 1 which means that we have two users *Alice* and *Bob* on the place u, a free ID 1 and an empty wavelet with ID 0 on place w where *Alice* and *Bob* are invited. An assignment $asg : \{user, txt, rng, o, n\} \to A$ with $asg(user) = Alice$, $asg(txt) = Hello\ Bob$, $asg(rng) = (0,0)$, $asg(o) = (0, \{Alice, Bob\}, \epsilon)$ and $asg(n) = (0, \{Alice, Bob\}, Hello\ Bob)$ satisfies the firing conditions of the transition *modify text*. By firing the transition *modify text* with assignment *asg* we obtain the follower marking

$$M' = (Alice, u) \oplus (Bob, u) \oplus, (1, id) \oplus ((0, \{Alice, Bob\}, Hello\ Bob), w)$$

where the assigned text *Hello Bob* has been inserted into the assigned wavelet.

Table 2. Signature $\Sigma\text{-}Wave$

sorts: bool, nat, mod, range, text, user, wavelet	
opns: true, false : $\to$ bool	next : nat $\to$ nat
start, end : range $\to$ nat	new : user nat $\to$ wavelet
addUser : user wavelet $\to$ wavelet	invited : wavelet user $\to$ bool
len : text $\to$ nat	sub : text range $\to$ text
insText : wavelet text nat $\to$ wavelet	remText : wavelet range $\to$ wavelet
logEntry : user range text $\to$ mod	
vars: free, next : nat; log : mod; rng : range;	txt : text; user, user$_1$, user$_2$: user;
o, n, r : wavelet	

In [25] we have shown how rule-based transformation of AHL-nets [18] in the sense of graph transformation [23] can be used to model dynamic changes in the structure of an Apache Wave platform, allowing us to delete or add features, leading to new platforms. Moreover, we analysed under which conditions different platform evolutions are compatible with each other such that each of the evolutions is applicable to the result of the other one.

Table 3. Carrier sets of $\Sigma\text{-}Wave$-algebra A

$A_{bool} = \{T, F\}$	$A_{nat} = \mathbb{N}$
$A_{user} = \{a, \dots, z, A, \dots, Z\}^*$	$A_{text} = \{a, \dots, z, A, \dots, Z, \dots\}^*$
$A_{wavelet} = A_{nat} \times \mathcal{P}(A_{user}) \times A_{text}$	$A_{range} = A_{nat} \times A_{nat}$
$A_{mod} = A_{user} \times A_{range} \times A_{text}$	

An example of a production (or transformation rule) *insertLog* for AHL-nets that can be used for the evolution of an Apache Wave platform is shown in Fig. 4. The production describes a local modification that removes a transition *modify text* and inserts a new transition *modify and log* and a new place *log*. Further, the newly created transition is connected to the former environment of the removed transition.

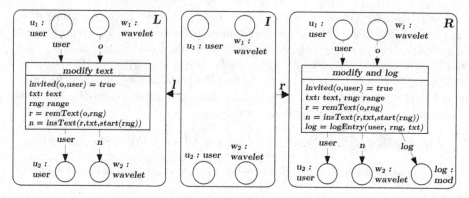

Fig. 4. Production *insertLog* for AHL-nets

The production can be applied to the AHL-net *Platform* in Fig. 1 via a match morphism $m : L \rightarrow Platform$, matching the *user* places to u and the *wavelet* places to w while the transition *modify text* is matched identically. The application of the production leads to a new AHL-net *Platform'* shown in Fig. 5 where the transition *modify text* has been replaced by *modify and log*, creating a log entry for every modification in a wavelet.

4   Modelling of Waves Using AHL-Processes and Instantiations

Now, we introduce AHL-process nets based on low-level occurrence nets (see [34]) and AHL-processes according to [21,20]. The net structure of a high-level occurrence net has similar properties like a low-level occurrence net, but it captures a set of different concurrent computations due to different initial markings. In fact, high-level occurrence nets can be considered to have a set of initial markings for the input places, whereas there is only one implicit initial marking of the input places for low-level occurrence nets.

Moreover, in a low-level occurrence net with an initial marking there is for any complete order of transitions, which is compatible with the causal relation (defined similar as in item 4 below for the high-level case), a corresponding firing sequence once there is a token on all input places. This is a consequence of the fact that in an occurrence net the causal relation is finitary. In the case of high-level occurrence nets an initial marking additionally contains data values, but in

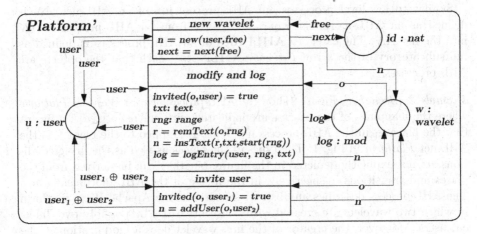

Fig. 5. Modified AHL-net *Platform'*

general some of the firing conditions in a complete order of transitions are not satisfied. Hence, even in the case that the causal relation is finitary, we cannot expect to have complete firing sequences.

In order to ensure a complete firing sequence in a high-level occurrence net there has to be an instantiation of the occurrence net (see [21]). In the following definition of AHL-process nets, in contrast to occurrence nets, we omit the requirement that the causal relation has to be finitary, because this is not a meaningful requirement for our application domain.

An AHL-process net K is an AHL-net $K = (\Sigma, P, T, pre, post, cond, type, A)$ such that for all $t \in T$ with $pre(t) = \sum_{i=1}^{n}(term_i, p_i)$ and notation $\bullet t = \{p_1, \ldots, p_n\}$ and similarly $t\bullet$ we have

1. (*Unarity*): $\bullet t, t\bullet$ are sets rather than multi sets for all $t \in T$, i.e. for $\bullet t$ the places $p_1, \ldots, p_n$ are pairwise distinct. Hence $|\bullet t| = n$ and the arc from p_i to t has a unary arc-inscription $term_i$.
2. (*No Forward Conflicts*): $\bullet t \cap \bullet t' = \emptyset$ for all $t, t' \in T, t \neq t'$
3. (*No Backward Conflicts*): $t\bullet \cap t'\bullet = \emptyset$ for all $t, t' \in T, t \neq t'$
4. (*Partial Order*): the causal relation $<_K \subseteq (P \times T) \cup (T \times P)$ defined by the transitive closure of $\{(p, t) \in P \times T \mid p \in \bullet t\} \cup \{(t, p) \in T \times P \mid p \in t\bullet\}$ is a strict partial order, i.e. the partial order is irreflexive.

AHL-process nets (with signature Σ and algebra A) together with AHL-net morphisms between AHL-process nets form the full subcategory **AHLPNets** $\subseteq$ **AHLNets**.

Note that an AHL-process net with a finitary causal relation is an AHL-occurrence net as defined in [21].

We define the sets of input places $IN(K) = \{p \in P_K \mid \nexists t \in T_K : p \in t\bullet\}$ and output places $OUT(K) = \{p \in P_K \mid \nexists t \in T_K : p \in \bullet t\}$ of an AHL-process net as the sets of places which are not in the post respectively pre domain of a transition.

Similar to low-level processes, an AHL-process mp of an AHL-net AN is defined as an AHL-morphism $mp : K \to AN$ from an AHL-process net K into the net AN. The category **AHLProcs** of all AHL-processes is defined as full subcategory of the arrow category **AHLNets**$^{\to}$ such that the objects are AHL-processes.

Example 2 (Scenario). Figure 2 shows an AHL-process *wave* : *Wave* $\to$ *Platform* where the mappings of the process are indicated with colons, e.g. $u_1 : u$ means that the place u_1 in the AHL-process net *Wave* is mapped to the place u in the AHL-net *Platform* in Fig. 1. The types of the places as well as the firing conditions are not explicitly depicted in the figure, but they can be derived from the places and transitions, respectively, in the image of the AHL-morphism *wave*. The AHL-process describes an abstract scenario in the Apache Wave platform in which two wavelets are created with consecutive IDs by possibly two different users. Moreover, the creator of the first wavelet does a modification to the wavelet, and it is open if this happens before or after the creation of the second wavelet. After that the creator of the second wavelet is invited to the first one, and does modifications to the first and then to the second wavelet.

Since the waves as well as the platforms may change at run-time, not only the rule-based transformation of platforms but also the modification of waves is an interesting aspect. In [25,27] we defined sufficient and necessary conditions for the composition and rule-based transformation of AHL-processes, allowing to model the modification of waves and scenarios. Based on the amalgamation of AHL-processes, analogously to the amalgamation of open net processes [35], we showed in [25] that AHL-nets have a compositional process semantics which makes it possible to separately analyse the interaction in smaller parts of large network systems consisting of different platforms. Moreover, the amalgamation allows to analyse the ability of users on different platforms to communicate with each other.

Furthermore, the extension of AHL-processes in [28] can be used to regain consistency between older waves and modified platforms, if the so-called *extension condition* is satisfied. Otherwise, in the case of minor changes the *process evolution based on action evolution* in [27] can be used to evolve the wave model according to the platform evolution, again leading to a consistent wave model.

For example, consider the platform evolution of *Platform* in Fig. 1 via production *insertLog* as described at the end of Sect. 3. We already have a scenario *wave* (see Example 2) corresponding to the original platform, but not to the modified one. However, we can obtain a valid scenario for the new platform by replacing all occurrences of the modified transition also in the AHL-process net *Wave'*. According to the results in [27] we can construct a production *insertLog*$^+$, containing three copies of the production *insertLog* that can be applied matching the different copies to the occurrences of *modify text*. The direct transformation leads to a new AHL-process *wave'* : *Wave'* $\to$ *Platform'* shown in Fig. 6 where according to the platform all modifications in the wave generate a log entry.

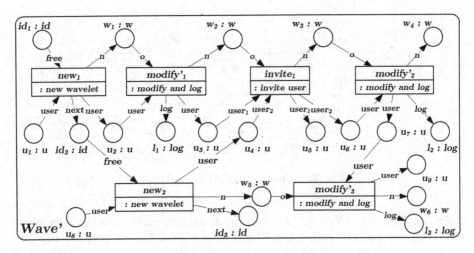

Fig. 6. Modified AHL-process $wave'$

Now, as described above, it is possible that there are different data-values and assignments for the AHL-process net $Wave$ which means that the AHL-process $wave$ models a set of different scenarios in the platform rather than a unique one. In order to obtain a model for a unique scenario with fixed data-values, we use instantiations of AHL-processes [21]. For this purpose we need the skeleton and flattening constructions for AHL-nets.

The skeleton $Skel(AN)$ of an AHL-net "forgets" the data part of the net, leading to a low-level place/transition (P/T) net with the same structure as the AHL-net. The flattening construction for AHL-nets also leads to a corresponding P/T net, but instead of forgetting the data part, all high-level information is encoded in the places and transitions.

Given an AHL-net $AN = (\Sigma, P, T, pre, post, cond, type, A)$ then the skeleton $Skel(AN)$ is defined by $Skel(AN) = (P, T, pre_S, post_S)$ with

$$pre_S(t) = \sum_{i=1}^{n} p_i \text{ for } pre(t) = \sum_{i=1}^{n} (term_i, p_i)$$

and similar for $post_S : T \to P^{\oplus}$. Given an AHL-morphism $f : AN_1 \to AN_2$ with $f = (f_P, f_T)$ then the skeleton of f is defined by $Skel(f) = (f_P : P_1 \to P_2, f_T : T_1 \to T_2)$.

Example 3 (Skeleton of an Algebraic High-Level Net). Figure 7 shows the skeleton $Skel(Wave)$ of the net $Wave$ in Fig. 2. The skeleton is a P/T net that has exactly the same structure as the high-level net $Wave$, but all high-level parts, i.e. the arc-inscriptions, the types and the firing conditions, are omitted.

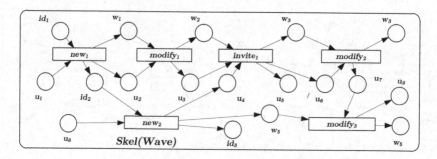

Fig. 7. Skeleton of the AHL-net *Wave*

Given an AHL-net $AN = (\Sigma, P, T, pre, post, cond, type, A)$ then the flattening $Flat(AN)$ is defined by a P/T net $Flat(AN) = (CP, CT, pre_A, post_A)$ with

- $CP = A \otimes P = \{(a, p) \mid a \in A_{type(p)}, p \in P\}$,
- $CT = \{(t, v) \mid t \in T, v : Var(t) \to A$ such that $cond(t)$ is valid in A under $v\}$, and
- $pre_A, post_A : CT \to CP^\oplus$ are the assigned pre and post domains as described in Sect. 3.

Given an AHL-morphism $f : AN_1 \to AN_2$ then the flattening of f is given by $Flat(f) = (id_A \otimes f_P : CP_1 \to CP_2, f_C : CT_1 \to CT_2)$ where $id_A \otimes f_P(a, p) = (a, f_P(p))$ and $f_C(t, v) = (f_T(t), v)$.

Example 4 (Flattening of an Algebraic High-Level Net). The instantiation *Inst* of the AHL-process *wave* shown in Fig. 3 is a subnet of the infinitely large flattening $Flat(Wave)$ of the AHL-net *Wave*. For a place p in the AHL-net, the possible data values $a \in A_{type(p)}$ are encoded in the places of $Flat(Wave)$, e.g. the place $(0, id_1)$ means that there is a token with value 0 on the place id_1. Analogously, the transition (new_1, v_1) (see Table 1 for the assignments) in the flattening means that the transition new_1 can fire with assignment v_1 if there are tokens 0 and A on the places id_1 and u_1, respectively.

Note that although the net *Wave* in Fig. 2 is an AHL-process net, due to assignment conflicts the flattening $Flat(Wave)$ is not a low-level process net. For instance, it is also possible that the wavelet with ID 0 is not created by user Alice (A) but by user Bob (B). This means that the transition new_1 is also enabled under an assignment v_1' which maps the variable *user* to B and thus there is also a place (B, u_1) and a transition (new_1, v_1') with pre domain $(0, id_1) \oplus (B, u_1)$, meaning that there is a forward conflict at $(0, id_1)$.

The above definitions of skeleton on flattening constructions constitute functors *Skel, Flat* : **AHLNets** $\to$ **PTNets** which preserve monomorphisms and pushouts as shown in [24]. Moreover, there is a natural transformation *proj* : $Flat \Rightarrow Skel$ that forgets the data-encoding of the flattening.

Now, given an AHL-process net K, an instantiation L of K is a subnet of the flattening $Flat(K)$ (i.e. there is an inclusion $in : L \hookrightarrow Flat(K)$) such that $proj(K) \circ in : L \twoheadrightarrow Skel(K)$ is an isomorphism. The category **Inst** of instantiations is given by pairs (L, K) such that L is an instantiation of K, and by pairs of morphisms (f_L, f_H) such that $in_2 \circ f_L = Flat(f_H) \circ in_1$.

An example of an instantiation is given by the P/T net *Inst* in Fig. 3 which is an instantiation of the AHL-process net *Wave*. The low-level P/T net *Inst* has the same structure as the high-level net *Wave*, and it is a subnet of its flattening, and therefore, models a part of its semantics. The instantiation fixes the data of the abstract scenario to the concrete case that user Alice (A) creates the first wavelet with ID 0, while user Bob (B) creates the second wavelet ID 1. Further, since the assignment contains mappings for all variables occurring in a firing condition of a transition, also the concrete text modifications and their positions in the wavelets are explicitly given in the instantiation.

In [24] also constructions for the composition and rule-based transformation of instantiations are given, however, with some minor restrictions. In addition, a pre image construction for instantiations is given in [24], providing for every instantiation L_2 of an AHL-process net K_2 and every AHL-morphism $f_H : K_1 \to K_2$ a unique instantiation L_1 and P/T-morphism $f_L : L_1 \to L_2$ such that (f_L, f_H) is an **Inst**-morphism. Moreover, it is shown in [24] that the category of instantiations of AHL-nets (without the restriction to AHL-process nets) has pushouts. These results and those for the functors *Skel* and *Flat* make it possible to easily transfer all the results for AHL-process nets also to their instantiations.

5   Conclusion

Algebraic high-level (AHL) nets are a well-known modelling technique based on Petri nets [11,10] with algebraic data types [33]. In this paper we have shown that AHL nets, AHL processes, and AHL transformations can be considered as integrated framework for modelling the evolution of communication platforms. In previous papers it was shown already how to use this framework to model communication platforms like Skype [29], Google Wave [25] and Apache Wave [27]. In this paper, in contrast to [27], we have considered also the instantiations of AHL-processes which are used to fix a choice of concrete data for a given AHL-process.

Moreover, we have shown by examples how to use the rule-based transformation of AHL-nets to model the evolution of Apache Wave platforms and scenarios, where platforms are modelled by AHL-nets and scenarios by AHL-processes. The evolution on both levels is defined by rule-based modifications in the sense of graph transformation systems [36]. While transformations of AHL-nets are introduced already in [18] the corresponding problem for AHL-processes is much more difficult as shown explicitly in [28].

In future work we want to consider interesting consistency and security requirements and study how they can be satisfied in our model based on the current integrated framework, or how to extend the model and/or the framework respectively. Moreover we will analyse what kind of properties can be preserved by evolution of platforms and scenarios.

References

1. Zilles, S.: Algebraic specification of data types. Project MAC Progress Report 11, 28–52. MIT (1974)
2. Goguen, J.A., Thatcher, J.W., Wagner, E.G., Wright, J.B.: Abstract data types as initial algebras and the correctness of data representations. In: Proc. of Conf. on Computer Graphics (1975)
3. Guttag, J.: The specification and application to programming of abstract data types. PhD thesis, University of Toronto (1975)
4. Ehrig, H., Kreowski, H.-J., Thatcher, J.W., Wagner, E.G., Wright, J.B.: Parametrized Data Types in Algebraic Specification Languages. In: de Bakker, J.W., van Leeuwen, J. (eds.) ICALP 1980. LNCS, vol. 85, pp. 157–168. Springer, Heidelberg (1980)
5. Hupbach, U., Kaphengst, H., Reichel, H.: Initial algebraic specification of data types, parameterized data types and algorithms. Technical Report 15, VEB Robotron ZFT, Dresden (1980)
6. CIP Language Group: Report on a wide spectrum language for program specification and development. Technical Report TUM-I8104, TU München (1981); also available as Springer LNCS 183
7. Petri, C.: Kommunikation mit Automaten. PhD thesis, Institut für instrumentelle Mathematik, Universität Bonn (1962)
8. Milner, R.: A Calculus of Communication Systems. LNCS, vol. 92. Springer, Heidelberg (1980)
9. Meseguer, J., Montanari, U.: Petri Nets Are Monoids. Information and Computation 88(2), 105–155 (1990)
10. Rozenberg, G.: Behaviour of Elementary Net Systems. In: Brauer, W., Reisig, W., Rozenberg, G. (eds.) APN 1986. LNCS, vol. 254, pp. 60–94. Springer, Heidelberg (1987)
11. Reisig, W.: Petrinetze, Eine Einführung. Springer, Berlin (1985)
12. Jensen, K.: Coloured Petri Nets: A High-Level Language for System Design and Analysis. In: Rozenberg, G. (ed.) APN 1990. LNCS, vol. 483, pp. 342–416. Springer, Heidelberg (1991)
13. Krämer, B.: Segras – a formal and semigraphical language combining petri nets and abstract data types for the specification of distributed systems. In: Proceedings of the 9th International Conference on Software Engineering. ICSE 1987, pp. 116–125. IEEE Computer Society Press, Los Alamitos (1987)
14. Krämer, B.: Concepts, Syntax and semantics of Segras, a specification language for distributed systems. PhD thesis, Technische Universtät Berlin (1989)
15. Hummert, U.: Algebraische High-Level Netze. PhD thesis, Technische Universtät Berlin (1989)
16. Reisig, W.: Petri nets and algebraic specifications. Theoretical Computer Science 80 (1991)
17. Dimitrovici, C., Hummert, U., Petrucci, L.: Semantics, Composition and Net Properties of Algebraic High-Level Nets. In: Rozenberg, G. (ed.) APN 1991. LNCS, vol. 524, pp. 93–117. Springer, Heidelberg (1991)

18. Padberg, J., Ehrig, H., Ribeiro, L.: Algebraic high-level net transformation systems. Mathematical Structures in Computer Science 80, 217–259 (1995)
19. Ehrig, H., Reisig, W.: An Algebraic View on Petri Nets. Bulletin of the EATCS 61, 52–58 (1997)
20. Ehrig, H., Hoffmann, K., Padberg, J., Baldan, P., Heckel, R.: High-Level Net Processes. In: Brauer, W., Ehrig, H., Karhumäki, J., Salomaa, A. (eds.) Formal and Natural Computing. LNCS, vol. 2300, pp. 191–219. Springer, Heidelberg (2002)
21. Ehrig, H.: Behaviour and Instantiation of High-Level Petri Net Processes. Fundamenta Informaticae 65(3), 211–247 (2005)
22. Ehrig, H.: Introduction to the Algebraic Theory of Graph Grammars (A Survey). In: Ng, E.W., Ehrig, H., Rozenberg, G. (eds.) Graph Grammars 1978. LNCS, vol. 73, pp. 1–69. Springer, Heidelberg (1979)
23. Rozenberg, G. (ed.): Handbook of Graph Grammars and Computing by Graph Transformation. Foundations, vol. 1. World Scientific, Singapore (1997)
24. Gabriel, K.: Composition and transformation of high-level petri net-processes. Diploma thesis, Technische Universtät Berlin (2009)
25. Ehrig, H., Gabriel, K.: Transformation of algebraic high-level nets and amalgamation of processes with applications to communication platforms. International Journal of Software and Informatics 5, Part1, 207–229 (2011)
26. Gabriel, K.: Algebraic high-level nets and processes applied to communication platforms. Technical Report 2010/14, Technische Universität Berlin (2010)
27. Gabriel, K., Ehrig, H.: Modelling evolution of communication platforms and scenarios based on transformations of high-level nets and processes. Theoretical Computer Science (2012)
28. Gabriel, K.: Modelling Evolution of Communication Platforms and Scenarios based on Transformations of High-Level Nets and Processes – Extended Version. Technical Report 2011/08, Technische Universität Berlin (2011)
29. Hoffmann, K., Modica, T.: Formal modeling of communication platforms using reconfigurable algebraic high-level nets. ECEASST 30, 1–25 (2010)
30. Google (February 2012), http://google.com
31. Apache Software Foundation (February 2012), http://apache.org
32. Apache Wave (February 2012), http://incubator.apache.org/wave/
33. Ehrig, H., Mahr, B.: Fundamentals of Algebraic Specification 1. Springer (1985)
34. Goltz, U., Reisig, W.: The Non-sequential Behavior of Petri Nets. Information and Control 57(2/3), 125–147 (1983)
35. Baldan, P., Corradini, A., Ehrig, H., Heckel, R.: Compositional Modeling of Reactive Systems Using Open Nets. In: Larsen, K.G., Nielsen, M. (eds.) CONCUR 2001. LNCS, vol. 2154, pp. 502–518. Springer, Heidelberg (2001)
36. Ehrig, H., Ehrig, K., Prange, U., Taentzer, G.: Fundamentals of Algebraic Graph Transformation. EATCS Monographs in TCS. Springer (2006)

Modeling Revisited

Herbert Weber

THESEUS Joint Research, Berlin, Germany
herbert.weber@fokus.fraunhofer.de

Abstract. Over the last two decades modeling has become a widespread engineering tool. Whereas object-oriented modeling dominated the discussions in software and data engineering, process-oriented modeling became prominent in business process modeling. Experience gained with both of these principal modeling techniques made us aware of shortcomings with both of them in their respective application environment. For instance, object-oriented modeling is seen as having its virtues now in rather low programming-level elaboration about systems, systems of systems, and complex infrastructures. In addition, object-oriented modeling is not easily understood by non-ICT professionals. Therefore, new needs become visible for modeling complex systems uniformly across numerous granularity, abstraction and virtualization levels. This article will introduce some arguments that will underpin the need for a fresh look at modeling in software and data engineering.

Keywords: Modeling, object-oriented modeling, process-oriented modeling, business process modeling, software engineering, data engineering, infrastructures, profiling, profiling methodology.

1 Introduction

Over the last decades modeling has become a widespread engineering methodology. Whereas object-oriented modeling dominated the discussions in software and data engineering, process-oriented modeling became prominent in business process modeling. Experience gained with both of these principal modeling techniques made us aware of shortcomings with both of them. For instance, object-oriented modeling is seen as having its virtues in rather low programming-level elaboration about systems. In addition, object-oriented modeling is not understood by non-ICT professionals.

Therefore, new requirements for modeling complex systems, systems of systems and entire Information and Communication Infrastructures uniformly will have to be taken into account. This article will introduce some arguments that will underpin the need for a fresh look at the modeling of information and communication infrastructures.

2 Modeling of Information and Communication Infrastructures

Modeling has become a widespread engineering methodology and is supported now by quite a selection of tools. Especially object-oriented modeling techniques as they

M. Heisel (Ed.): Krämer Festschrift, LNCS 7365, pp. 26–35, 2012.

have been defined in the "Unified Modeling Language (UML)" have gained a high level of recognition and widespread use. UML supports, in both, data engineering and software engineering, tasks and activities and has become a kind of lingua franca in these two disciplines.

More recent developments, however, seem to demand other modeling techniques: Techniques to model entire information and communication infrastructures in a uniform way. Their modeling requires the collaborative action of ICT professionals and ICT nonprofessionals that tend to look at ICT infrastructures in different ways and demand hence uniform modeling techniques across different levels of granularity, different levels of abstraction and different levels of virtualization of information and communication infrastructures that they both will be able to understand and use. To meet this challenge to uniformly model information and communication infrastructures, for example, on a "user level" and on a "developer level" will be the motivation for the introduction of another than an object-oriented modeling technique.

Modeling entire information and communication infrastructures becomes a necessity in quite a number of endeavors like analyzing   infrastructures for the purpose of their

- understanding by new users

or for the purpose of the

- integration of new systems into infrastructures
- outsourcing of part of an infrastructure to service providers
- replacement of systems by externally offered services
- monitoring of infrastructures during their operation

etc.

The need for this kind of a retrospective modeling of information and communication infrastructures can, for example, be explained with the currently running "Future Internet Public-Private Partnership (FI-PPP)" of the European Commission in its 7th Framework Program:

"Prior investments into the development of infrastructures in Europe funded either nationally or within the framework programs of the European Union may be exploited in the FI-PPP. Making the assets that they represent available to wherever there may be an interest in their use is of utmost importance. For that purpose existing infrastructures need to be analyzed to reveal their assets and to describe them uniformly to enable their proper understanding and to enable their reuse wherever and whenever possible."

Assets of interest may be of different kinds:

- Concepts: i.e., models, designs, architectures, terminologies, taxonomies, ontologies, etc.
- Data: i.e., unstructured, semi-structured or structured information, geo data, business data, health care data, etc.
- Systems: i.e., software systems, hardware systems, communication systems, etc.
- Infrastructures: i.e., communication infrastructures, information management infrastructures, service management infrastructures, etc.

Knowing and understanding the capabilities that these assets provide will then enable the discovery of

- differences and/or commonalities between infrastructures
- transfer opportunities for parts of an infrastructure into another infrastructure
- standardization opportunities for interfaces within an infrastructure
- reuse opportunities for an infrastructure in other application domains
- customization opportunities for infrastructures

etc.

The great variety of capabilities of infrastructures is demanding a systematics for the capability analysis process and the description of capabilities embedded in infrastructures that is formal enough to enable the comprehensive analysis and understanding of infrastructures and is informal enough to allow non-ICT professionals to make use of them.

An example for the modeling of information and communication infrastructures as a monitoring exercise arose in the THESEUS Program funded by the German Federal Government on "New Technologies for the Internet of Services". The program led to the development of more than 20 demonstrators, prototypes, and experimental systems, for different purposes with different approaches and for different applications. Their analysis, comparison, and evaluation demand for a modeling technique that could be easily understood and applied by developers with different backgrounds.

All these artifacts have been described on three different levels of abstraction:

- as "landscapes" that identify the building blocks that constitute the artifacts and the relationships existing between the building blocks;
- as "blueprints" that identify the "capabilities" provided by the building blocks and hence describe what the artifacts are able to deliver;
- as "specifications" that identify the characteristics of the implementation of the capabilities in terms of "functions".

The modeling technique that has been introduced and is now used in the two projects explained above is called "Profiling".

3   Profiling

Profiling is meant to be a methodology that will lead to the development of a sustainable knowledge base containing all relevant information required to govern the documentation, continuous evaluation and evolution of information and communication infrastructures. Therefore, profiles are recorded in a way to support the detection of impacts resulting from changes at one "place" upon other "places" in the information and communication infrastructure.

Profiling is hence a methodology for the description of computing artifacts and their respective application environment. In many instances information on those artifacts and application environments is not known since it has not been systematically acquired and recorded or – if some information exists – it is not complete or outdated. Also, where this information exists it may be distributed across numerous documents that describe the information in terms of different notations. Profiling is, therefore, developed to enable a uniform description of all the information of concern. It is hence a notation that may be used across a set of different competence domains like information and communication technologies, applications of information and communication technologies, business settings in which applications of information and communication technologies exist, and even of societal settings that relate to the use of applications of information and communication technologies. As different as the artifacts of concern may be and as different as their descriptions might be in the end, stakeholders interested in these artifacts will only take notice of them if their descriptions are simple and easy to read.

Profiling is, therefore, a methodology to

- uniformly document societal, economic, and technical artifacts
- enable the communication about the different artifacts in a common language

Profiling provides for these purposes a notation that will be formal enough to

- enable the comparison of artifacts to reveal similarities, differences, etc.
- enable the evaluation of artifacts to reveal inconsistencies, incompatibilities, etc.

and that will be informal enough to allow its use by professionals with different backgrounds.

Profiling may hence be understood as a methodology that relates to other (formal or semiformal) description techniques as depicted in the following diagram:

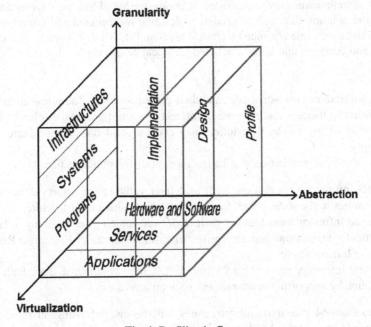

Fig. 1. Profiling in Context

The diagram indicates that infrastructures and artifacts constituting infrastructures will be characterized along three different dimensions:

- The "Abstraction Dimension" denotes the fact that artifacts may be seen to exist and can be described at different abstraction levels: Artifacts may be implemented, they may be designed, and they may be "profiled".
- The "Granularity Dimension" denotes the fact that artifacts may be seen as being decomposable/composable into building blocks like programs, systems, and infrastructures.
- The "Virtualization Dimension" denotes the fact that artifacts may be seen, for example, as consisting of devices, as services provided by these devices, or as applications that have been built by using services provided by the respective devices.

Information and communication infrastructures may be of a considerable size and complexity. Acquiring information about them may be a very cumbersome and tedious job. It is, therefore, of utmost importance to clearly define beforehand the purpose for which a profiling will be conducted to minimize the effort and to restrict the profiling to the appropriate level of detail.

Profiling will also have to be conducted in a very disciplined way that enables its stepwise completion. This stepwise completion is proposed here to take place over three different stages. In order to enable the profiling for different purposes, the different stages will be defined to gradually increase the expressiveness of the notation to describe profiles:

It starts out with a very limited set of terms and concepts that will suffice in the profiling for some more administrative and less technical characteristics of information and communication infrastructures. It continues by adding new terms and concepts to the notation that will be needed to describe information and communication infrastructures on some advanced technical level and it will end with the introduction of terms and concepts that allow a detailed technical description.

Stage 1

Stage 1 introduces infrastructures and their properties on an "administrative level". This is meant to indicate that they are of interest to a – not necessarily clearly defined – community of users. The description may even suggest that infrastructures are in short supply.

Stage 1 differentiates between infrastructures of different nature like

- Societal Infrastructures that are built to deliver value to the society at large or to communities in the society like, for instance, a health care infrastructure
- Economic Infrastructures that are built to deliver value to the economy at large or to particular institutions and enterprises like, for instance, an Enterprise Resource Planning Infrastructure
- Technical Infrastructures, like a Corporate ICT Infrastructure, that are built to deliver value by supporting economic and societal activities

It can be assumed that most infrastructures will be encompassing all three of the above types in an integrated fashion.

The description of information and communication infrastructures in stage 1 will be based on a number of "Infrastructure Attributes". The "Infrastructure Attributes" will serve in the identification and basic characterization of the respective information and communication infrastructure.

"Infrastructure Attribute"
- Stakeholder
  Who has an interest in the information and communication infrastructure
  - Owner
  - Provider
  - Operator
  - User
  - Developer

etc.

- Objective/Purpose
  What is the objective/purpose of the existence of the information and communication infrastructure in terms of its
  - Availability for its User
  - Availability for the interfacing with other information and communication infrastructures
  - Availability for the interoperation with other information and communication infrastructures

etc.

Stage 2

Stage 2 introduces "Actionable Artifacts" as the building blocks of information and communication infrastructures. "Actionable Artifacts" are introduced as a common descriptive term and concept for the many different types of building blocks that constitute an information and communication infrastructure. These common descriptive terms and concepts indicate that all "Actionable Artifacts" will be described uniformly by a cross-cutting concept of a "Capability".

The description of information and communication infrastructures on stage 2 will be based on the concept of a "Capability". Capabilities are denotations for what an Actionable Artifact is capable of doing – what actions it is capable of conducting.

Capabilities are understood as "Stimulus Action Response Sequences": A stimulus invokes an Action and the conduct of the Action results in a response. This enables the description of all types of infrastructures introduced in stage 1 in exactly the same way: Societal and Economic Infrastructures will be stimulated to invoke one or a number of Actions conducted by human beings or societal/economic organizations and will deliver a response in the same way as Computing Artifacts that enable the invocation of programs that get executed and deliver a response.

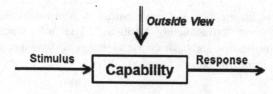

Fig. 2. Capability Model

Capabilities are an "outside" view at an Actionable Artifact. They do not reveal information on how the Actionable Artifact conducts Actions. They hence represent an advanced technical description of information and communication infrastructures. As such they serve all those stakeholders that intend to understand what potential value the respective information and communication infrastructure of Actionable Artifacts might have for them.

Since Capabilities represent the potential value of Actionable Artifacts to their stakeholders, they also serve in the mapping of stakeholder requirements and capabilities provided by the Actionable Artifacts. For the selection of Actionable Artifacts for their use it will, however, be impracticable to analyze Actionable Artifacts for all their Capabilities but rather for desired sets of Capabilities.

In order to support this capability-based analysis for Actionable Artifacts, the Profiling Methodology provides for the "Capability-based Classification" of Actionable Artifacts. This classification may relate back to the differentiation between the different types of infrastructures and may distinguish between

- Societal Capabilities
- Economic Capabilities
- Technical Capabilities

as it was introduced for the profiling in stage 1.

The classification of Capabilities may, however, also relate to other "Capability Attributes" that might be necessary to characterize Capabilities.

Stage 3

Stage 3 introduces "Actions" as "Abstract Implementations" of Capabilities. They represent the "inside" view at Actionable Artifacts. In order to serve as abstract implementations for Capabilities, Actions will be characterized with a set of five different "Action Attributes":

- Objectives/Purposes of the Actions
- Stakeholders of the Actions
- Deliveries of the Actions
- Enablers of the Actions
- Processes that govern the conduct of the Actions

These five Attributes are meant to answer the following questions about Actions:

- Why is the Action being defined (Objective/Purpose)?
- Who has an interest in that Action (Stakeholder)?
- What is the Action providing as a response (Delivery)?

- With what support can the Action be conducted (Enabler)?
- How is the Action being conducted in steps (Process)?

It is obvious that these Action Attributes are not necessarily independent of each other. The relationships that may exist between them will be depicted in the following graph:

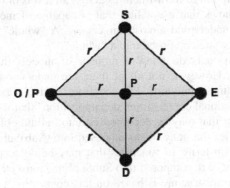

Fig. 3. Function Specifications

The description of information and communication infrastructures in stage 3 is – as one can easily conclude – meant to be used for a very detailed description of their Actionable Artifacts.

Their full description is preferably structured in a tabular form in which the rows of the table represent an Action and the columns represent the Action Attributes.

| | | **Attributes** | |
	AA_1	AA_2	AA_3
A_1	val	val	val
A_2	val	val	val
A_3	val	val	val

Fig. 4. Artifact-Attribute Relationships

4   Structuring of Profiles

The Profiling Methodology will have to be applicable at different granularity levels as, for example, on the level where an infrastructure will be described in terms of its building blocks that may be off-the-shelf available commercial systems or it may be necessary to profile them on a more detailed level where the building blocks are, for instance, "data management functions" or "communication protocols". The different levels will usually also correspond to particular professional communities that are concerned about their respective model and that may not even care for another community that is concerned about another level. The Profiling Methodology allows this separation of concerns but will not allow different notations for the different levels to enable uniform description of infrastructures across all levels of refinement.

Past experience shows that a notation that is capable of meeting these demands must be known and understood almost universally. A "whole" will be decomposed into "parts" and "parts" are composed into a "whole".

Computing professionals do know a number of models that support compositions/decompositions. However, not all of them are understood and understandable outside of the computing community. We, therefore, restrict ourselves to a model that is usually called "functional composition/ decomposition" that would look at an infrastructure as an artifact that may be decomposed into building blocks whose building blocks offer capabilities that may be decomposed into (Sub)SubCapabilities that are, in turn, implemented in terms of functions that may be decomposed into SubFunctions that, in turn, may be decomposed into SubSubFunctions, etc.

The profile of an infrastructure is based on this concept of a breakdown structure for artifacts, capabilities, and functions. For their characterization they will be associated with "artifact attributes", "capability attributes", and "function attributes". The representation of infrastructures and their characteristics may then be comprehensively represented in a tabular form as depicted below.

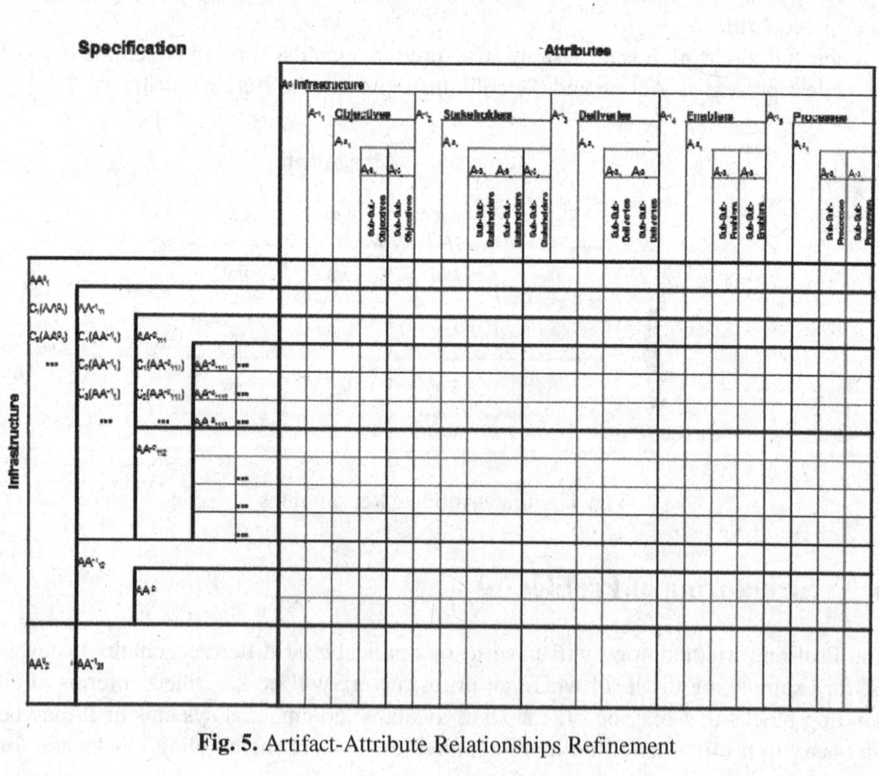

Fig. 5. Artifact-Attribute Relationships Refinement

Profiling is possible only with the information provided by the owners of infrastructures. Some of the owners may have and may be ready to provide lots of information, some others may not have or may not want to provide information. The methodology is, therefore, not demanding for an equally detailed description of all infrastructures of concern but will leave it to the discretion of the infrastructure owners to deliver the information that is felt to be exhaustive from the owner's point of view.

5   Conclusion

Profiling is not a new modeling technique but rather a revival of the modeling of artifacts as breakdown structures in much the same way as it was practiced in the early days of software engineering. It looks at artifacts by identifying and specifying their capabilities in terms of functions and function decompositions/ compositions.

Insofar, however, it is a departure from now predominant object-oriented modeling. This retreat to semantically simpler models has been provoked by the insight that non-programming professionals do have a hard time understanding object orientation in much the same way as it was hard for programming professionals at the time of its invention.

Profiling is collecting much less information about artifacts as object-oriented models but it is exactly that reduction of information that is needed to model large infrastructures of "industrial" size. It is obvious that an all encompassing model of such an infrastructure as a documentation would not be possible for the sheer effort that it would require to describe it as a UML model. Profiling is meant to enable exactly this but not only as a one 4-page "architecture diagram" but as a description that could be driven to that level of detail that is required for the purpose it is meant to serve.

The methodology has been and will be used in profiling exercises of considerable size and has – for its simplicity – gained immediate acceptance by IT nonprofessionals and professionals.

Acknowledgement. The modeling technique described above is borrowing ideas from very many researchers and practitioners who have worked on subjects like "structured design", "functional modeling", "object-oriented modeling", etc. for decades. It would be unfair to mention only some of them in a bibliography so to not exceed the available space in this paper. The paper is largely based on a technical report produced in the context of the "Future Internet Public-Private Partnership" Project of the European Union as Deliverable D3.1 and Deliverable D3.4 of the Project "INFINITY - INfrastructures for the Future Internet commuNITY".

A Conceptual Framework and Experimental Workbench for Architectures

Marco Konersmann and Michael Goedicke

paluno - The Ruhr Institute for Software Technology,
University of Duisburg–Essen
Gerlingstraße 16, 45127 Essen, Germany
{marco.konersmann,michael.goedicke}@paluno.uni-due.de

Abstract. When developing the architecture of a software system, inconsistent architecture representations and missing specifications or documentations are often a problem. We present a conceptual framework for software architecture that can help to avoid inconsistencies between the specification and the implementation, and thus helps during the maintenance and evolution of software systems. For experimenting with the framework, we present an experimental workbench. Within this workbench, architecture information is described in an intermediate language in a semantic wiki. The semantic information is used as an experimental representation of the architecture and provides a basis for bidirectional transformations between implemented and specified architecture. A systematic integration of model information in the source code of component models allows for maintaining only one representation of the architecture: the source code. The workbench can be easily extended to experiment with other Architecture Description Languages, Component Models, and analysis languages.

1 Motivation

Current approaches for software architecture development propose to develop software architecture specifications using sophisticated languages, to analyze the architecture, and eventually to implement it using modern software component technologies (cf. [1]). Following these best-practices thus leads to at least two representations of the software architecture: the specification and the implementation. The specification is an abstract, precise description of the architecture, which lacks implementation details. The implementation includes the architecture and any other implementation detail of the software. Architecture analysis can introduce further representations, when architectures are transformed into analysis languages.

The simultaneous existence of more than one representation of the architecture makes it harder to maintain because all representations have to be kept consistent. Else, faults might be introduced during maintenance and evolution when developers rely on outdated or false information. To avoid such faults, we present a conceptual framework for software architecture, that ensures the consistency between architecture representations.

M. Heisel (Ed.): Krämer Festschrift, LNCS 7365, pp. 36–52, 2012.

The framework is accompanied by an experimental workbench. The experimental workbench is the technical platform for the framework. It can be used for experimenting with the features of the framework, and for viewing and editing architectures in arbitrary Architecture Description Languages (ADLs) and Component Models (CMs). In this work an ADL is any language used to describe a software architecture on a higher level of abstraction than the implementation code of current programming languages.

The remainder of this paper is structured as follows: In section 2 we discuss how other approaches relate to the problem. In section 3 we present our framework. Section 4 presents the experimental workbench for software architectures, which is based on the framework. Section 5 shows the benefits of the workbench in a small example. We discuss our results and identify future work in section 6 before we conclude in section 7.

2   Related Work

Managing multiple representations of software design and specifically architecture has been subject to other fields of research. Closely related to the paper at hand is the field of Model-Driven Software Development (MDSD) (e.g. [2]), model execution (e.g. [3,4]), and round trip engineering (e.g. [5]). In this context we differentiate these approaches regarding the abstraction levels that they focus on and the possibility of bidirectional transformations between representations of the design or architecture.

In MDSD abstract domain specific models of the software to be developed are created with domain experts. These domain models are refined with detailed technical models that are not relevant to the domain, but to the platform that will run the software. Such models are often the basis for automated code generation. The generated code has to be enriched with implementation details. Model-Driven Architecture (MDA) [6] is a MDSD approach by the Object Management Group (OMG)[1]. In MDA Platform-Independent Models (PIM) are the domain models. Platform-Definition Models (PDM) are the basis for translating PIMs into Platform-Specific Models (PSM). PSM can be run on their corresponding platform.

MDSD concentrates on deriving code from models. The specification (PIM, PDM, and PSM) and the code are two representations of the architecture that are independently subject to evolution and maintenance. Changes in the specification can be taken over automatically in the implementation. When the architecture changes in the implementation, these changes cannot be automatically taken over in the specification. MDSD bridges the gap between the abstraction levels of the representations, but changes can only be carried over one way, from the abstract specification to the detailed source code.

Model execution (e.g. Executable UML [3,4]) reduces the representations to the specification. The specifying model is enriched with clear semantics. Thus the models can be executed. In these approaches, typically less abstract models

---

[1] http://www.omg.org

are used, that can be easily translated into programming language semantics, e.g Unified Modeling Language (UML) class diagrams or state charts. Model execution thus does not bridge the gap between abstraction levels.

Round trip engineering describes techniques to synchronize models and code. Changes in the models can be automatically translated into the corresponding code, and changes in the code can be automatically translated into the corresponding model. The models used in round trip engineering are very detailed, technical models, e.g. UML class diagrams [7] or state charts. Round trip engineering thus allows for two-way synchronization, but does not bridge the gap between abstraction levels.

In this section we have shown that the current approaches do not solve the problem that we have identified in section 1, because the combination (1) bridging the gap between abstraction levels, and (2) allowing bi-directional synchronization between code and model, is not addressed by these approaches.

3   A Conceptual Framework for Architectures

To address the problem, we now present a conceptual framework for architectures. An overview of the artifacts of the framework and their relationships is given in figure 1. The main goal of the framework is to support the maintenance and evolution of software architectures. The development of the framework pursues three objectives:

1. It is ensured that the architecture implementation and specification are consistent.
2. The architecture can be viewed and edited using arbitrary ADLs and their respective editors, and deployed using arbitrary CMs.
3. Analyses can be performed over the architecture to evaluate its quality and validity.

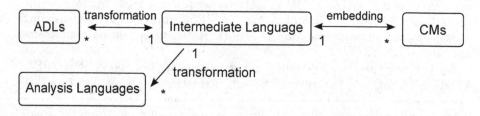

Fig. 1. Overview of the conceptual framework for architectures

The realization of objective 1 avoids that faults are introduced during maintenance and evolution. As shown in section 2, having only the specification does not solve the problem. In our framework the only persistent representation is the implementation. In our approach we assume that the architecture will be implemented using a well-defined CM, e.g. using Enterprise Java Beans [8] of the Java Enterprise Edition (JEE) [9].

CMs and ADLs differ in their features and their abstraction level (cf. [10]). CMs include implementation details, and typically only define the structure of the system formally. ADLs do not include implementation details, but typically include aspects besides the structure, e.g. behaviour or quality (cf. [10]).

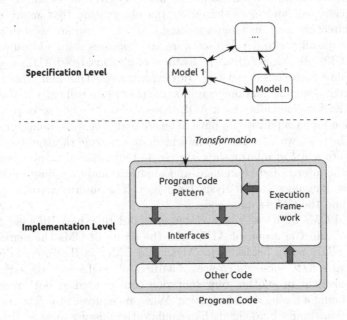

Fig. 2. An overview of the embedded models approach: Model elements are represented using program code patterns. The code patterns provide interfaces for interacting with arbitrary other code. An execution engine understands the embedded specification and executes the embedded model. (Source: [11])

To achieve objective 1, the abstract architecture information of ADLs is explicitly integrated into the source code that forms the CM. This is performed using the *embedded models* approach [11]. The architecture is thus explicitly accessible at design time and at run time and at the same time specification and implementation. In the embedded models approach rules are defined how to systematically and explicitly integrate this information into the implementation, utilizing program code patterns. Figure 2 gives an overview about the structure of the embedded models approach. Models in the specification level are transformed into program code patterns on the implementation level. In the architecture framework, the models on the specification level are the models expressed in ADLs. Program code patterns in the architecture framework are based on the patterns introduced by the CMs in use, enhanced with information that cannot be expressed in the CM, e.g. utilizing typed meta data such as annotations in Java [12]. The program code patterns provide interfaces to arbitrary program code that is not part of the architecture description, but represents the implementation details. An execution framework is used to execute the model code. In the architecture framework, the execution framework is based on the existing execution frameworks of the CMs, e.g. application servers. These have to be enhanced to understand the semantics of the embedded architecture information. An example of an embedded model is given in section 5.

The objectives 2 and 3 are based on the observation that many different ADLs, architecture analysis languages, and CMs exist and are used in practice. The framework allows to develop software architectures using almost arbitrary ADLs and CMs. To achieve this, the features of all considered ADLs need to be embedded into each considered CM. However, many ADLs and CMs exist for many different domains, and one can imagine that more will exist in the future. Defining rules for embedding each ADL in each CM does not seem realistic, as one definition for each pair would have to be created. The same holds for analysis languages. Instead, we introduce an intermediate language that reduces the $n{:}m$ relationship to a $n{:}1{:}m$ relationship. We create bidirectional mappings between ADLs and the intermediate language, and unidirectional mappings between the intermediate language and analysis languages. The intermediate language is embedded into the CM's source code.

ADLs and CMs both describe architectures, but they have different features (cf. [10]). Within the group of ADLs and the group of CMs the features also differ. The relationship between the ADLs and CMs via the intermediate language has to reflect these differences. Features of ADLs and CMs that have a direct equivalent in another representation can be used in both representations by defining a model transformation. When no equivalent exists, a complex transformation should be defined that emulate the missing feature, if possible. An example for a complex transformation is the feature of hierarchical architectures: In such architectures *composite* components have other components as children. These children are hidden from the parent component's context. The interfaces of parent components are delegated to their children's interfaces and vice versa. The children are interconnected via their interfaces. When an ADL is chosen that allows for hierarchical architectures and a CM is chosen that only allows flat architectures, the CM does not have a direct equivalence of the parent and child relationship. It might possible to emulate such a behaviour using only the concepts available in the CM. In that case a complex transformation can be used. If the feature cannot be emulated, the feature cannot be used in the first place. If the feature is mandatory to be used (e.g. because it is a core concept of the language), but it cannot be expressed in the second representation the representations are incompatible. This means that choosing the first representation excludes the latter from being chosen.

To consider this aspect, the meta model of the intermediate language is modular. In the framework this modularity is currently described using an orthogonal variability model (OVM) [13, p. 72ff.]. When an ADL or a CM is chosen for working with the architecture, the ADL's or CM's features define the configuration of the variability model. The variability model defines which modules in the meta model of the intermediate language are active, and which other representations are compatible. Figure 3 shows an example of this dependency: The features identified for ADLs and CMs include the variation point *Component Hierarchy*. The variation point is expressed with a triangle. The variants of this variability point are *Hierarchical* denoting a hierarchical component model, and *Flat*, denoting the absence of hierarchy. The variants are mutually exclusive, as denoted by the *[1...1]* expression at the variation point. When choosing an ADL with a hierarchical component model, the variant *Hierarchical* is activated. Consequently the reference in the meta model of the intermediate language is available.

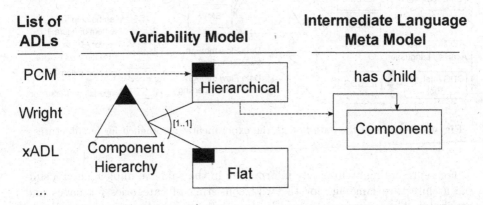

Fig. 3. The Intermediate Language has a variable meta model. Depending on the chosen ADL or CM, features of the meta model are activated or not. The dashed arrow from the list of ADLs to the variability model means that the ADL PCM has a hierarchical component model. The dashed arrow from the variability model to the meta model means that choosing the variant *hierarchical* enables the reference in the meta model.

In this section we presented our conceptual framework for ADLs. In the next section, we present an experimental workbench for architectures, which is based on this framework.

4 An Experimental Workbench for Architectures

We developed an experimental workbench for architectures based on the conceptual framework. The workbench allows to experiment with architectures, using different ADLs, CMs, and analyses. An overview of the workbench is given in figure 4. The core of the workbench is a Semantic MediaWiki (SMW)[2]. A semantic wiki contains pages with informal information enriched with typed key-value pairs of structured information (attributes). Pages can be grouped into categories. This semantic information can be subject to queries for systematically

---

[2] http://semantic-mediawiki.org

finding information in the wiki. The wiki provides flexibility in the information structure and a REST[3] [14] interface for accessing the information with arbitrary clients. This renders the SMW useful for experiments.

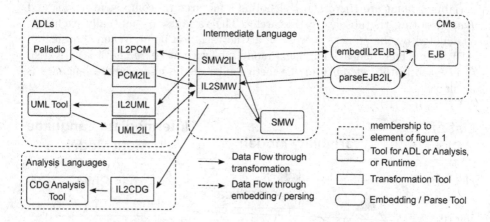

Fig. 4. Overview of the data flow in the experimental workbench for architectures

For representing architecture information in the wiki, we implemented a simple architecture language for the wiki consisting of categories for pages and attributes. The language has the role of the intermediate language in our framework. The language is presented in figure 5 and should be seen as initial approach for further experiments with the conceptual framework for architectures. The language consists of *components*, *interfaces*, and *operations*. Operations are atomic entities that have a name. Interfaces comprise a set of operations. Components have *required* and *provided* interfaces, and *common parameters*, which are required interfaces that are also provided (cf. [15]). Components instantiate child components that are identified by names. Thus a hierarchy of components is defined. Child components are connected to each other using common interfaces. This means that two components can be connected to each other when one provides the interface that the other component requires. Interfaces of children can also be delegated by the parent. A delegated provided interface is not connected to a required interface, but is provided by the parent to its context. Delegated required interfaces of children are also required by the parent. Delegated common parameters of children are common parameters of the parent. With that language, static structures of architectures can be defined. SMW allows arbitrary additional attributes to be attached to pages.

The information in the wiki can be transformed into ADLs and into analysis languages. To address ADLs we implemented bidirectional transformations between the intermediate language and a subset of the UML, and a subset of the Palladio Component Model (PCM) [16]. Despite the name "Palladio Component Model",

---

[3] Representational State Transfer.

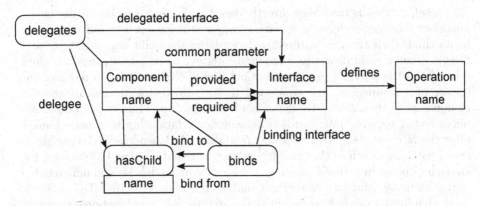

Fig. 5. The definition of the intermediate language in the semantic wiki. The rectangles represent categories of pages, with their attributes below. Rounded rectangles represent so-called internal objects. These are attributes that can take multiple values and references. The arrows between categories and between categories and internal objects are references. The role of the reference is labeled at the arrow. The line between a category and an internal object shows that the internal object is defined by the category.

the PCM is regarded as an ADL here, because it is used to describe architectures on a higher level of abstraction than the implementation code. We can thus transform architectures defined in the wiki into these languages, and use their respective editors to modify the architecture. In the case of PCM, the Palladio Simulator[4] can also be used to execute performance tests on the architecture. These tests require more information than the current intermediate language provides. When this information is given in PCM, and the architecture is transformed into the intermediate language, this additional information is added to the respective pages using attributes. Currently that information remains unused in other representations.

To realize the transformation, we parse the wiki data and store it as an Ecore model. Ecore is the meta model used in the Eclipse Modeling Framework (EMF) [17]. For UML an Ecore meta model exists in the Eclipse UML2 project[5]. The PCM meta model is also defined in Ecore using EMF (cf. [18]). The transformations between the Ecore models is realized with ATL, the model-to-model transformation tool of the Eclipse Modeling Project[6].

To address analysis languages, a unidirectional transformation has been developed from the intermediate language to a simple component dependency graph (CDG). The CDG is a directed graph that consists of *components* and *dependency* relations between the components. Figure 6 shows an example of an architecture and its CDG. The dependency relationship from component *Shop* to

---

[4] http://www.palladio-simulator.com

[5] http://www.eclipse.org/modeling/mdt/?project=uml2#uml2

[6] http://www.eclipse.org/modeling/

ShoppingCart means that *Shop* directly depends on *ShoppingCart*. A direct dependency is defined as follows: When a component delegates a provided interface to its child, then the parent directly depends on the child (e.g. *WebShop* and *Shop*). When a child delegates a required interface to its parent, then the child depends on the parent (e.g. *ShoppingCart* and *WebShop*. When a required interface of a component *A* is connected to the provided equivalent of another component *B*, then *A* directly depends on *B* (e.g. *Shop* and *ShoppingCart*. An unconnected required interface is a dependency relationship to a node named after the interface (e.g. *WebShop* and *IDatabase*. A dependency relationship is typed with the interface that the dependency is based on. The CDG allows for analyzing the architecture regarding cycles in the dependencies and unreachable components, by using standard graph analysis techniques. As the CDG does not carry all information that is relevant to the architecture, a bidirectional transformation is not possible. To realize the transformation between the intermediate language and the CDG, we use the model transformation tool ATL. The CDG is realized as an Ecore model.

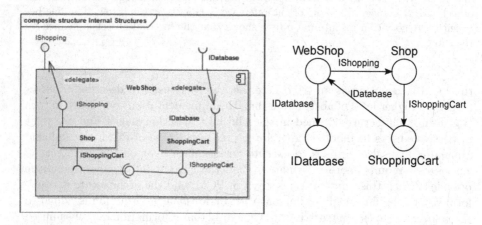

Fig. 6. The left side shows an example architecture expressed in UML. The right side shows its component dependency graph.

For executing the architectures defined in the intermediate language, we embedded the intermediate language into Enterprise Java Beans (EJB) [8]. The embedding ensures that the architecture definition is correctly and precisely implemented, and that changes to the implemented architecture can be included in the architecture definition in the wiki. In the following, the embedding of the language shown in figure 5 is described.

The component in the intermediate language is a page with a name. In EJB, we chose to use singleton beans as components. Singleton beans exist exactly once during the run time of the system. Using more than one component instance is not possible using this pattern. The pattern is shown in figure 7.

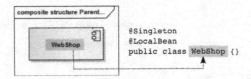

Fig. 7. The pattern for a component

Figure 8 shows the patterns for required and provided interfaces as well as common parameters of components. Provided interfaces are represented as EJB bean interfaces. Required interfaces are represented as required bean interfaces. These required bean interfaces are injected by the execution environment. Common parameters are interfaces that are required and provided. Thus the interface operations delegate the execution to the required interface. The pattern for an interface and its operation is not shown. They are represented as interfaces and their operations in Java.

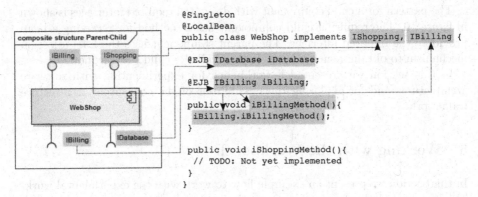

Fig. 8. The pattern for required and provided interfaces, and common parameters of components

Figure 9 shows the pattern for child components with delegated provided interfaces and delegated common parameter interfaces. Child components are are injected to the parent using the EJB injection mechanism. Children and their interfaces are in a Java package named after the parent. In addition to the pattern for provided interfaces, the pattern for delegated provided interfaces delegates the execution of the interface operations to the child component. Delegated common parameter interfaces also use this pattern, but additionally define and call a method of the child component that provides to the child the reference to the implementing bean.

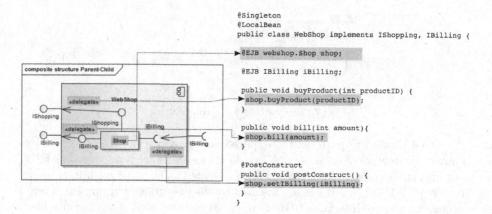

Fig. 9. The pattern for child components with delegated provided and common parameter interfaces

The pattern for a child component with delegated required interfaces is shown in figure 10. The requiring child component has a method for receiving a bean providing the required interface. The parent component uses the EJB injection mechanism to obtain a such a bean. It then calls its child's setter method.

In this section we presented a workbench for experimenting with software architectures and for exploring the possibilities of the conceptual architecture framework.

5   Working with the Workbench

In this section we present an example how to work with the experimental workbench presented above. The transformation and embedding steps are not shown in this example because they are executed by command line programs. As a first step we implemented a small example architecture in UML using the Eclipse UML tool. The example architecture is shown on the left side of figure 11. It contains the composite component *WebShop* that provides the interface *IShopping* and requires the interface *IDatabase*. The interface *IBilling* is a common parameter. The interface *IShopping* and the common parameter *IBilling* are delegated to the child component *Shop*. Another child component is *Shopping-Cart*, which requires the interface *IDatabase*. This requirement is delegated to the parent component. *Shop* and *ShoppingCart* are connected by the interface *IShoppingCart*.

The architecture is then transformed into the intermediate language in the SMW. Figure 12 shows a screenshot of the *WebShop* component representation in the SMW. The presentation of the data can be arbitrarily designed. As the next step, the architecture is embedded into EJB source code. The representation of the parent component in the resulting source code is shown on the right side of figure 11.

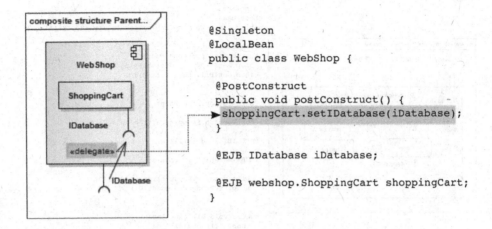

Fig. 10. The pattern for a component with a delegated required interface

During the evolution of the system a change in the architecture takes place: The common parameter *IBilling* is now a provided interface delegated to a new child component *Billing*. The change happens in the source code of the EJB component model. The UML model and the EJB implementation of the new architecture are shown in figure 13. The right side of the figure shows the changed EJB implementation. After transforming the embedded model into UML via the intermediate language, the new architecture can be seen in UML on the left side of figure 13.

6   Discussion

In this section we discuss our ongoing work regarding the conceptual framework and the experimental workbench, and the results presented in this paper.

6.1   Conceptual Framework

With the framework we strive to achieve three objectives. The first objective is to ensure that the architecture implementation and specification are consistent. To achieve this objective we use bidirectional transformations between ADLs and the intermediate language, and the embedded models approach to integrate the architectural information in the intermediate language with the source code of CMs. Both techniques can be used to transfer information consistently. The model transformation is a deeply researched and well understood field. However, one has still to be careful when defining bidirectional transformations. Some languages might have features that are hard to integrate with the features of other languages. The embedded models approach is not that mature. Embedded models are currently only researched regarding behavioural models, specifically state machines and process models. Architecture definitions are more complex

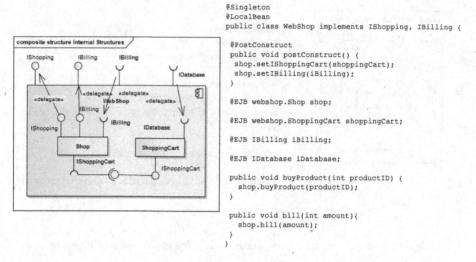

```
@Singleton
@LocalBean
public class WebShop implements IShopping, IBilling {

  @PostConstruct
  public void postConstruct() {
    shop.setIShoppingCart(shoppingCart);
    shop.setIBilling(iBilling);
  }

  @EJB webshop.Shop shop;

  @EJB webshop.ShoppingCart shoppingCart;

  @EJB IBilling iBilling;

  @EJB IDatabase iDatabase;

  public void buyProduct(int productID) {
    shop.buyProduct(productID);
  }

  public void bill(int amount){
    shop.bill(amount);
  }
}
```

Fig. 11. The example architecture in UML on the left side, and embedded into EJB on the right side

than these models. Behavioural models are just one aspect of software architecture. Several viewpoints have also to be considered, e.g. static and dynamic structure, communication, deployment, and quality aspects. The complexity of architectural description is a challenge yet to address in the embedded models approach.

The second objective is that the architecture can be viewed and edited using arbitrary ADLs and their respective editors, and deployed using arbitrary CMs. This objective is addressed by the intermediate language and the bidirectional transformations between the ADLs and the intermediate language, as well as the embedded models approach. Instead of defining patterns for embedding each ADL in each CM, potentially in several programming languages, the intermediate language is embedded into the CMs, and transformations are defined between ADLs and the intermediate language. This reduces the effort for adding new ADLs and CMs to work with the framework. However, the variability of the intermediate language is a challenge. ADLs and CMs have different features, and even a feature such as a component hierarchy may be differently realized. E.g. in one ADL a child component is a static component that is defined in its parent. In another ADL a child component may be a named instance of a component that is defined in the same scope as the parent. This has to be addressed when the variability model of the intermediate language is elaborated.

For the framework to be useful, it should be possible to adapt the intermediate language to further progress in the area of architecture descriptions. To achieve this, the intermediate language should be modular and thus allow extensions in the future.

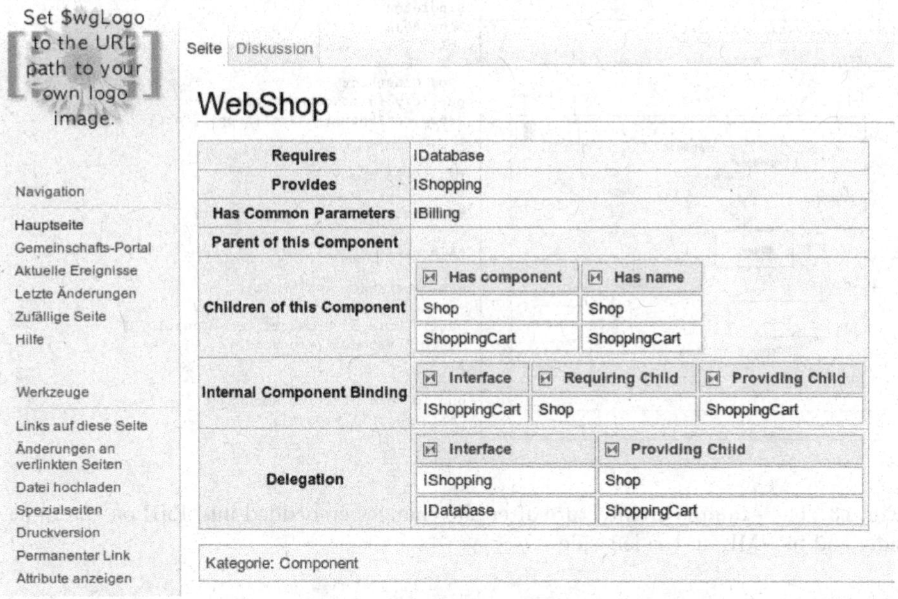

Fig. 12. The *WebShop* component of the example architecture in the SMW

The third objective is that analyses can be performed over the architecture to evaluate its quality and validity. This is addressed by defining unidirectional transformations between the intermediate language and analysis languages. Some types of analysis can also be performed using ADLs, e.g. performance analyses using the PCM. Some kinds of analysis can also be performed using the implementation. E.g. stress tests using the embedded architecture and a stress test driver. Here complex dependencies may be introduced for executing such analyses: Some analyses, such as performance tests require detailed information about the system's behaviour and e.g. its deployment. Such information is only available from some ADLs. These complex dependencies can be addressed by identifying which variants of the meta model of the intermediate language are necessary for an analysis language.

As we elaborated, the objectives stated in the beginning of this paper are addressed and it seems we can successfully achieve the objectives. However, we have found challenges to reach the objectives we have identified, that are addressed in our ongoing work.

6.2   Experimental Workbench

The experimental workbench has been developed to experiment with, evaluate, and refine the framework. The use of the SMW is helpful for testing new language constructs, because it allows arbitrary data to be added to pages. However, the language presented in this paper is far from being useful for realistic case studies

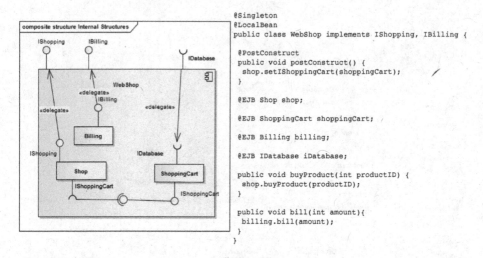

Fig. 13. The example architecture after the changes embedded into EJB on the right side, and in UML on the left side

and needs to be refined. Also, the variability aspect of the intermediate language is currently not taken into account in the SMW.

The architecture representation in the SMW contradicts the idea to have only one persistent representation, because the architecture is persistent in the code and in the SMW. In the long run, the SMW should not store persistent architecture information. Instead, a transformation (bi- or unidirectional) could be developed from the intermediate language that is embedded in a CM to the SMW in terms of an ADL or analysis language. The SMW could provide a good basis for documenting the architecture, as it allows for arbitrary information to be added to elements, including informal text and figures.

7   Conclusion

We have presented our approach that helps to avoid faults due to inconsistencies between architecture specifications and their implementation. In contrast to related work shown in section 2, our approach is based on the idea to have only the source code as persistent representation of the architecture, while still bridging the gap between the different abstraction levels of the specification and the implementation of software architecture. Using the embedded models approach, the architecture information is explicitly integrated in the source code and accessible at design and run time. The conceptual framework allows for modifying the architecture with arbitrary Architecture Description Languages and Component Models, as long as transformations and embedding mechanisms have been defined for these languages. The modeled architecture can be analyzed using languages that are embodied in the framework using transformations. An intermediate language has been introduced to reduce the effort of defining transformations between architecture descriptions.

We have also presented an experimental workbench for architectures that is based on the conceptual framework. The workbench allows for experimenting with architectures, and elaborate the framework. It uses a semantic wiki as a core, that contains the architectural information and allows for arbitrary extensions of the intermediate language. The workbench also includes a set of programs to transform the architecture information into ADLs and analysis languages, and to embed the architecture in CMs. Currently the workbench supports a subset of UML and the Palladio Component Model as ADLs, a component dependency graph as analysis language, and an embedding into Enterprise Java Beans as Component Model. We showed how to use the workbench in a simple example.

As future work we plan to address the challenges identified in the discussion in section 6. In addition, we plan to develop a tool suite for unifying the definition of transformations between the intermediate language and ADLs and analysis languages. We also want to research more deeply the possible patterns and mechanisms for embedding architecture information. Another challenge is the question, how to manage the architecture when in one system more than one ADL or CM is used.

References

1. Taylor, R.N., Medvidovic, N., Dashofy, E.M.: Software Architecture: Foundations, Theory, and Practice. Wiley Publishing (2009)
2. Brown, A., Conallen, J., Tropeano, D.: Introduction: Models, Modeling, and Model-Driven Architecture (MDA) Model-Driven Software Development. In: Beydeda, S., Book, M., Gruhn, V. (eds.) Model-Driven Software Development, pp. 1–16. Springer, Berlin (2005)
3. Luz, M.P., da Silva, A.R.: Executing UML Models. In: 3rd Workshop in Software Model Engineering, WiSME 2004 (2004)
4. Mellor, S.J., Balcer, M.: Executable UML: A Foundation for Model-Driven Architectures. Addison-Wesley Longman Publishing Co., Inc., Boston (2002)
5. Nickel, U.A., Niere, J., Wadsack, J.P., Zündorf, A.: Roundtrip Engineering with FUJABA. In: Proc of 2nd Workshop on Software-Reengineering (WSR), Bad Honnef, Germany (2000)
6. Mukerji, J., Miller, J.: Technical Guide to Model Driven Architecture: The MDA Guide v1.0.1. Technical report (2003)
7. OMG: OMG Unified Modeling LanguageTM (OMG UML), Superstructure, Version 2.4.1, Object Management Group (August 2011)
8. Sun Microsystems, Inc.: JSR 318: Enterprise JavaBeans™3.1 (December 2009), http://jcp.org/en/jsr/detail?id=318
9. Sun Microsystems, Inc.: JSR 316: Java™Platform, Enterprise Edition 6 (Java EE 6) Specification (December 2009), http://jcp.org/en/jsr/detail?id=316
10. Müller, M., Balz, M., Goedicke, M.: Representing Formal Component Models in OSGi. In: Engels, G., Luckey, M., Schäfer, W. (eds.) Software Engineering. LNI, vol. 159, pp. 45–56. GI (2010)

11. Balz, M.: Embedding Model Specifications in Object-Oriented Program Code: A Bottom-up Approach for Model-based Software Development. PhD thesis, Universitat Duisburg-Essen (May 2011)
12. Sun Microsystems, Inc.: JSR 175: A Metadata Facility for the Java^{TM} Programming Language (2004), http://jcp.org/en/jsr/detail?id=175
13. Pohl, K., Böckle, G., van der Linden, F.: Software product line engineering - foundations, principles, and techniques. Springer (2005)
14. Fielding, R.T.: Architectural Styles and the Design of Network-based Software Architectures. PhD thesis, University of California, Irvine (2000), http://www.ics.uci.edu/~fielding/pubs/dissertation/top.htm
15. Schumann, H., Goedicke, M.: Component-oriented software development with pi. Technical Report 1/94, Department of Mathematics and Computer Science, University of Essen (1994)
16. Reussner, R., Becker, S., Happe, J., Koziolek, H., Krogmann, K., Kuperberg, M.: The Palladio Component Model. Technical report, Chair for Software Design & Quality (SDQ), University of Karlsruhe (TH), Germany (May 2007)
17. Steinberg, D., Budinsky, F., Paternostro, M., Merks, E.: EMF: Eclipse Modeling Framework 2.0, 2nd edn. Addison-Wesley Professional (2009)
18. Becker, S., Koziolek, H., Reussner, R.: Model-Based Performance Prediction with the Palladio Component Model. In: Proceedings of the 6th International Workshop on Software and Performance, WOSP 2007, pp. 54–65. ACM, New York (2007)

Virtual Computing:
The Emperor's New Clothes?

Djamshid Tavangarian

University of Rostock
Research Group Computer Architecture
Rostock / Germany
djamshid.tavangarian@uni-rostock.de

Abstract. Recently, advances in networks, processors and storages for computer architectures have affected computer organization systems leading to a me-
tamorphose of traditional systems. The increasing demands for well adapted
computer infrastructure and different services along with advances in IT industry have motivated researchers to extend the possibilities of virtuality and virtual mechanism in a wide area of computing problems in order to better respond
to daily work and business opportunities to produce high quality services and
products. Therefore, we call all these processes *Virtual Computing (VC)*. In this
paper, a thorough survey of VC is presented including definitions, characteristics, challenges, issues, and novel potentials to enhance organization methods in
the field of computer architecture. Exemplarily, we describe two application
fields, energy efficiency and cloud security, to demonstrate new ways of optimization of overall system's architectures using virtualization.

Keywords: Virtualization, Virtual Processors and Storages, Virtual Organization, ICT, Collaborative Networks.

1 Introduction

Virtualization and concepts of virtualization have been existed for many decades.
Today, they are used in many technical and non-technical disciplines. There are different and sometimes very complex concepts, projects and products with a variety of
features available. Virtual machines, virtual environment, virtual society, virtual mobility, virtual life, virtual money etc. are a few examples in a wide range of application fields. Gartner`s Hype Cycle for Virtualization covers the most important topics
of it and their technical processes as well as the short and long term developments of
virtualization [1] [2] [3].

In the field of computing, virtualization is the creation of a virtual rather than a
physical version of particular components or processes. Virtualization technologies
are used to combine or divide resources to realize transparent operation environments,
such as hardware (e.g. servers, storage devices or network resources, etc.) and software (e.g. operating systems, applications, drivers, etc.) partitioning or aggregation,

M. Heisel (Ed.): Krämer Festschrift, LNCS 7365, pp. 53–70, 2012.

partial or complete machine simulation, emulation, time-sharing, resource sharing, etc. and also important applications like server consolidation, storage virtualization, supporting multiple operating systems, system migration, increase in energy efficiency, secure computing platforms, etc. [4]. These concepts and technologies are based on the underlying physical architectures and their organizational principles on different abstraction levels.

This paper will present an overview of the most important known methods of virtualization and new possibilities of virtualization for modern technological developments in the field of computer architectures and analyze the important features. It will show novel potentials to enhance new computing systems and their respective architectures and services. Exemplarily, the paper describes two application fields to demonstrate new ways of optimization of overall system's architectures using virtualization. The first one focuses on energy efficient system organization for computing centers and cloud computing infrastructure under consideration of whole components in environments like server, storage, and network consolidation, etc. The second one introduces some basic concepts to realize a novel kind of secure data storage in a cloud computing environment using virtualization technologies. Furthermore, the paper demonstrates the increase of efficiency by applying virtualization in the two presented fields.

2   Abstraction Levels

We describe a computer, like all complicated systems, at different abstraction levels. The levels reach from the view of the simple-minded user down to the level of the hardware and circuits and physics lying underneath. The great success in the use of computers is that the operation of a computer in one of that levels is extensively regardless of the underneath lying levels. Therefore, a user must only know the level which is relevant for him. For example, a user of a word processing system needs no programming or operating system knowledge and a programmer does not need to know the logic structure (gates or flip flops) of the hardware by which his program is carried out. This fact is important for virtualization because virtualization processes can be accomplished transparently for the users in several levels. Each level has different criteria with advantages and disadvantages [20].

The advantage of abstraction is for example the upward compatibility to save the portability of applications, which allows for instance the use of available programs on a new computer.

The architecture of computing systems generally consists of the hardware that actually executes instructions, system software, which represents the organization of the system, and the applications to execute user´s tasks (Fig. 1). Therefore, there are several different logical levels of abstraction regarding the existing software in computer architectures. Looking at the levels from top to bottom, the abstraction decreases and more and more details of a specific computer become visible.

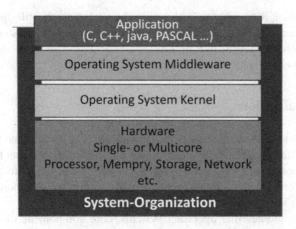

Fig. 1. Abstraction levels in a computer system

At application or user level, the programs present the user application with a customized appearance to the user's task. At this level, the software developers use high-level languages (such as C, C++, C#, Pascal, Java etc.). A high level programming language can be mapped with a different compiler to the given or to another machine where it should show the same behavior. In this case, the term *source compatibility* is used.

The operating system (OS) level consists of software which provides the basic functions for the operation of a computer [12]. It manages resources such as memory, input and output devices and controls the execution of programs. The OS thus forms the link between the computer hardware and the user's application software. Virtualization inside an OS is used for different processes like virtual processes, virtual timer etc. In this paper, we will discuss the whole virtualization of an OS.

The kernel of an OS is its central component. In the kernel, the process and data organization is determined to have a basis for the execution of all other software components of the operating system. The kernel is the lowest software layer of the system and has direct access to the hardware. Common requirements for a core system are parallel processing of different tasks (multitasking), adherence to time-critical limits, openness to diverse applications and extensions. Parts not associated with the kernel are called *userland*.

High level programming languages have relatively little to do with the underlying machine. A compiler generated from the high-level language programs into to a machine executable instructions which corresponds to the mnemonic instruction of the machine.

The hardware of the system consists of one (single-core) or more processors (multi-core processor), different kinds of memory and storages, network and I/O units for data transfer and communication with the outside world.

The system organization consists of programs and tools belonging to all abstraction levels to operate and control all sequences and processes related to the architecture of the system. It can be extended by different tools resulting from virtualization processes.

A virtualization is possible in each level. The next chapters will discuss the different virtualization concepts for hardware levels, like processor and storage, as well as the different software levels, like application or operation system level. However, first we will define virtualization and the features of virtualization.

3   Virtualization

The primary goal of *virtualization* is the decoupling of software from the hardware to be able to allocate the available resources of the individual systems to a given task. So, virtualization is a technique for mapping of the logical functions into to physical structures of computing resources to simplify the way in which other systems, applications, or end users interact with those resources. It is also a hiding of the physical characters of resources like operating systems, core components of CPU, memory, disk space, network connectivity, etc. for better organization of systems. Virtualization allows the placement of specific virtual environments, from which each of it contains only the necessary services for their task. With the virtualization, it is possible to get defined system environments for the execution of a given task [1] [3].

Virtualization of IT components makes it possible to transparent by increase the efficiency, flexibility and availability of computing systems. Thus, on one physical machine a web server, a mail server, and an FTP server can run at the same time. But for security reasons this is generally not recommended. If one of the three services is compromised, the entire server will be affected. However, if each of these services has the own virtual machine, isolated from others on the same physical server, it is only the affected virtual machine to be replaced. A further advantage is server consolidation. The virtual machines are assigned exactly the resources needed for a particular task. Changed requirements do not require changing the hardware [11].

In the context of virtualization often the term *emulation* is used. Emulation is defined as the functional reproduction of a system by another one. The new system receives the same data, executes the same programs and achieves the same results as the original system. Thus, an emulator is a system that imitates another. The emulated system is not isolated while operated, so it is not a virtualization. Examples here are commercial emulators such as DOSBox or the free projects QEMU and Bochs Plex86 [32] [33] [34]. The difference is that they emulate the complete hardware of a PC, which normally needs huge computing power.

In contrast to (hardware) emulation, the *para-virtualization* provides interfaces to the physical hardware. The critical CPU instructions, which respond directly to the hardware, must first be rewritten in the host system and therefore need not be intercepted and replaced by more elaborate procedures. A lean program, the *hypervisor* (*virtual machine monitor*, *VMM*), is responsible for the scheduling tasks and resources of the virtual machine [2] [6] [13]. The disadvantage is that the guest operating systems must be adapted. Only processors with hardware virtualization technology (Intel's Vanderpool, AMD's Pacifica) allow running of unmodified guest systems. This is called the *full virtualization* or some time as *hardware-assisted virtualization*. The latter is not to be confused with the hardware emulation. One advantage of full virtualization and especially para-virtualization is the much higher execution speed.

Another advantage is the live migration of virtual machines from one host system to another, which is important for server virtualization. The guest systems are continuously available, even if one of the hosts must be shut down for maintenance.

There are two types of hypervisor:

The *type-1 hypervisor* runs directly on the hardware and provides the guest systems with the available resources. Typical examples are Xen (open source), VMware ESX and Microsoft Hyper-V.

The *type-2 hypervisor* runs on an operating system that provides I/O resources. A typical example is the Kernel-based Virtual Machine (KVM). KVM supports full virtualization. Full Virtualization supports different systems like VirtualBox, VMware Player, VMware Workstation and VMware Server.

There are different types of virtualization regarding the levels of abstraction, which can partly be combined with each other and differ in the technical concepts. In the following chapters we will discuss such most important virtualization concepts which we will use for an optimization of selected systems and applications.

3.1　Server Virtualization

The *server virtualization* plays an important role and is the basis for a wide range of applications from demand-oriented IT to cloud computing [13] [25]. The concepts for server virtualization, also called partitioning, can be divided into two basic layers of virtualization (Fig. 2, Fig. 3):

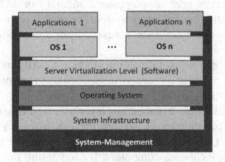

Fig. 2. Server virtualization

- the server virtualization software as a platform with the different operating systems above the virtualization software (Fig. 2) and
- operating systems of the applications above a substrate.

Both types can be combined.

In the first case, *virtual servers*, the virtualization can be implemented directly on the system operation system and the relating hardware platform (Fig. 2). The result of this virtualization is called *virtual machines* (*VM*). In many cases, these virtual servers inherit properties of the underlying physical hardware. Some of these properties are for example processor type, bit-orientation in main memory, and the type of I/O adapter cards. Such virtual servers can be installed for different types of available operating systems. Each virtual machine is an instance of the physical machine that gives users an illusion of accessing the physical machine directly. It represents also a fully protected and isolated copy of the underlying system.

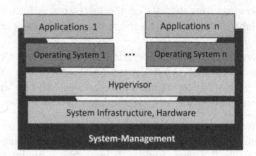

Fig. 3. Hypervisor-based server virtualization

The next case of virtualization, hypervisor-based virtualization, is implemented at a hardware level virtualization layer that can run on the guest operating systems (Fig. 3). The virtualization layer implements functions exclusively for the assignment of physical resources to virtual servers. It runs directly on the real hardware. If the appropriate processor technology supports several levels of privileges, they can achieve a very good isolation of the virtual server.

Fine-grained resources such as processors, memory or I/O adapters can thereby (often without rebooting the operating system) be added or removed. In some cases, the runtime environments control the accesses from a common pool of resources to achieve a balanced load.

A disadvantage is that, depending on the product, a partly modification of the guest operating system is necessary (para-virtualization). As mentioned before, modern processors support virtualization in hardware.

The *physical partitioning virtualization layer* as a next possibility of server virtualization enables the partitioning of servers through a separation of the underlying physical assemblies. Compute cluster architecture is an example for such systems with parallel working local-area computers. By separating the real components, they are fully isolated and cannot interfere with each other. Individual components, e.g. systems consisting of processors and memory units can be dynamically and/or remotely added or removed without rebooting the operating system.

3.2 Application Virtualization

The main purpose of application virtualization (Fig. 4) is to isolate applications from their surroundings so that no conflicts with other programs or the operating system occur [5]. This simplifies system management and improves security. Application virtualization software which runs in data centers looks as locally installed applications on the desktop machine. These applications are running against each other in isolated environments. Since only a small number of operating system instances is needed, usually the system overhead compared to the hypervisor-based virtualization solution can be reduced. In the application virtualization is possible that multiple, mutually isolated applications run on a shared (virtualized multitasking) operating system (Fig. 4b, 4c). Also an application virtualization is possible in a cluster architecture, e.g. in the remote computing center of a cloud (Fig. 4c).

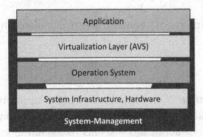 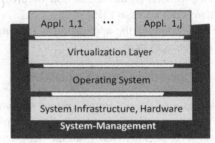

a.) Application virtualization in a desktop system, e. g. with the help of application virtual software (AVS)

b.) Application multitasking virtualization

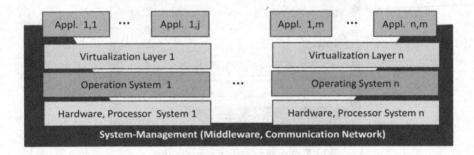

c.) Application virtualization in a cluster architecture

Fig. 4. Different categories of application virtualization

For the virtualization layer usually an Application Virtualization Software (AVS) is used (Fig. 4a). This software controls access to external objects, devices, and system resources like registry database or file systems [36] [37]. If the application tries to write in a locked directory, access is either blocked or redirected transparently to the application in a virtual environment. Physically, the virtual application is in a directory that is usually set in the configuration. When the virtualization layer is turned off, the application disappears and all of changes made by application.

The degree of virtualization is different for different solutions. For some products, it is possible to define the extent of isolation. For example, it can often define which directories are excluded from virtualization. For example, the user directory can be released for write access, so the user can store files on his PC.

The most known examples are java virtual machine (JVM) and .Net common language runtime (CLR).

The difference to desktop and server virtualization is that the hardware is virtualized by a "native" operating system, but that only one abstraction layer between applications and the operating system will be necessary. In contrast to traditional desktop programs, an installation of programs on the native underlying operating system is not necessary (Fig. 4a).

In all solutions the application is running in an environment which is isolated by the operating system.

3.3   Operating System Virtualization

In the case of the *operating system virtualization* (OS Virtualization), the kernel of the operating system will be installed in a position to create multiple isolated environments (Fig. 5). This view from the perspective of applications seems like stand-alone operating systems but in fact it runs on the same OS [9] [10] [38].

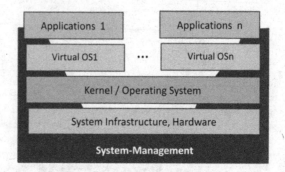

Fig. 5. Operation system virtualization

A virtualized operating system provides isolated environments. It is available and looks from the perspective of the application as own operating system. The virtual environments inherit properties and functions of the underlying operating system, such as the version of the operating system, patch levels or system libraries. The environments are independent name spaces, file systems, users, software installation and network addresses.

3.4   Storage Virtualization

Storage virtualization extends the storage environment with a logical, virtual layer that decouples the data storage of user's application from the physical architecture [8] [35] [38]. In a storage network using virtualization, the memory components can be transparently added or removed without the running processes (user's work or applications) are affected thereby. This makes it possible to divide or combine storage sub-devices and memory components, regardless of the limits and structure of given hardware. With storage virtualization the user gets better utilization of storage spaces and more flexibility; it makes maintenance easier; removing a disk from a RAID [40] system without data loss or execution interruptions, backup and data migration can be simplified, control of access rights and the organization of the storage environment is practicable, etc. All these factors can be addressed by means of virtualization according to content rather than on the technical features.

While virtualization hides the complexity of the technical storage infrastructure from users, applications, and administrators, the use as well as the administration of the system is greatly simplified. This is particularly true for very large storage environments such as Storage Attached Networks (SAN): SANs often have historically grown over the years, thus created a heterogeneous infrastructure. With proper techniques of storage virtualization, e.g. by special controllers, heterogeneous environment can be consolidated through integration of all components and subsystems to a large storage system which virtually can be seen as a homogeneous system. Often this is also the only economical way to resolve interoperability issues between systems from different vendors or with different technical realizations.

Due to the complexity of today's storage systems, the storage virtualization techniques are implemented at different levels and with different techniques. A small selection of such methods are: host-based as a function of the operating system, e.g. as a file system or logical volume manager, as RAID controllers implemented inside the storage devices, network-based systems, e.g. a Fiber Channel protocol with a mix of hardware, networking of storage subsystems and its software implementation. With SANs, depending on where the virtualization layer is placed three approaches are common: integrated into the SAN within dedicated virtualization servers (in-band approach), decoupled from the memory stream of the LAN (Out-of-band) or in intelligent switches.

3.5   Multi-core Processor Virtualization

Today, multi-core processors, as dual- or quad-core processors, are a part of usual servers, desktops, mobile devices like tabs and smart phones. The penetration of this new generation of processors increases continuously in the area of complex and software-intensive systems.

Virtualization and multi-core processors fit together well: virtualized systems can be almost completely equipped with one or more separate CPU core(s). Thus, there is less mutual influence, and each system can utilize the present hardware fully. For this Intel and AMD introduced an additional, higher privileged mode called *root mode*. This mode has more rights than the known user and kernel modes. This additional layer controls the virtualization and allows that a (normal) operating system does not notice it. At the same time, it allows the hardware implementation (Intel-VT or AMD-V) efficient use of all available CPU cores.

This layer be used to control the usage model, the visibility of the existing interfaces, and the emulation of any other devices as a console port for network communication, etc. The root mode virtualization allows completely new application scenarios that were previously not impossible.

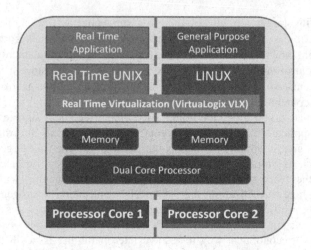

Fig. 6. Using a multi-core processor for real time application

An interesting topic is the use of different operating systems for the entire system. Here, several sub-systems (real-time systems included) control various aspects of the overall solution while they are running on the same hardware (Fig. 6). This can separate working areas. Therefore, the reliability of the overall system is increased. If an error occurred, the influence of it is locally oriented because a complete application with various tasks runs on a single and separate part of the hardware on different virtual machines. In addition, the underlying operating systems can be optimized for the given tasks, and it may remain in spite of various requirements in only one common device.

Another field is the virtualization of real time applications using several cores within a multi-core. At first impression, we can say that real-time and multi-core produce conflict in general. This is due to the fact that the real-time support of a system is defined as the possibility that the period between the occurrence of an event and the system's response to this incident has to be calculated. With multicore processors, this calculation is difficult because the equation gets additional parameters:

- *System Architecture:* depending on the configuration with two or more processors, it should be noted that the response time of some parameters such as memory allocation and cache architecture (cache alignment, cache, location etc.) is hard to calculate.
- *Real Parallelism:* unlike in the past, processes in the system are no longer pseudo-parallel, but actually executed in parallel. This requires finer granularity and improved locking mechanisms. Finally, functions can now be run truly parallel, offset only by a few op-codes on different cores. Thus, the same interrupt service routine can for example be executed in parallel.

These additional parameters introduce a chaotic moment in the calculations, which becomes almost insurmountable. Hardware virtualization solves this dilemma: A real-time hypervisor allows the real-time operating system to use one of the cores, while the other cores are available for standard operating system. This can be ensured by a clean separation between the control and user interface. However, hardware virtualization is not possible without loss of time. Thus, always remains the task to test the end system and to ensure correct response times. In general, virtualization with the high performance of modern CPUs and chipsets permits to take its full advantage.

4   Applications Using Virtualization

There are a huge number of virtualization methods in all abstraction levels of computing system architectures. Meanwhile, we generally know how virtualization works and which benefits we can get using various virtualization methods. In the above chapters we discussed some selected and the commonly used virtualization methods using the today's available modern hardware environments with muticore processors and structured storages. Recently, the virtualizations are used to optimize the systems regarding different aspects like energy consumption, security, transparency etc. In the following we will discuss some of the applications and concepts using virtualization methods to improve the system characteristics.

4.1   Server Virtualization for Energy Improvement in Computing Centers

Many data and computing centers (DCCs) use virtualization techniques for efficient utilization of modern server resources. Migrating virtual machines across physical hosts is a powerful strategy to facilitate fault management and system maintenance in such virtualized environments. Currently often manual migration of virtual machines is employed in data centers. Automatic live migration for moving virtual machines during runtime between physical hosts in an automatic manner might be a technology with a multitude of use cases in future data centers.

Modern data centers deploy virtualization for several components, such as servers, network, and storage [11]. Server virtualization, which can be seen as a technique for aggregating several virtual machines on a small number of physical servers, is able to execute different operating systems and application software. But especially this advantage of virtualization – the improved utilization of hardware by running many virtual machines (VMs) on less physical hosts – is also its disadvantage [13]: If there are problems with one physical host, these problems affect many virtual servers usually implying service downtimes. Even if the administrator wants to change a hardware component of the physical host or the entire host itself, there may occur a service downtime of many virtual machines [16].

To reduce or even avoid such problems, migration techniques are commonly used in current data and computing centers [17]. But we can use such advantages resulting of an combination of virtualization and dynamic and life migration for different applications, e.g. to improve energy efficiency in a DCC because energy consumption of DCCs has been increasing continuously during the last years due to rising demands of computational power especially in current Grid- and Cloud-Computing systems.

One promising approach of reducing this energy consumption is the consolidation of servers by virtualization. Many low loaded computer systems are virtualized and run on few physical servers to reduce the number of energy-consuming computers by turning off the empty servers. At present, this consolidation is usually done statically, thus, the administrator of a DCC manually migrates many virtual machines with low load onto one physical server which may lead to overload when the workload rises unexpectedly. Dynamic server migration that adapts to the number of running physical machines to the current workload overcomes these problems. Physical machines can be highly loaded and in case of further rising load virtual machines are migrated to other physical server systems that have been switched on. Such dynamic load aggregation approaches are rarely used and typically only consider few criteria for migration. A classification of migration criteria for live migration of a virtual machine in load aggregation environments and proposals for an algorithm for combining many different kinds of migration criteria to a clustering-based metric are presented in [17]. Thus, the novel load aggregation algorithm optimizes energy consumption as well as other migration criteria like runtime performance of applications. The migration related criteria have been categorized in that concept into four classes that have been the basis for developing a clustering algorithm to optimize distribution of applications (in this case in form of virtual machines) to physical machines. The clustering algorithm targets a minimal number of physical machines hosting all virtual machines and also examines relationships between machines that improve the execution time by employing hardware or software properties like e.g. communication between applications of different virtual machines. As a result it is possible to optimize the energy efficiency up to 50 % in a data and computing center.

4.2   Energy Optimized Storage Systems

A new method regarding the storage organization for better energy efficiency in a data center with the help of virtualization uses the following important characters of the stored data: the stored data can be divided into several different categories. According to our investigations in one of our running projects [17], we could for an example state that over 50% of data are not used for longer periods, like 3 months or more (long term date). Approximately 30% of the data are accessed in medium periods, like between 6 weeks to 3 months (medium term data). In fact, only a small proportion (approximately 20%) is used more frequently (short time data). Such percentages of those parts are dynamic and differ from one application to other but similar in magnitude. Therefore, in an application with such data structure it is possible to organize the storage architecture in three virtualized partitions for both read and write operations. The first partition, the smallest but the fastest part of the storage, will be used for the short term data. This partition is realized e.g. with Solid-State-Drives (SSDs) which are faster but more expensive than disk drives. The second partition with a medium size of storage and medium access time, like fast disk drives, is used for the medium term data. The third partition of the storage with the biggest storage capacity but cheap storages is used for the long term data. This form of organization results in a hierarchical structure of the storage (Fig. 7), we call it *Hierarchical Storage Virtualization (HSV)*. The virtualization layer consists of a directory with all necessary information about the usage of data and makes data access transparent for the processors and the whole system.

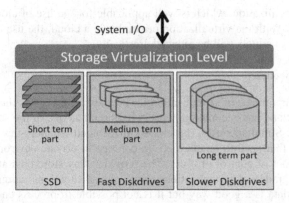

Fig. 7. The Architecture of a Hierarchical Storage Virtualization (HSV)

To save energy, we can turn off the long term part of the storage. If the data from this partition are to be accessed, the storage part is turned on. The short term part is realized with SSD components which are very fast in comparison to the next parts which are disk drives. So it is possible to get better energy efficiency of the storage combined with in general better I/O performance. Depending on the dimensions of the data in medium part of the storage it is possible to put it in standby mode which leads to less energy consumption but to faster wake up process.

4.3   Cloud Virtualization

Cloud computing is a popular concept of information technology, which is becoming increasingly important. Actually, cloud computing concepts do not belong to new technologies but it rather integrates all aspects and links of distributed computing e.g. virtualization, management, billing, etc. in a holistic approach for different applications.

One aspect is the abstraction of applications, tools, services, and physical infrastructure. For users and clients, the cloud provides SLAs (System Level Agreements) which define availability, performance, response times, and cost as primary criteria. The management, remote access, and proper operation of the infrastructure, resources and/or applications are in responsibility of the cloud provider. The cloud infrastructure is both local (as private cloud) and remote (as public cloud), or combination of both (hybrid cloud), for example a combination of customer's own data center as well as the external computing facilities on the Internet.

In addition, this operation concept of the cloud infrastructure allows scaling the resources dynamically and demand-oriented to help adapting any existing bottlenecks and/or peak performance requirements. This on-demand approach refers not only to resources on the hardware environment but also on the dynamic provision of infrastructure, software components, or applications in all areas.

The application fields of virtualization in cloud computing are e.g. server virtualization, virtualization of collection of servers, desktop virtualization, storage virtualization, and application virtualization. Virtualization for cloud computing offers excellent starting points for the consolidation of the infrastructure. It is especially usable for commercial and enterprise applications. According to IDC, for example, the desktop virtualization, which is well applicable for the use of cloud, will become very important. With the virtualization principles in a cloud, the use of resources and the work with computers will be reduced drastically.

4.4   Cloud Security

The growing importance of virtualization for business processes is the subject of safety management and has become immensely important as one of the success factors of the cloud [39]. Simultaneously, the cloud's distributed technologies have additional security issues that need to be clarified. In contrast to private environments, the data in a cloud are out of control of users. The provider may store data around the world with different grades of virtualizations, laws, social situations, administrations, etc. Encryption of data is a good way but it is not possible to process encrypted data for calculations. The data have to be decrypted before processing within a program on the computing infrastructure of the cloud. Therefore, we need additional and/or alternative methods for user's data and processes within virtualized environments which run fully under user's control.

In this chapter, we will introduce new ideas and procedures for a comprehensive coverage of security issues in a cloud environment with decentralized and remotely accessible appliances and computers. The approach refers to three sections, each to be implemented systematically by the appropriate components and processes:

- **Security of Stored User Data**

    Security of user data can be achieved by new models and algorithms in their storing process. These algorithms use splitting methods of user data regardless of encryptions. Encryption can take place as usual. The algorithms for data-splitting therefore offer new ways to provide additional security. For data security, the data are extended by a partitioned data structure. A small but important part is stored in the local area (private cloud, desktop, mobile device etc.). The large remainder is stored in the central virtual area (Fig. 8). In the central virtual area the data are not complete. If the user needs the data, the remote data will be accessed to complete the whole data in the private part and to process all data together. To process the data in the cloud the next section will give more details.

- Structured Partitioning
    Original data
    Central stored data
    Locally stored data

- Unstructured Partitioning
    Original data
    Central stored data
    Locally stored data

Fig. 8. Partitioning regarding to the stripping with regular and irregular (random) data portions

A partitioning can be done by a stripping and/or selection. By stripping the data is partitioned with regular or irregular repeats (Fig. 8). Here, the selected data items are separated and stored in the local area. The rest is stored in the central area (Fig. 8). Selection means to select the most important parts of the data which should be stored in the home area. For an automation of the selection process special algorithms are needed.

- **Security of Applications**

The security of an application during execution is carried out with the help of a so-called splitting of software structures of an application and runs as a virtual distributed program. This is an application divided into several parts and spread under full control of the user running. Few by user defined or selected processes can run on the user's local computer and the rest of the processes run on the central computers. Thus, it is not possible to determine which parts are already processed or what kind of results have emerged.

In general, the application can be executed over Internet, in a distributed environment on local computer systems (desktop, mobile appliances, server farms, clusters, multiprocessor systems, etc.) and on the central infrastructure.

The processing of an application is divided between a bigger part in the central infrastructure and a smaller part in the local computers according to their available resources (processing power, memory, and communication bandwidth). The aim is to prevent the complete execution of the application in the central region so that a tracking of the processes in the central region (which is out of user's control) is avoided. The full results are available in the local part only. In case of a clever partitioning of the applications, no sufficient results in the central area are available for third parties. For this approach, the application is to be prepared to allow the user to choose proper portions of the program (Fig. 9).

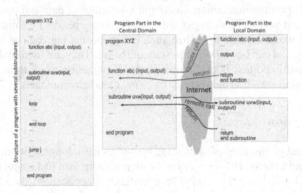

Fig. 9. Distributed execution of a program with the help of Remote Procedure Calls

The program section in the central area includes functions and subroutine calls but they run in the local area. The routines are placed in the local area. The calls can be made, for example, by remote procedure calls. When calling and at the end of the processes, only the subroutine's input and output parameters are transferred. Regarding to the data partitioning described in the above section the most important data is placed in the local part for further local processing.

To automate the process, some research and development works are needed. The most important question is to find solutions which are very individual for the customer of a cloud. But in principal it is possible to choose an arbitrary part of a program and convert it to a subroutine with some extensions to deliver the necessary parameters for an execution in the local area. We are currently working on these topics with good expectations.

- **Communication Channel**

  The communication channel is the third sensitive part of security. A sensitive data transfer is normally done between local computers and the cloud via Internet as a point-to-point communication. With the same philosophy, we divide the data to be transferred in several (e.g. two) parts. One part consists of security information for safety-relevant data (especially keywords) and another part are the working data which are user's encrypted data. The transmission will be executed over separate channels with different technologies and providers. For example the smaller part, the key words, are transmitted by a channel with lower bandwidth (like UMTS, GSM, etc.). The encrypted data are transmitted by a broadband channel (Wi-Fi, DSL, etc.). This results in an addition to the previously known encryption method that enhances the security of data transfer to a large extent.

  This approach is principally not new and is used in several areas, for example, in the area of telebanking with mobile TANs. The mobile TANs are, in context of the data encryption for the cloud, the keywords. Furthermore, there are also protocols that were developed specifically for such applications, such as multi-homing process, and SCTP (Stream Control Transport Protocol). This reflected the nature of the use and sharing of data into a new model for improving the security of data transmission.

A combination of all three methods, data partitioning, program partitioning, and communication channel partitioning, delivers a complex structure of data and process organization which make it very difficult to get sensible processing results for third parties. There are more R&D works needed to realize such environments but each of the above methods are known and can be classified as state of the art. They are used in different applications. The most important R&D subject is the combination of all three concepts in a virtualized world to get a holistic security for using cloud environments.

5   Conclusion

Virtualization and partitioning of computing resources has a long tradition, especially for mainframe manufacturers. However, virtualization is more than just a new term for existing concepts because it covers a much broader field of applications than before. Meanwhile, all operating system vendors want such capabilities in their systems because virtualization is a powerful concept to realize easy environments for the users who work with applications. Therefore, from the user's view virtualization can be understood as abstraction of tasks. The user is able to focus on own applications independently from the hardware and software as well as from the place of the application and if necessary without long installation procedures.

The potential of virtualization is great in the field of computing. Meanwhile we have different methods and broad areas which are using virtualization in several contexts. Therefore, we can say that we currently have a research field named virtual computing which uses the known methods of virtualization (old clothes) to find alternative ways, concepts, and algorithms (tailoring new *real* clothes!) for optimizing and realization of new and available systems.

In this paper, we introduced the most important examples of virtualization methods using computers. Based on that, we discussed the optimization of two important application and problem areas (enhancement of energy efficiency in computing and data center and cloud security with the help of virtualization in their virtual worlds). Both application areas will deliver new research aspects and new benefits for users as well as for vendors.

We think there are many additional scientific fields which are candidates for the optimization and/or realization of systems using virtualization. For example, it is possible to extend the above described methods of energy efficiency in computing centers to the software of an application or to the software and structure of operating systems to get more energy efficient systems. So we hold the belief that such a paper could actually stimulate the readers to analyze new developments in the area of virtualization, use of it and help put them in perspective.

References

1. Wolf, C., Halter, E.M.: Virtualization: From the Desktop to the Enterprise. Apress (2005)
2. Kelbley, J., Sterling, M., Stewart, A.: Hyper-V: Insider's Guide to Microsoft's Hypervisor. NetApp (2009)
3. Nanda, S., Chiueh, T.: A Survey on Virtualization Technologies (2005), http://www.ecsl.cs.sunysb.edu/tr/TR179.pdf
4. White, J., Pilbeam, A.: A Survey of Virtualization Technologies With Performance Testing (2010), http://arxiv.org/abs/1010.3233
5. Application virtualization, Softricity, http://www.softricity.com/products/systemguard.asp
6. Windows Server 2008 Hyper-V: Insider's Guide to Microsoft's Hypervisor, MS (2009)
7. Gartners Hype Cycle Virtualization, http://virtualization.info/en/news/2010/09/paper-gartner-hype-cycle-for-virtualization-2010.html
8. Massiglia, P., Bunn, F.: Virtual Storage Redefined. Technologies And Applications For Storage Virtualization. Veritas Software Corporation (2003)
9. Surbone, L.M., et al.: Operating System-Level Virtualization. Alphascript (2009)
10. Barham, P.: Xen and the art of virtualization. In: Symposium on Operating Systems Principles. ACM Press (2003)
11. Huff, M.: Why Virtualize? Whitepaper (January 2009), http://www.technologent.com/Documents/WhyVirtualizev_Jan09.pdf
12. Silberschatz, A., Galvin, P.B., Gagne, G.: Operating System Concepts, 6th edn. John Wiley & Sons, Inc. (2002)
13. Beckereit, F., et al.: Server-Virtualisierung 1-3, Bitkom (2009)
14. Rose, R.: Survey of System Virtualization Techniques, http://citeseer.ist.psu.edu/720518.html
15. Xenoppix (2004), http://unit.aist.go.jp/itri/knoppix/xen/indexen.html
16. VMware Inc. How VMware Virtualization Right-sizes IT Infrastructure to Reduce Power Consumption (2008)

17. Versick, D., Tavangarian, D.: Reducing Energy Consumption by Load Aggregation with an Optimized Dynamic Live Migration of Virtual Machines. In: Proceedings of the 2010 International Conference on P2P, Parallel, Grid, Cloud and Internet Computing, pp. 164–170. IEEE (2010)
18. Usermode Linux Community Pages, http://usermodelinux.org/
19. Usermode Linux, http://usermodelinux.sourceforge.net/
20. Xen, http://www.cl.cam.ac.uk/Research/SRG/netos/xen/index
21. Kramer, J.: Abstraction – the key to Computing,
    http://www.sofismo.ch/links/kramer-abstraction.pdf
22. XenSource, http://www.xensource.com/
23. Litke, A., et al.: Managing service level agreement contracts in OGSA-based Grids. Future Generation Computer Systems, vol. 4(4). Elsevier (2008)
24. MacLaren, J.: Towards Service Level Agreement Based Scheduling on the Grid, rpc48.cs.man.ac.uk (2004)
25. Steinder, M., et al.: Server virtualization in autonomic management of heterogeneous workloads. In: 10th IFIP/IEEE International Symposium on Integrated Network Management, IM 2007, Munich (2007)
26. Mosharaf, N.M., Chowdhury, K., Boutaba, R.: A survey of network virtualization. The International Journal of Computer and Telecommunications Networking 54(5) (2010)
27. Semnanian, A.A., et al.: Virtualization Technology and its Impact on Computer Hardware Architecture. In: 8th International Conference on Information Technology New Generations (ITNG), as New Generations (ITNG), Las Vegas (2011)
28. Connectivity in the Virtualized Datacenter: How to Ensure Next-Generation Services, Fluke (2010),
    http://www.broadcom.com/collateral/wp/
    Virtualization-WP300-R.pdf
29. Virtualisierung mit Xen,
    http://hssonne.cs.unisb.de:8080/lehrstuhl/SS2005/Seminar_Akt
    uelle_Technologien/library/03_Ebert_RamanauskasSoftwareVirtu
    alisierung.pdf
30. Rimal, B.P., et al.: A Taxonomy and Survey of Cloud Computing Systems. In: 5th International Joint Conference on INC, IMS and IDC, Seoul (2009)
31. Hilbrich, R., Gerlach, M.: Virtualisierung bei Eingebetteten Multicore Systemen: Integration und Isolation sicherheitskritischer Funktionen. In: 4th International Workshop on Multicore Software Engineering, IWMSE 2011, Waikiki, Honolulu (2011)
32. http://qemu-buch.de/
33. Culler, D., Singh, J.P., Gupta, A.: Parallel Computer Architecture: A Hardware/Software Approach. The Kaufmann Series in Computer Architecture and Design (1998)
34. Staunstrup, J., Wolf, W.: Hardware/Software Co-Design: Principles and Practice. Springer (2010)
35. Tanenbaum, A.S.: Modern Operating Systems, 2nd edn. Prentice Hall (2001)
36. Zheng, R., Liao, X.: A Novel Virtual Grid Experiment Method in MedIm Grid. In: IEEE/IFIP International Conference on Embedded and Ubiquitous Computing, EUC 2008 (2008)
37. http://hdsurvivor.blogspot.com/2006/10/application-
    virtualization-future-of.html
38. Laadan, O., Nieh, J.: Operating System Virtualization: Practice and Experience, CS Columbia (2008), http://systems.cs.columbia.edu/files/wpid-systor
    2010-osvirt.pdf
39. Müller, K.R.: IT-Sicherheit mit System. Springer (2011)
40. Patterson, D.A., Chen, P., Gibson, G., Katz, R.H.: Introduction to redundant arrays of inexpensive disks (RAID), COMPCON Spring 1989. IEEE (1989)

Linked Compute Units and Linked Experiments: Using Topology and Orchestration Technology for Flexible Support of Scientific Applications

Frank Leymann

Institute of Architecture of Application Systems (IAAS)
Universität Stuttgart
Leymann@iaas.uni-stuttgart.de

Abstract. Being able to run and manage applications in different environments (especially in clouds) is an urgent requirement in industry. Such portability requires a standard language to define both, the structure of an application as well as its management behavior. This paper sketches the main ingredients of such a language and explains its underlying concepts. Next, the concept of linked compute units is introduced providing verifiability of the results of data-intense work. Considering human beings in this concept results in linked social compute units. The benefits of describing scientific applications by this concept are worked out. The resulting vision of being able to run in silico experiments everywhere and its supporting high-level architecture is presented.

1 Introduction

The extensive focus on data is a major shift in science [HTT09]. This data must be shared and often connected with other data sources in order to allow reproducibility of research results [HB11]. In case data has been produced by software (like simulation software, for example) making this software (publicly) available and linking it to this data and also to the input data sources will significantly increase the reproducibility of research results. For this purpose, this software and all its prerequisites (i.e. the overall *application*) must be defined accordingly.

The definition of an application can be done based on a standard specification language called TOSCA (Topology and Orchestration Specification for Cloud Applications) [TOSCA]. The specification not only allows defining the structure of an application (its so-called *topology*) but also its management behavior (by means of so-called *plans*). Plans are workflows (a.k.a. *orchestrations* in the SOA domain) that realize functionality like (i) provisioning an application, i.e. installing, deploying and configuring all of its associated software components and setting up its infrastructure, (ii) updating selected components, or (iii) moving data associated with the application or some of its components. The topology, its associated plans, and the artifacts required to actually run the overall software is included in a corresponding *package*. Thus, a package not only contains the software of the actual business logic of interest, but also all prerequisite software (or links to this software, respectively).

M. Heisel (Ed.): Krämer Festschrift, LNCS 7365, pp. 71–80, 2012.

In cases in which data has been produced or has to be analyzed by software, linking the package of this software to the data extends the model of linked data with infrastructure elements required to produce or verify the data; we call this extended model *linked compute units*. Especially in data-intense science linked compute units provide a significant step forward towards reproducibility of scientific results. Linked compute units will also contribute to significantly increase trust in research results that are based on data and simulations. By also considering humans involved we present the concept of linked experiments that additionally support folding in skills etc required to solve a data- or compute-intense scientific problem.

2   TOSCA Conceptual Overview

The Topology and Orchestration Specification for Cloud Applications (TOSCA) is a language to define both, the overall structure of an application as well as its management behavior in a format called *service template* (see Figure 1).

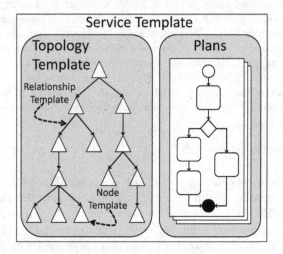

Fig. 1. Structure of a Service Definition

The overall structure of an application is defined as a *topology template*. A topology template describes all the kinds of ingredients of an application (so-called *node templates*) as well as the kinds of relations between these ingredients (so-called *relationship templates*). Node templates are considered as vertices and relationship templates as edges of an acyclic directed graph that make up the topology of an application. Examples of node templates are programs encoding the logic of a proper application, a JEE container for a program (that is offered as an EJB), a database system required by the program as persistent store, data definition scripts to set up the database structure of the program in the database system, and an operating system for the JEE container as well as for the database system. Examples of relationship templates are deployed_in specifying that a program is deployed in a JEE container, or hosted_by specifying that a JEE container is hosted by an operating system. Both, node templates as well as relationship templates are typed by referring to corresponding node types and relationship types; we ignore this indirection here for the sake of conciseness.

Node templates are descriptions of the ingredients of an application, but they are not the actual ingredients themselves. Basically, a node template defines the potential properties of an actual ingredient as well as the operations that can be used to manage the ingredient. In order to materialize such an actual ingredient the corresponding node template must be instantiated. When instantiating a node template its properties get values assigned. For example, a node template representing a JEE container has an IP_Address property; when instantiating the node template the corresponding JEE container receives a concrete IP address. Also, the cardinality of a node template within a topology template is defined. This cardinality controls the minimum and maximum number of instances of that node template in an instance of the topology template. For example, a service template may define that its included JEE container has a cardinality of 2 to 5 instances. Instantiating a service template means to set the cardinalities of the node templates of its topology template, and to set the properties of the instances of these node templates.

Node templates have an interface that describes the operations made available by a node template for the purpose of managing its instances. For example, the JEE container node template has operations for starting and stopping its instances, for deploying a program on them and so on. These operations can be invoked by tasks of plans (see Figure 2) of a containing service template for managing the instances of its node templates individually, and, thus, for managing corresponding applications (i.e. instances of a topology template) as a whole.

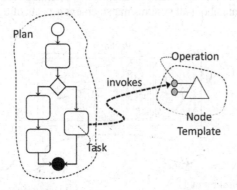

Fig. 2. Relation Between Tasks and Operations

A *plan* is a workflow that executes in the context of an instance of a service template, e.g. it has access to the actual property values of the instances of the node templates of the topology template. More precisely, the tasks that make up a plan use the operations of the interfaces of the node templates of the topology template. Such a task passes input to an operation, thus triggering actions on an instance of a node template. On completion of the operation it passes its output back to the task, such that this data is available for further tasks of the plan. For example, a task may use the deploy() operation of the JEE container node template passing as input both, the identifier of the concrete JEE container on which an EJB should be deployed as well as the EJB itself; the `deploy()` operation returns the actual state of the deployed EJB.

In order to create an instance of an application described by a service template a special plan called *build plan* must be run. The build plan orchestrates the actions required to create the instances of the node templates by invoking proper operations, setting values of the properties of the node templates by passing the actual values as parameters of the operations, running tasks repetitively in order to reflect the cardinalities specified for certain node templates in a topology template etc. In general, the values to be passed to the operations may come from various sources: for example, some values may be contained in the input message starting the build plan, or the build plan itself may contain tasks that interact with human beings requesting corresponding values, respectively. Once the build plan completes successfully, the application is provisioned and can be used. While the application is provisioned several maintenance actions might be required: for example, the database underlying the application must be backed up, or a fix to the underlying operating system must be applied. These kinds of maintenance actions are performed by plans that are collectively referred to as *management plans*. Finally, when the application should be de-provisioned a *termination plan* is performed.

Typically, people (like system administrators) understanding the overall structure of an application and its needs in terms of management and administration specify both, its topology template as well as its plans. Application developers focus on the logic aspects of an application, often passing management requirements to administrators as well as structural information about the application. Sometimes, the roles of developers and administrators may coincide: for example scientific applications are often developed by people that also take care about all systems management aspects of it.

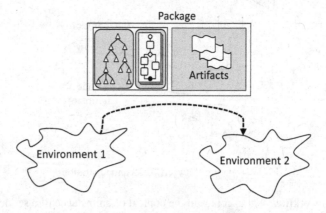

Fig. 3. Packages and Their Exchange

Once the service template of an application has been specified, the artifacts required to execute and manage the application have to be identified. For example, the code of the application logic might be an EJB, the implementation of the operations of the JEE container might be a JAR file, or the implementation of the operating system might be in a virtual image, respectively. All these artifacts are combined with the topology template and the plans into a *package* that can be exchanged between environments (see Figure 3). In essence, a receiving environment will parse the package, identify the contained artifacts, store them and make them available for the plans (especially the build plan), and run the build plan of the service template. After that, the application is ready for use.

The name of the specification indicates that TOSCA is applicable to cloud applications only. But this is not the case: Any kind of application can be described by TOSCA, and a corresponding package can be created. The package may then be exchanged and processed as sketched before. Neither the sending nor the receiving environment might be a cloud environment: what is required at the receiving side is a new middleware component (called *topology container*) that can receive packages, parse packages, and process them. A tooling environment to create such packages (similar to the ones described here) as well as the use of packages to support the movement of applications across environments is described in [LFM11].

Note that "exchange of packages" may have different realizations. For example, the package might be sent to the receiving environment and stored there in some sort of catalogue, for example, instead of immediately processing it. Users may browse the catalogue, find interesting packages, and ask for running the corresponding build plan (so-called "self-service"). We will discuss this kind of usage later in section 4.

3   Compute Units

The concept of a social compute unit (SCU) has been introduced in [DB11]: it is a collection of socially networked humans that provide "compute power" to solve a given problem based on the individual skills of the participating humans as well as software tools that support them. The ingredients of an SCU can be dynamically discovered, composed, and installed.

No details are given in [DB11] about how the software tools are provided, discovered, or installed. We propose to use TOSCA in order to specify the software tools (like any other application) of an SCU. Software tools can be made available as a corresponding package for being composed into an SCU. TOSCA supports the inclusion of documentation elements in each element of a service template. Such documentation elements may be used to specify metadata about the elements of service templates supporting their proper discoverability for composing SCUs. Furthermore, TOSCA is extensible, thus allowing defining new typed metadata for enhanced discoverability of software tools for an SCU. Finally, the problem of how to install software tools that are composed into an SCU now has a simple solution: the build plan of the service template of the corresponding package is executed to install (and configure...) the software tool.

In Figure 4, the social compute unit U_1 is shown. U_1 consists of three human beings one of which is linked to an application depicted as a package. A social compute unit may explicitly include all other resources (like data sets or documents) that are critical for solving the given problem. In Figure 4, we show a data set as such a resource. U_1 includes one particular data set required for solving the problem U_1 has been composed for.

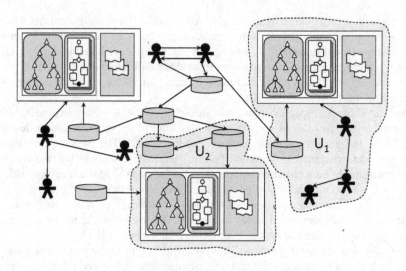

Fig. 4. Extended Social Compute Units

U_2 is another collection distinguished in Figure 4. It consists of two data sets and an application. Because this collection does not include a human being, we refer to it just as a *compute unit*. Compute units may be turned into social compute units by adding human beings to them; vice versa, social compute units can be turned into compute units by having all human beings leaving them. Thus, compute units may be perceived as granules of reuse for composing social compute units. And compute units may be considered as residuals of the work performed by social compute units. The following sections will motivate compute units and their relations to social compute units.

4   Linked Compute Units

Since centuries, the two main approaches of gaining scientific insight are performing experiments and developing theories. A few decades ago, simulations (i.e. computations) became a third established approach to cope with situations where the equations making up a theoretical model are too complicated to be solved analytically: simulations approximate solutions that are hard to determine purely analytically and, thus, gain insight based on computations – this is referred to as the 3rd paradigm of science [HTT09]. When using simulations, potentially huge data sets are often generated that must be analyzed to gain results. Similarly, using large instruments (like large telescopes or particle colliders) also results in huge data sets that are to be analyzed. Often, this analysis takes place at some later point in time, i.e. the data sets have to be maintained. Compared to simulations, which emphasize the importance of computations, large instruments emphasize data in itself as a fundamental aspect of science in addition to the software proper required for the analysis of the data. This new focus on data and the corresponding data processing pipeline is a separate approach for gaining insight, referred to as the 4th paradigm of science [HTT09].

To allow for the verification of research results that are based on data or computations, both, this data as well as all required software (like the simulation software producing the data or software for analyzing the data) must be made available: without the corresponding software, data-intense research results cannot be verified. In case data is made available, it is often associated with other data sets that also must be made available to allow for verification: for example, the data that served as input for a simulation producing the data at hand must be accessible. Furthermore, explicit relations between these data sets must be established easing the comprehension of the dependencies between the data: for example, it must be specified that one data set has been the input for a computation producing another data set. For this purpose RDF links [RDF] may be used, especially to specify the semantics of these relations. The resulting concept of data sets related to each other via links is referred to as *linked data* [HB11].

In [B06], guidelines for linking data have been provided: (i) each data set is to be identified by a URI, (ii) this URI can be dereferenced, (iii) dereferencing will return the data (ideally encoded in a standard format), and (iv) a data set provides links to its related data sets. This way, a "global data space" will evolve [HB11]. Thus, a scientist has to identify all relevant data via a URI. This URI must in fact be a URL that allows using the protocol of its schema (e.g. HTTP, FTP) to retrieve the data, and the retrieval must return this data, ideally in a widely used format (typically dependent on the domain). Finally, the scientist establishes links between the data sets provided, also pointing to data sets that are perhaps relevant but provided by someone else.

Using the linked data concept is a key step forward towards reproducibility of data-intense research results. But what is still missing in this concept is making the software available that is required for reproducibility (e.g. software for the generation, analysis, visualization etc of data). We propose to make this software available as packages. Similar to data, each package is identified by a URI, that can be dereferenced, which will return the package, and packages and data will be linked. What results is a compute unit introduced in the section before extended by links relating its included artifacts – we call this a *linked compute unit*.

This way, data and corresponding software is jointly published. By adding corresponding links the relations between data and software is specified. To verify (or audit...) research results a single URI is required that provides "the entry" into this collection. Based on this entry URI all the other entities required for the verification can be discovered by following links: a link originating at an entity points to another entity by specifying the URI of its target. This URI is dereferencable, i.e. the entity identified by the URI can be retrieved; this link may be source of further links that can be followed again, etc. If a URI identifies data this data can be retrieved; if a URI identifies a package (of an application, software, computation...) this package can be retrieved and "installed". "Installation" basically means to drop the package into a topology container (cf. section 2) that will process it: i.e. the topology container will identify the build plan of the package and run the build plan resulting in an installed (i.e. ready to execute) instance of the corresponding application (or software, computation...). Figure 5 illustrates this. The application may now be used with data sets D_1 and D_2 as input, as specified by the linked compute unit U. This situation would correspond to $D'_1=D_1$ and $D'_2=D_2$; for successful verification the expectation is $D'_3=D_3$. But of course the application can be used with other input data (i.e. $D'_1 \neq D_1$ or $D'_2 \neq D_2$) producing new results establishing trust in the application itself, or producing new insight, respectively.

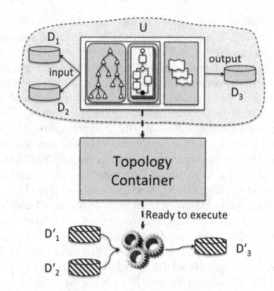

Fig. 5. Processing Linked Compute Units

5   Linked Experiments

Often, when data is produced in experiments human beings must collaborate. For example, astronomers configure a large telescope, database engineers define strategies to store and maintain the captured data, software engineers change or develop software to analyze the captured data at a later point in time, physicists discuss the analysis results of the data, mathematicians determine proper parameterization of simulation runs, and so on. Typically, such people are specialized having dedicated skills and a corresponding team must be discovered and composed: thus, these people match the concept of a social compute unit [DB11].

We propose to identify people of a social compute unit by means of URIs too. Also, people are linked expressing relationships between them or the other ingredients of the social compute unit. For example, a person might be linked to a package indicating that this person has created the package; a person might be linked to a data set specifying that this person owns and maintains the data set; two people might be linked expressing that the first person requires input by the second person; and so on. Note, that instead of a concrete person being a member of a social compute unit an abstract role may be defined. Such a role may again be identified by a URI, which is dereferencable. When dereferenced, a description of the kind of person required (e.g. in terms of skills need) is returned. By adding people or roles to a linked compute unit and linking these people or roles to the other ingredients of the linked compute unit a *linked social compute unit* results.

A linked social compute unit may be seen as a template for solving problems that require the combined power of socially networked humans, software tools, and data resources. Allocating the required people, installing the software tools, and making the data resources available can solve "an instance" of the problem. "Allocating people" means to either request the identified person directly or to first discover team candidates by means of the criteria specified in a role definition and requesting one of them to join the team in a second step. "Installing a software tool" means to install the derefenced package as described before. "Making data available" means to dereference the identified data source.

When work is performed within an instance of the problem new data may be produced and added to the linked social compute unit as well as linked to other elements of the linked social compute unit. Also, some team members may leave the linked social compute unit, others might join. This way, a linked social compute unit is dynamic. The fact that URIs uniquely identify all elements of a linked social compute unit makes it easily traceable, i.e. the elements leaving or joining it are canonically identified (and are dereferencable). Once the problem has been solved, the team members might leave the linked social compute unit and a linked compute unit remains. This residual can be used later on to verify, analyze, or audit the results of the work performed.

We propose to call the application of the concept of a linked social compute unit to science a *linked experiment*. The people (either directly identified or indirectly identified via a role definition) are scientists or other people required to perform an experiment. The software tools are simulation packages, data analysis tools etc. The data sets are data available at the start of the experiment. When performing the experiment new data may be produced. Once the experiment is finished the remaining linked compute unit establishes trust in the scientific insight gained (as sketched before).

Both, linked experiments and linked compute units are granules of reuse. Linked compute units provide data and tools to base new experiments (or simulations etc) on. Linked experiments in addition even provide team structures that have been proven in the past to successfully perform a certain kind of experiment (or simulation etc).

In some areas of science initial steps towards realizing the concept of linked compute units are already taken. For example, the myExperiment website [myExp] shares hundreds of workflows relevant in the area of life science. A scientist may download such a workflow from the website and install it in the corresponding workflow system manually. Perhaps this requires that this workflow system first must be downloaded, installed, configured manually, which in turn might imply that the environment required by the workflow system (i.e. an application server) has to be set up before, and so on. By providing a package that includes the workflow system and its prerequisites as well as the appropriate workflows, setting up the workflow environment as well as the workflows will be a simple automated task.

Of course, this requires the ubiquitous availability of a topology container in the corresponding environment. Since this is a single component only that can bootstrap and set up all other environments provided as packages, requiring such a component is a tolerable prerequisite that supports problem solving and especially experiments.

6 Summary

The concept of linked compute units and linked social compute units introduced in this paper support both, the verifiability of results of data-driven actions as well as the reusability of proven settings in solving data-driven problems. The application of these concepts in science has been presented as linked experiments. These new concepts are based on social compute units, linked data, and topology and orchestration technology from cloud computing, which are combined to extend their area of applicability.

References

[B06]   Berners-Lee, T.: Design Issues – Linked Data, W3C (2006),
           http://www.w3.org/DesignIssues/LinkedData.html
[BPMN]   Business Process Model and Notation (BPMN) Version 2.0, OMG (2012),
           http://www.omg.org/spec/BPMN/2.0/
[DB11]   Dustdar, S., Bhattacharya, K.: The Social Compute Unit. IEEE Internet Computing 15(3) (2011)
[HB11]   Heath, T., Bizer, C.: Linked Data – Evolving the Web into a Global Data Space. Morgan & Claypool (2011)
[HTT09]   Hey, T., Tansley, S., Tolle, K.: The Fourth Paradigm – Data-intensive Scientific Discovery, Microsoft Research. Redmond, WA (2009)
[JAR]   JAR File Specification,
           http://docs.oracle.com/javase/1.4.2/docs/guide/jar/jar.html
[LFM11]   Leymann, F., Fehling, C., Mietzner, R., Nowak, A., Dustdar, S.: Moving Applications to the Cloud: An Approach based on Application Model Enrichment. International Journal of Cooperative Information Systems 20(3) (2011)
[myExp]   MyExperiment Website, http://www.myexperiment.org/workflows
[RDF]   Resource Description Framework (RDF): Concepts and Abstract Syntax, W3C (2004),
           http://www.w3.org/TR/2004/REC-rdf-concepts-20040210/
[TOSCA]   TOSCA Topology and Orchestration Specification for Cloud Applications, OASIS (2011), http://www.oasis-open.org/committees/tc_home.php?wg_abbrev=tosca

Pattern-Based Context Establishment for Service-Oriented Architectures*

Kristian Beckers, Stephan Faßbender, Maritta Heisel, and Rene Meis

paluno - The Ruhr Institute for Software Technology
University of Duisburg-Essen, Germany
firstname.lastname@paluno.uni-due.de

Abstract. A context description of a software system and its environment is essential for any given software engineering process. Requirements define statements about the environment (according to Jackson's
terminology). The context description of a Service-Oriented Architecture is difficult to provide, because of the variety of technical systems
and stakeholders involved. We present two patterns for SOA systems
and support their instantiation with a structured method. In addition,
we show how the pattern can be used in a secure service development
life-cycle.

Keywords: SOA, requirements engineering, secure software development.

1 Introduction

Nowadays Service-Oriented Architectures (*SOA*) as part of Service-Oriented
Computing (*SOC*) is a well known paradigm with raising importance [15,14].
The subject of SOC is vast and enormously complex, and SOC is based on
many concepts which have their origin in diverse disciplines. SOA and software
engineering (*SE*) for SOA are among the most important research fields for
SOC [14].

Still, there are some open issues when dealing with SOA. One of them is security [16,14]. Assurance of security of a SOA is much more complicated than for
other architectural styles. Since the single services used are normally distributed
and loosely coupled over the Internet, standardized protocols for link-up are
needed [5]. Another field for security issues is the fact that in common SOA
scenarios, not a single person or company controls all infrastructure and services
that are orchestrated [16,14]. Hence, when dealing with security for SOA, we
not only have to face the usual security problems as in other IT systems, but
additionally multilateral settings with many stakeholders in a distributed environment have to be considered, which even more complicates finding a solution.

---

* This research was partially supported by the EU project Network of Excellence on
  Engineering Secure Future Internet Software Services and Systems (NESSoS, ICT-
  2009.1.4 Trustworthy ICT, Grant No. 256980).

M. Heisel (Ed.): Krämer Festschrift, LNCS 7365, pp. 81–101, 2012.

The big number of very heterogeneous stakeholders also complicates the fulfillment other objectives, such as compliance, performance, or usability. For example, when considering compliance, each stakeholder may introduce new regulations to be met by the SOA. Such a regulation can be a law, which protects this stakeholder, or requires the stakeholder to ensure a certain functionality. Additionally, most of the stakeholders, like service providers, have a contractual relationship to the SOA to be developed. In a previous paper [3], we have argued that for legal requirements engineering, it is crucial to capture the stakeholders and the entire context of an IT system.

To sum up, from a software engineer's perspective, there is a need for a continuous and integrated method to consider multiple stakeholders and their different objectives in a SOA development life cycle. This method should be transparent in means of documentation and traceability to make it possible, for example, to trace a compliance regulation down to the measures taken to accomplish it.

This requirement sounds simple, but when looking at standard SE life cycles, such as Microsoft SDL [10] or CLASP [13], we see that there are so many steps with dependent in- and outputs to be performed, that achieving this requirement is very challenging.

Achieving transparency between requirements of a stakeholder, measures and proof that the measures have been implemented, means using methods that are aware of traceability for each activity or transformation or refinement. For some steps and some parts of, for example, security, such methods already exist, but missing an appropriate approach at one point brakes the whole trace. Hence, it is an important goal to analyze the whole SE life cycle, find the gaps and propose possibilities to bridge those gaps. It is surprising that in most cases the description of the very first steps of such a life cycle is deficient. How to capture and describe the setting of a problem and to structure the context of the system-to-be is often missing. But this information is of crucial importance for understanding the problem and performing requirements engineering.

Hence, in this paper, we focus on establishing the context of a SOA application, which forms the basis for all later development steps, especially considering security.

The rest of the paper is organized as follows. Section 2 describes a small use case in the field of media publishing, which we use to illustrate our ideas in this paper. In Sect. 3 we give a brief background about SOA and its layers. Two patterns and the corresponding textual templates are introduced in Sect. 4. The patterns and templates help to establish the context of a SOA. Section 5 introduces a method to instantiate the patterns and templates. A short overview of the application of our method to our case study is presented in Sect. 6. Finally, we outline the use of our method in the context of Microsoft SDL [10] and CLASP [13] in Sect. 7, and we give a short conclusion in Sect. 8.

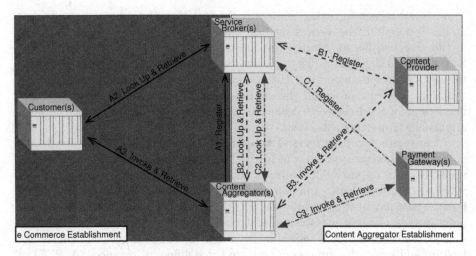

Fig. 1. SOA Scenario
A=Business Case,B=Content Provider Integration,C=Payment Gateway Integration

2   Running Example

As our running example, we have chosen a media publishing setting. In this setting, there are customers, who want to retrieve certain media. For example, this media can be a piece of software, a video or movie, a song, or an e-book. On the other side, we have various content providers. A small content provider may offer only one media type and only a small selection of media to choose from. In contrast, a big publisher usually offers all media types and a large selection of media.

The main problem in the relationship between customers and content providers is that on the one hand the customers prefer a uniform search and access interface and do not want browse a big number of different shops, with different access technologies, credentials, and so on. A second problem for customers is to oversee the whole market. Customers might not even know the right content providers for very special media. On the other hand, not all content providers are able or willing to set up and maintain a shop infrastructure with essential functionality such as billing.

The business idea of our example is to introduce a content aggregator as a mediator between these two sides. The aggregator collects the offers of different content providers. These joined offers are then made available to the customers.

The content aggregator decides to choose a SOA to realize its business, because of the dynamics in this setting. There is huge number of providers. The aggregator wants to be able to find and integrate these providers at run-time. Moreover, the access for the content providers to the content aggregator should be as simple as possible. Therefore, services are reasonable. Services enable the providers to wrap their existing technologies and use standard protocols.

A second reason for using services is the fact that the content provider has no direct access to the devices the customers use to search for media. A device in this case can be, for example, a smartphone, a settop box, or a tablet PC. So the content aggregator has to ensure that the customer can find the solution the aggregator provides. And the content aggregator has to ensure that the technology used for providing the solution can be easily adapted for each device. Services are a good choice to achieve both goals. In Sect. 3, we provide detailed arguments supporting this claim.

A last reason for using services would be the large number of different banks and online payment systems, which have to be integrated to fulfill the payment needs. But this requirement is already addressed by so-called *payment gateways*, which aggregate all banks and make payment functionalities available at a single point. These payment gateways offer their functionality also by services. At this point, we use the best practice already established in the market.

The resulting scenario is shown in Fig. 1. The figure shows the common service look up and invocation process. There are three different instances (A, B, C) of the Register, Look Up & Retrieve, and Invoke & Retrieve sequences in our scenario. The content aggregator queries a service broker to find content providers (Arrow B2 in Fig. 1) and payment gateways (C2) to establish its business. Content providers (B1) and payment gateways (C1) registered themselves at the service brokers before. At run-time, the content aggregator invokes the services of the providers (B3) and gateways (C3). Note that the set of gateways will be quite static and slowly evolving as there are not that many payment gateways, and establishing the needed service-level agreements (SLAs) and trust cannot be achieved on the fly. In contrast, the set of content providers can be different for each business process invocation. The market of providers is changing fast, and standard SLAs can be used, so service invocation can be done automatically. To realize the business case, content aggregators register their service at a service broker (A1). The customers are now able to find the aggregators (A2) and search for and retrieve (A3) the desired content.

3   Background

In this section, we give a definition of our notion of SOA and how a SOA is structured.

3.1   SOA Definition

Various definitions of SOA exist, because the SOA concept spans a wide field of research areas and technologies. However, there is a common understanding about some core characteristics of SOA. First, a SOA is modular with a high autonomy of its parts, not only in the sense of interaction within the architecture, but also in the sense of e.g. autonomous stakeholders and development teams [5,14,15]. Second, services have a coarse granularity, encapsulating more or less complex tasks. As a result, a single service is a complex product [5].

Third, SOA is process-driven [5]. In most cases, a service performs one activity of a business process [1]. Hence, a SOA has to be designed to fulfill business requirements and goals [15]. Fourth, the services of a SOA have to be loosely coupled [14]. The business processes to be supported by a SOA change frequently. In consequence, a SOA has to evolve dynamically [14]. Hence, the services are loosely coupled to enable dynamic (re)assembly. Fifth, the re-usability of services is high [15,14,1]. The re-usability is a result of the autonomy of services and the loose coupling between them. Sixth, a SOA is a distributed system [14,5]. The reasons are that business processes cross the border of one enterprise [16] and that services can be offered by third-party service providers [14]. Seventh, SOA is technology-independent [14,5]. SOA is meant to integrate highly heterogeneous services, which means that the used technologies to implement the services can differ. Summarizing, SOA can be characterized as a process driven, modular, technology-independent, dynamic and distributed system, which relies on reusable, autonomous, loosely coupled and coarse-grained services.

3.2   SOA Layers

A SOA spans different layers, shown in Fig. 2. The first and top layer is the Business Domain layer, which represents the real world. It consists of Organizations, their structure and actors, and their business relations to each other. The second layer is the Business Process layer. To run the business, certain Processes are executed. Organizations participate in these processes. A process can be executed within one organization or across organizations' borders. These processes are supported by Business Services, which form the the Business Service layer. A business service encapsulates a business function, which performs a process activity within a business process. Besides atomic business services, there are also composite business services, which rely on other business services. These services are built by composing other business services. All business services rely upon Infrastructure Services, which form the fourth layer. The infrastructure services offer the technical functions needed for the business services. These technical functions are implemented especially for the SOA or expose interfaces from the Operational Systems used in an organization. These operational systems, like databases or legacy systems, are part of the last SOA layer at the bottom of the SOA stack. Each of the presented layers in isolation is complex and a field for research on its own. Combining these layers and devising a SE method to span the layers is a great challenge in the field of SOA research [14].

4   Patterns for SOA

We now introduce two patterns, which help us to describe the setting of a SOA, namely a SOA layer pattern, and a SOA stakeholder pattern. They are used to structure the information about the problem at hand. The patterns are based on the insights we gave in Sect. 3. In Sect. 4.1, we present a pattern, which uses the SOA layers to structure the SOA itself. Based on this pattern, we present an extended pattern in Sect. 4.2, which adds different kinds of stakeholders.

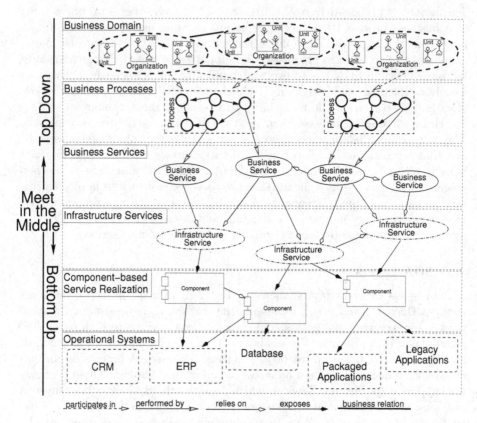

Fig. 2. SOA Layers (based on [14,2])

4.1 SOA Layer Pattern

The layers presented in Sect. 3.2 form a generic pattern to describe the essence of a SOA. Three approaches for instantiating this pattern are possible, as shown in Fig. 2. When building a SOA from scratch, a Top Down method should be used. The existing information about the organizations and processes and the related requirements can be refined to an architecture comprising business services, infrastructure services, components and operational systems. Note that for the early SE phases such as requirements engineering, not all layers are of relevance. For example, the operational systems are chosen in later phases. A Bottom Up approach is of use when evolving existing systems. When the re-description and the reuse of already productive systems is the focus, one would collect the existing artifacts in the IT landscape, describe the existing processes they support and elicit the involved organizations. For developing a new SOA based on existing systems, a Meet in the Middle method is reasonable.

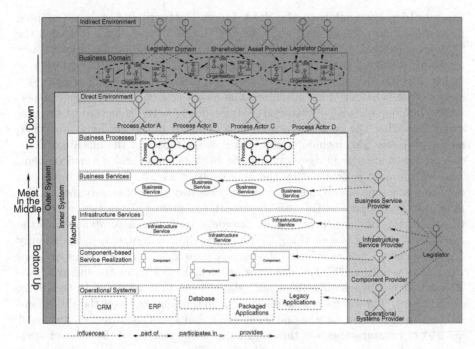

Fig. 3. Stakeholder SOA Pattern

4.2 SOA Stakeholder Pattern

An IT System is not an end in itself. It interacts with its environment and changes the environment. The way it changes the environment is based on the requirements it has to meet. The source for most of these requirements are stakeholders. There are direct stakeholders, who interact with the system, and indirect stakeholders, who do not have a direct relation to the system but to one or more direct stakeholders [7]. To know and consider all of these stakeholders is crucial for software engineering.

For a SOA, the knowledge about the environment and the stakeholders is even more a key to success than for other architectures. Conventional applications are often built for a generic use case, which was obtained by generalizing a set of usage scenarios. To use such an application, the environment has to be adapted to a generic use case. Thus, it often happens that organizations are built around their systems. Changing an organization is costly, and processes that are built to meet IT requirements are often inefficient. In contrast, one major aim of SOA is to enable organizations to build IT systems, which follow their business processes. To reach this aim, it is necessary to be able to adapt a certain single scenario and consider its peculiarities. Hence, the scenario for which a SOA is built has to be described in detail.

Stakeholder Extension to the SOA Layer Pattern. In Fig. 3, we adapted problem-based methods, such as problem frames by Jackson [9], to enrich the SOA layer pattern with its environmental context. According to Jackson's terminology, a system consists of a Machine and its environment. The white area in Fig. 3 spans the SOA layers that form the machine. The business processes describe the behavior of the machine. The business services, infrastructure services, components, and operational systems describe the structure of the machine. Note that the business processes are not part of the machine altogether, as the processes also include actors, which are not part of the machine. Thus, the processes are the bridge between the SOA machine and its environment. The environment is depicted by the gray parts of Fig. 3. Unlike Jackson, who only considers one environment, we distinguish two kinds of environments. The light gray part spans the Direct Environment, comprising all entities, which participate in the business processes or provide a part, like a component, of the machine. An *entity* is something that exits in the environment, independently of the machine or other entities. The direct environment reflects Jackson's environment definition [9]. The dark gray part in Fig. 3 spans the Indirect Environment. It comprises all entities not related to the machine but to the direct environment. The business domain layer is one bridge between the direct and indirect environment. On the one hand, some entities of the direct environment are part of organizations. On the other hand, some entities of the indirect environment influence one or more organizations. The machine and the direct environment form the Inner System, while the Outer System also includes the indirect environment.

The entities we consider in this paper are stakeholders. Information assets, for example, are put aside. There are two general classes of stakeholders [7]. The direct stakeholders are part the direct environment, and the indirect stakeholders are part of the indirect environment. We derived more specific stakeholders from the direct and indirect stakeholders, because these two classes are very generic. Process Actors and different kinds of Providers are part of the direct environment. Legislators, Domains, Shareholders and Asset Providers are part of the indirect environment. In Fig. 3, the resulting stakeholder classes are depicted as stick figures.

Process actors are part of an organization. A process actor can represent an entire organization, a role within this organization, or a specific person. This depends on the usage of the pattern and the level of detail needed when used. A process actor participates in one or more business processes. In some cases, a process actor does not only influence other actors through the process, but also influences them directly. For example, one actor can be the supervisor of another actor. This information should be elicited as it can impact the requirements one actor has. In general, process actors are the source of most of the requirements a machine has to fulfill.

In contrast, providers are stakeholders that are not directly involved in the business process. However, they provide a part of one layer within the machine. There are Business Service Providers, Infrastructure Service Providers, Component Providers and Operational Systems Providers. A provider can be a representative for a whole group of providers, or be a specific one. This also depends on the usage scenario, as for the process actors. The requirements and goals of the providers can be ignored for conventional applications. The reason is that the user of a part a provider offers gains full control of this part in traditional scenarios. For example, a development library once bought is a property of the buyers afterwards. They can change it according to their needs and can be sure that the provider has no influence on the library any longer. This scenario changes for a SOA. Providers are selected at run-time, and in most cases the parts offered by providers remain under their full control. In this scenario, the requirements, goals and other properties of those providers have to be considered. Moreover, the selection of providers can have an impact on other requirements. For example, when a certain information has to remain within one country, all providers from other countries will deny the fulfillment of this requirement. In general, providers introduce only few new requirements, but they have a large influence on already existing requirements.

Legislators represent the jurisdiction of an area. Areas can be very different in size and significance. For example, there are states, like Hessen, there are nations, like Germany, and there are unions like the European Union. The laws of such areas can be interconnected. Then they build a hierarchy with defined scopes. Or they are unrelated, and therefore they can be conflicting. The influence of a legislator is a very strong one. No organization can disobey a law without facing serious consequences. But to be compliant to laws is a complex goal. In general, laws are formulated imprecisely, defining high-level goals. Thus, for every action organizations take, they have to be aware of the relevant laws, and they have to take these laws into account for the problem at hand. For a SOA, one has to know which legislators are of relevance, which laws they enacted related to a SOA, and how to transform these laws into requirements for the SOA.

Domains represent another part of the environment of organizations. The term domain is used in the meaning of business domain. A domain comprises organizations of similar structure, purpose and goals. Domains often introduce specific regulations like standards. In some cases, these regulations are as binding as laws. Other regulations are more a kind of best practice collections. And as legislators enact laws, which aim at special domains, identifying domains helps to find relevant laws. To consider a domain is important, because describing knowledge and regulations of relevant domains sharpens the view on the organizations.

A Shareholder brings in a certain asset and gets a share of the organization in exchange. In most cases the asset is money. The exchange implies that the asset is owned by the organization afterwards. The share of the organization ensures a specified degree of influence for the shareholder. Shareholders are the primary source of business goals of an organization.

Asset Providers cede a material or immaterial asset to one or more organizations. Unlike shareholders, they remain owners of this asset, and therefore a long-term contractual relation is established. Such a contract implies a certain influence on the organization. Besides a direct relation, there are also cases where organizations have to avoid the improper use of assets they do not know beforehand. For example,when intellectual properties are stored on a file hosting platform, the filehoster must enable the owners of these intellectual properties to delete the intellectual properties. Thus, asset providers and their influence on organizations also depend on the relevant legislators.

Knowledge about Stakeholders. The pattern shown in Fig. 3 only captures an important, but small, part of the information about the stakeholders. Hence, we provide *templates* for all stakeholders to document the information to be completed. The templates are textual patterns, which structure information about stakeholders. The structure of these templates applies for all stakeholders of a given kind.

Table 1 and Table 2 show the templates. The first entries are the same for both templates. They capture the name or identifier of the stakeholder at hand, a short description to clarify its properties and position in the environment, and the motivation of interacting in our scenario. The last entry is about the level of abstraction, which is used to describe the stakeholder. Is it a specific stakeholder, who represents a group of homogeneous stakeholders, or a generic stakeholder that is used as placeholder for a group? For the direct stakeholder template (Table 2) there is an additional option for stakeholders, which describe roles within an organization.

For the indirect stakeholder template (Table 1), there are two more general entries. The first entry describes the influence the indirect stakeholder has on the target organization(s) or provider(s). The second entry describes the relation to other indirect stakeholders. Besides these general entries for an indirect stakeholder, Table 1 also shows entries, which are specific for a special kind of indirect stakeholder. For a legislator, there is an entry for the law candidates, which might be of relevance. For a domain, there is an entry about the domain-specific regulations. For shareholders, the description of the shares they own has to be added. And for the asset provider, the assets have to be described.

For the direct stakeholder template (Table 2), there are two additional stakeholder kind-specific entries. The first kind specifies the process and activities the process actors participate in. The second kind specifies the process participants that these stakeholders have a influence on.

5   A Knowledge Elicitation Method for SOA

We have developed a method to instantiate the patterns shown in Figs. 2 and 3 and the associated templates. We divide the method in an information structuring and a stakeholder elicitation phase.

Information Structuring Phase. For structuring the information necessary to design a SOA according to the SOA layer pattern (see Fig. 2), we suggest a meet in the middle procedure. The reason is that the business services and

Table 1. Template for Indirect Stakeholder

Name What is the name or identifier of the stakeholder?

Description Which important properties does the stakeholder have? What characterizes the stakeholder? What is its place in the environment?

Motivation Which objectives does the stakeholder follow? Why does the stakeholder influence the organization(s) / provider(s)?

Kind

☐ **Specific** Is the stakeholder a real entity? Is the stakeholder not used to represent a group?

☐ **Representative** Is the stakeholder a real entity? Is this stakeholder used as proxy for a group of homogeneous stakeholders?

☐ **Group** Is the stakeholder not a real entity? Is this stakeholder used to describe for a group of homogeneous stakeholders?

Influence

On	Description	Severity
Which organization / provider is influenced?	Which kind of influence? What kind of enforcement? What is the base for the influence?	What is the rating for the severity of the influence?

Relation to other stakeholders

To	Description
Which other indirect stakeholder is related to the stakeholder at hand?	Which kind of relation?

optional entries

. . . .

Law candidates *(Legislator)* Which laws which might be of relevance for the actual SOA to be developed?

Domain-specific regulations *(Domain)* Which domain-specific regulations including, for example, standards and best practice do exist?

Shares *(Shareholder)* Which kind of shares owns the shareholder? How many of them are property of the shareholder?

Assets *(Asset Provider)*

Asset	Description	Provided To
What are the assets owned by the asset provider?	What are the properties of the asset? How can it be characterized?	To which organization is the asset provided?

infrastructure services layers are intertwined with the business elements. Therefore, we need information both about the technology-related and the business-related layers. Furthermore, our method provides validity checks for the relations between the different layers.

Table 2. Template for Direct Stakeholder

Name What is the name or identifier of the stakeholder?

Description Which important properties does the stakeholder have? What characterizes the stakeholder? What is its place in the environment?

Motivation Which objectives does the stakeholder follow? Why does the stakeholder influence the organization(s) / provider(s)?

Kind

☐ **Specific** Is the stakeholder a real entity? Is the stakeholder not used to represent a group?

☐ **Representative** Is the stakeholder a real entity? Is this stakeholder used as proxy for a group of homogeneous stakeholders?

☐ **Group** Is the stakeholder not a real entity? Is this stakeholder used to describe for a group of homogeneous stakeholders?

☐ **Role** Can this stakeholder be shared through groups of heterogeneous stakeholders? Are there well-defined rights and permissions for this stakeholder?

optional entries

....

Takes Part In *(Process Actor)*

Process	Activity
In which process does the actor participate?	Which activity does the actor enact?

Influence *(Process Actor)*

On	Description
Which other actor is influenced by the actor at hand?	Which kind of influence does the actor at hand have to the target actor?

The external input for all steps of this phase (see Fig. 4) is the Unstructured Scenario Description. The SOA Layer Pattern is an additional external input for the first step Describe Organizations. It is instantiated layer by layer in separated steps, based on the Unstructured Scenario Description.

In the step Describe Organizations, we have to collect all relevant organizations. For each such organization, we have to collect statements about this organization, describing it further. Next, we have to analyze these statements if they describe business relations between organizations. Last, we have to check for inconsistencies. For example, we have to ensure that no organization is isolated. Being isolated means that there are no business relations to other organizations. In case we find an isolated organization, this organizations is either not of relevance for our scenario, or we are missing important information.

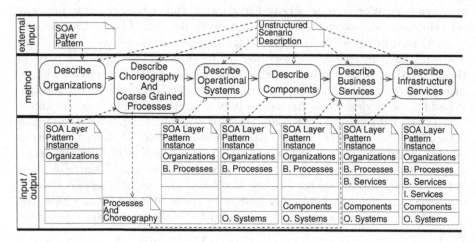

Fig. 4. Description Structuring Phase

In the next step **Describe Choreography And Coarse Grained Processes**, we have to structure the interaction between organizations. Additionally, we structure the available information about internal processes of organizations. The input for this step is the partly instantiated **SOA Layer Pattern**. We start with the organizations and their choreography. The choreography describes the interaction between the organizations. We recommend to document the choreography using an appropriate notation. For example, UML and SoaML collaboration diagrams [12] can be used. UML and SoaML activity diagrams are of use for more detailed interaction and internal process descriptions. The described processes do not have to be complete, but processes and process steps already mentioned or explained in the scenario description should be captured by such diagrams. Next, we have to ensure the coherence of the **SOA Layer Pattern** instance for finishing the step **Describe Choreography And Coarse Grained Processes**. The interactions described by the choreography should reflect the business relations found for the organizations. Moreover, the detailed process descriptions must be coherent at the points of transitions between organizations.

For the step **Describe Operational Systems**, we look for statements mentioning IT systems already used within one of the organizations. The operational systems found have to be analyzed for those, which are to be replaced, and those, which should be wrapped in the new SOA. Only the latter kind of operational system should be added to the **SOA Layer Pattern** instance.

At least one component should be described in the step **Describe Components** for each operational system. Whenever for an operational system there is no statement about a component, which should be re-used, the information is missing in the **Unstructured Scenario Description**, or the operational system is unnecessary. Note that components can exist, which are not part of an operational system, but are already mentioned in the scenario description. But to be sure not to miss any relevant operational system, for each component mentioned in the Unstructured Scenario Description, we have to check if it exposes such a system.

Up to this point, we have structured the business and the technical parts of the description. Next, we close the gap between those parts. We search for statements, which describe business services, for the step Describe Business Services. We add those services to the business service layer. For each business service, we have to check if there is a corresponding process step in the processes described in step Describe Orchestration And Coarse Grained Processes. If such an activity is missing, it should be added. Additionally we have to check if the business service at hand directly exposes a component, which is already part of the SOA Layer Pattern instance. Last, we have to check whether the business service at hand is atomic or a composition of other business services. If it is a composition, the business services used to compose it have to be added to the business service layer, too.

The procedure for Describe Infrastructure Services is almost the same. One difference is that infrastructure services are mapped to business services instead of activities within the process, and that they can be orphans. It is not necessary that an infrastructure service is used by an already known business service. The reason is that infrastructure services may provide a more general functionality.

Stakeholder Elicitation Phase. In this phase (see Fig. 5), we elicit the stakeholders of our SOA. Therefore, we inspect each element of the SOA Layer Pattern instantiated in the previous phase. First, we instantiate the direct system environment (see Fig. 3). We start with the organizations given in the SOA Layer Pattern Instance. For each process related to an organization, we identify the process actors, which act on behalf of the organization in this particular process. There has to be at least one process actor for each organization-process-relation. For all process actors, we have to instantiate the corresponding Direct Stakeholder Templates. Finally, we have to establish the relations between associated process actors.

Next, we inspect each business service, infrastructure service, component and operational system, whether there are already known provider(s) or not. When the providers are already known, we instantiate Direct Stakeholder Templates for them and add them and the corresponding relations to the SOA Stakeholder Pattern instance.

Further, we instantiate the indirect system environment. We also start with the organizations. We analyze for each organization at hand, if there are relevant legislators, domains, shareholders and asset providers. For each identified indirect stakeholder, we instantiate the corresponding Indirect Stakeholder Template, and we add the indirect stakeholder and their relations to SOA Stakeholder Pattern instance. We repeat this procedure for all providers we find in the direct system environment.

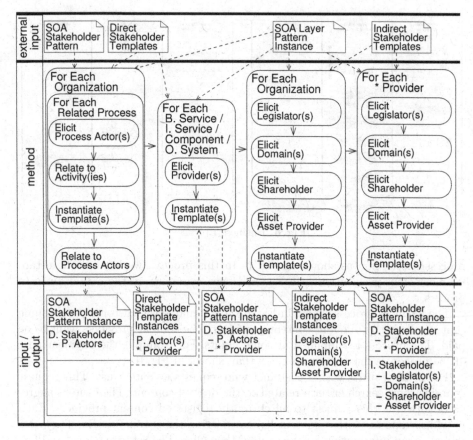

Fig. 5. Stakeholder Elicitation Phase

6 Using the Method

We now apply the presented method to the use case described in Sect. 2. We derive the organizations Customer, Content Aggregator, Content Provider and Bank from the description in Sect. 2. While the Content Aggregator only represents the specific aggregator for whom the SOA has to be developed, the other organizations represent groups. The Content Aggregator is the mediator between Customer and Content Provider. Hence, the business relations reflect this mediation. To accomplish payment, all organizations have business relations to Banks.

Next, we have to structure and describe the choreography and coarse grained processes. Figure 1 already shows a high level choreography. We refine this choreography further and find three major processes: The Content Look up process, in which Customer, Content Aggregator, and Content Provider take part, the Content Delivery process, in which also these three organizations take part, and the Content Payment process, in which all organizations take part. We refine the choreography and these major processes further and end up with an integrated

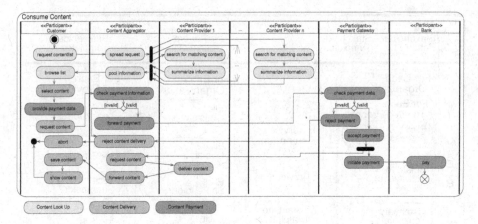

Fig. 6. Business Process

process description as shown in Fig. 6. In this process, we left out the establishment steps as mentioned in Fig. 1. Hence, we focus on the actual business process.

The business process shown in Fig. 6 should enable the customer to consume content offered by different content providers. The content providers want to be paid. The process is simplified at some points. For example, the payment part of the process is much more complex than shown in Fig. 6.

The process starts with a customer who requests a content list. This request contains some search criteria related to the desired content. The content aggregator forwards this request to all currently registered content providers. Each provider responds with a content list considering the search criteria. They also add payment information for the content they offer. The lists are pooled and forwarded to the customer. Note that for this step the activity diagram is simplified. In a real setting, there would be a need to model some sort of timeout and how to deal with it. Next, the customer selects the desired content, provides payment data, and requests the content from the aggregator. The aggregator checks if the payment information is valid. This means that a validity check is executed that decides if the order matches the payment information. If it is not valid, the content delivery is rejected. Otherwise the payment information is forwarded to the payment gateway. The gateway checks if the payment data is valid. The difference between payment data and payment information is that the payment data contains the payment information and the order data. In case the data is invalid the request is rejected and aborted. If the data is valid, the payment is initiated by the payment gateway and fulfilled by the bank. The payment gateway also acknowledges the request, and the content aggregator contacts the relevant content provider. This provider sends the requested content to the aggregator, who forwards it to the customer. The costumer saves and consumes the content.

We skip the description of the operational systems and the components, because our scenario is a new development of a SOA, and no already existing technologies are mentioned in the scenario description.

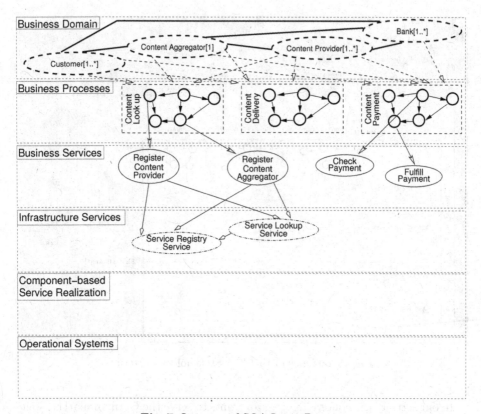

Fig. 7. Instance of SOA Layer Pattern

As mentioned business services, we find Register Content Provider, Register Content Aggregator, Check Payment, and Fulfill Payment. Register Content Provider and Register Content Aggregator rely on the infrastructure services Service Registry Service, and Service Lookup Service. All in all, we obtain the instance of the SOA Layer Pattern shown in Fig. 7.

The result of the stakeholder elicitation phase of our method (Fig. 5) is depicted in Fig. 8. For the Direct Environment, we identified four process actors and two providers. Customer, Content Provider and Bank are stakeholders representing a group. The members of these groups can change dynamically in our scenario, and the members are not that homogeneous that we can refine them further, for example, in roles. For the Content Provider we would be able to do so, but since the processes are to be designed, there is no information we can collect in this early stage. Payment Gateway and Service Broker were already mentioned in the initial unstructured scenario description, but as there is no decision for a specific provider up to this point, they also represent groups.

For the Indirect Environment we identify Germany, Europe and the USA as legislators, Media and Finance as domains, and GEMA, VG Wort and Content Owner as asset providers.

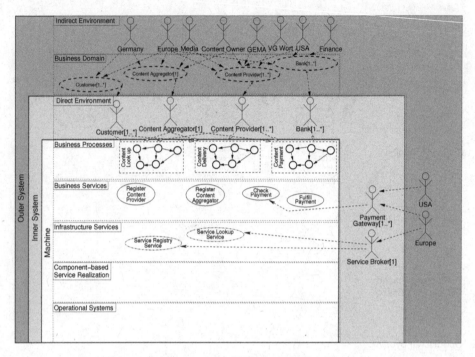

Fig. 8. Instance of the SOA Stakeholder Pattern

In our setting, the content aggregator wants to serve the German market, so it is likely that also the customers are from Germany. Thus, the legislator Germany has to be introduced. And as Germany is a part of Europe, Europe has also to be introduced. Since the big media companies reside in the US, we also add USA. To add USA is also necessary for the Payment Gateway, because some important gateways reside in the US. For the Service Broker, we take the decision to aim for a European one.

In Germany, there exist two special kinds of asset providers, besides the Content Owner, which directly plead themselves against content provider and aggregator. GEMA and VG Wort are right distributors, who plead all media owners against media consumers in Germany.

The content aggregator and the content provider are part of the Media domain. Bank is part of the Finance domain.

For reasons of space, we do not show instances of the stakeholder templates (Tables 1 and 2).

7   Using the SOA Patterns in Secure Software Development Life-Cycles

The well-known security development life-cycles (SDL) approaches Microsoft SDL [8,10] and the Comprehensive, Lightweight Application Security Process

(CLASP) by the Open Web Application Security Project (OWASP) [13] define processes to develop secure software. Gregoire et al. [6] compared both methods and derived the following phases: *Education and Awareness*, *Project Inception*, *Analysis*, *Design*, *Implementation*, *Testing and Verification*, and *Deployment and Support*.

The education and awareness phase of both SDLs can benefit from our pattern-based approach due to a structured security education of SOA. Security experts can use the instantiated patterns and templates to explain the security requirements of the stakeholders, as well as threats and attacks by pointing out their relations to other stakeholders or SOA elements in the patterns.

In the project inception phase of the Microsoft SDL, our patterns can be used to define the roles in the project, which are stakeholders in our patterns. The CLASP approach focuses on security metrics. The instantiated patterns and templates can also be useful for eliciting, e.g., the number of assets in the SOA.

The SOA context description is useful as a starting point for defining security requirements for each stakeholder. The CLASP SDL has always considered security requirements in this phase, while the Microsoft SDL only considers security requirements in a recent update [10]. The SOA patterns can help in the elicitation of security requirements. For example, the relation of a stakeholder to a part of the SOA might reveal a security issue, e.g., for the owner of a media content in the SOA, an integrity security goal, and a corresponding requirement might be needed.

In the design phase, both approaches demand a specification of the architecture-to-be and also threat modeling. Our patterns can be used as a starting point for deriving a SOA architecture. CLASP emphasizes designing a security architecture. This is an extension of the software architecture with security features. These security features can be checked against the security requirements elicited using the SOA patterns. Moreover, CLASP defines an activity for assessing the security of third-party software that shall be integrated into the architecture. The instantiated patterns can support the identification of these third-party components. Microsoft SDL presents a product risk assessment activity, which determines where to focus security efforts. The instantiated SOA patterns can also support this activity for an initial high level risk analysis.

We do not see any use for the patterns in the implementation and testing and verification phases. However, deployment and support can benefit from our patterns. Both require documentation of security, e.g., in the form of manuals. The instantiated patterns and the templates can be used as part of this documentation.

8   Conclusion

We presented *patterns for the context establishment of Service Oriented Architectures*. This approach serves as a proof-of-concept that context descriptions of complex software systems can largely benefit from patterns. Our approach comprises the following main benefits:

- Domain(here: SOA)-specific context establishment based on patterns
- Systematic pattern-based identification of all stakeholders and technologies involved
- Easing the burden of setting up an initial description of a SOA
- The approach has the potential to improve the outcome of service development within a SOA environment

The work presented here will be extended to support requirements elicitation and design description of SOA in a software engineering process. We plan to identify relations between our patterns and specific tasks in typical processes.

In addition, we intend to develop a general method to integrate our SOA patterns as a pre-phase for context establishment into existing security requirements engineering approaches, e.g., KAOS [4], Secure-Tropos [11] and Security Engineering Process using Patterns (SEPP) [17].

References

1. Arsanjani, A., Ghosh, S., Allam, A., Abdollah, T., Gariapathy, S., Holley, K.: SOMA: a method for developing service-oriented solutions. IBM Systems Journal 47(3), 377–396 (2008)
2. Arsanjani, A., Zhang, L.-J., Ellis, M., Allam, A., Channabasavaiah, K.: Design an SOA solution using a reference architecture. Technical report, IBM (2007), http://www.ibm.com/developerworks/library/ar-archtemp/
3. Beckers, K., Faßbender, S., Küster, J.-C., Schmidt, H.: A Pattern-Based Method for Identifying and Analyzing Laws. In: Regnell, B., Damian, D. (eds.) REFSQ 2012. LNCS, vol. 7195, pp. 256–262. Springer, Heidelberg (2012)
4. Darimont, R., Delor, E., Massonet, P., van Lamsweerde, A.: GRAIL/KAOS: an environment for goal-driven requirements engineering. In: Proceedings of the 19th International Conference on Software Engineering (ICSE), pp. 612–613. ACM, New York (1997)
5. Dijkman, R.M., Dumas, M.: Service-oriented design: A multi-viewpoint approach. International Journal on Cooperative Information Systems 13(4), 337–368 (2004)
6. Gregoire, J., Buyens, K., De Win, B., Scandariato, R., Joosen, W.: On the secure software development process: CLASP and SDL compared. In: Proceedings of the Third International Workshop on Software Engineering for Secure Systems, SESS 2007, pp. 1–7. IEEE Computer Society, Washington, DC (2007)
7. Gürses, S., Berendt, B., Santen, T.: Multilateral Security Requirements Analysis for Preserving Privacy in Ubiquitous Environments. In: Proceedings of the Workshop on Ubiquitous Knowledge Discovery for Users, pp. 51–64 (2006), www.ecmlpkdd2006.org/ws-ukdu.pdf
8. Howard, M., Lipner, S.: The Security Development Lifecycle: SDL: A Process for Developing Demonstrably More Secure Software. Microsoft Press (2006)
9. Jackson, M.: Problem Frames. In: Analyzing and Structuring Software Development Problems. Addison-Wesley (2001)
10. Microsoft. Microsoft Security Development Lifecycle Simplified Implementation of the Microsoft SDL. SDL 1-2, Microsoft (2010), http://www.microsoft.com/download/en/details.aspx?displaylang=en&id=123%79

11. Mouratidis, H., Giorgini, P.: Secure tropos: a security-oriented extension of the tropos methodology. International Journal of Software Engineering and Knowledge Engineering 17(2), 285–309 (2007)
12. Object Management Group, Needham, MA, USA. Service oriented architecture modeling language 1.0 - Beta 2 (December 2009),
    `http://www.omg.org/spec/SoaML/1.0/Beta2/PDF`
13. OWASP. CLASP (Comprehensive, Lightweight Application Security Process). Technical report, The Open Web Application Security Project, OWASP (2011)
14. Papazoglou, M.P., Traverso, P., Dustdar, S., Leymann, F.: Service-oriented computing: a research roadmap. Int. J. Cooperative Inf. Syst. 17(2), 223–255 (2008)
15. Perepletchikov, M., Ryan, C., Frampton, K., Schmidt, H.W.: Formalising service-oriented design. Journal of Software 3(2), 1–14 (2008)
16. Rodríguez, A., Fernández-Medina, E., Piattini, M.: A BPMN extension for the modeling of security requirements in business processes. The Institute of Electronics, Information and Communication Engineers (IEICE) Transactions 90-D(4), 745–752 (2007)
17. Schmidt, H., Hatebur, D., Heisel, M.: A pattern- and component-based method to develop secure software. In: Mouratidis, H. (ed.) Software Engineering for Secure Systems: Academic and Industrial Perspectives, ch.3, pp. 32–74. IGI Global (2011)

Cloud Blueprints for Integrating and Managing Cloud Federations

Michael P. Papazoglou

European Research Institute in Service Science, Tilburg University, The Netherlands
mikep@uvt.nl

Abstract. Contemporary cloud technologies face insurmountable obstacles. They follow a pull-based, producer-centric trajectory to development where cloud consumers have to 'squeeze and bolt' applications onto cloud APIs. They also introduce a monolithic SaaS/PaaS/IaaS stack where a one-size-fits-all mentality and vendor lock-in prevail. As a consequence consumers cannot mix and match functionality from diverse tiers of the cloud stack – horizontally or vertically – dynamically configuring it to address their needs.

This paper presents an approach that overcomes these obstacles by providing an innovative reference architecture, an enhanced cloud delivery model which breaks down the rigidity of the cloud stack and transforms it into modular and easily combined components, and a complete integration and management environment that offers integration-as-a-service functionality.

Keywords: Cloud computing delivery models, cloud integration, cloud management, cloud service abstraction mechanisms, cloud service composability, service contracts.

1 Introduction

The cloud abstraction model delivers a shared pool of configurable computing resources (processors, storage, applications, etc.) that can be dynamically and automatically provisioned and released. Cloud capabilities are defined and provided as three levels of service offerings: Software as a Service (SaaS), Platform as a Service (PaaS), and Infrastructure as a Service (IaaS) where users of cloud-related services are able to focus on what the service provides them rather than how the services are implemented or hosted. The service models, and the fact that cloud computing is discussed in terms of the creation, delivery and consumption of cloud services, mean that cloud computing supports service orientation.

While cloud computing is on the surface a very simple concept — the consumption and/or delivery of services from the cloud — there are many open issues regarding the delivery types of cloud computing and the scope of deployment. With the traditional cloud delivery models, prototyping a new system generally leads to uncontrollable "islands of clouds" that result from the fragmentation of the market where a multiplicity of vendors provides individual segregated IaaS/PaaS/SaaS functionalities that prevent any combination of

M. Heisel (Ed.): Krämer Festschrift, LNCS 7365, pp. 102–119, 2012.
© Springer-Verlag Berlin Heidelberg 2012

on-premises and off-premises applications, processes, resources and data in a coordinated fashion.

This makes it impossible to develop integrated solutions, which are typical of cloud federations, where public cloud-based services need to be combined with internal application components to create a composite application using Web-based APIs. As a result, we are now experiencing a proliferation of "cloud silos", fragmenting what should be a more open computing environment and thus posing a major barrier for the adoption of cloud computing. As a result of the above, enterprises looking at transforming their IT operations to cloud-based technologies face a non-incremental and potentially disruptive step with frequent release fixes, patches, enhancements, and serious integrative efforts, which essentially prevent SME cloud infrastructure providers from entering the cloud provisioning market. This is impacting both end-user (consumer) organizations and the providers of cloud services as it hinders them from adjusting dynamically to new business requirements.

What is needed is a solution that leads to the creation of an open, competitive cloud market, in which cloud capabilities can be procured, allocated, and provisioned on demand by the consumer, irrespectively whether these capabilities are local or remote. These cloud solutions are typical of a cloud federation, which, according to business analysts, is the next step forward in the evolution of cloud computing [1,7,13].

This approach is central to the cloud blueprinting, which is examined in this paper. It offers the best-possible economic model and maximum agility as it improves the effectiveness and productivity in cloud development activities and enables enterprises of all sizes to bring new products and services to the market more rapidly.

Before we highlight some of the features of Cloud-Sourcing, we shall review in some depth the major obstacles for federated clouds that Cloud-Sourcing aspires to solve.

2   Cloud Integration Obstacles

A *cloud federation* comprises an assembly of IT resources spanning various cloud providers and diverse (public or private) clouds where each part can be independently selected by the developer and then put together, on demand, by the cloud provisioning system over the Internet [6,12]. In this way, consumers, providers and enterprises will be able to choose freely among a pool of service providers, and service providers will be able to use from other providers any kind of cloud capability – irrespective whether this capability in at the level of infrastructure (IaaS), platform (PaaS), or application (SaaS) – to allow a federation to handle exceptional loads on their own offerings.

Federating disparate cloud computing infrastructures with each other allows disparate cloud resources and capabilities-capacity, monitoring, and management to be shared, much like power from a power grid. This means that regardless of whether the cloud resources are local or remote they must work together. This approach requires serious integrative efforts into existing infrastructure architecture. Unfortunately, federations of public and private clouds cannot become a reality unless integration issues, such the ones highlighted earlier, are overcome.

Cloud integration goes well beyond the use of common APIs. It needs to fuse interoperability with portability and effective cloud resource management. Cloud integration requires, in addition to common APIs, clear separation of concerns (and control), flexible mappings of cloud resources to services, higher-level forms of abstraction to automate the allocation of resources and to allow for resource sharing and management at a finer level of granularity. It also requires creating a cloud solution with one of its portions running on internal systems, and another portion delivered from the external cloud environment in which on-going data exchanges and process coordination occur between the internal and external environments.

When it comes to integrating cloud resources across organizational boundaries, and integrating multiple stakeholders, contemporary cloud technologies face insurmountable obstacles – since they have not been designed with cloud integration in mind. Their major drawbacks can be summarized as follows [18].

– They follow a bottom up (or pull) producer-centric trajectory to development. Consumers try to 'squeeze and bolt' applications onto existing standard cloud APIs without being able to consider the broader application picture and needs. By shifting the burden of conformity to the consumer, the provider basically requires the user to meet its needs, not the other way around. What is more, consumers are left with the burden of installation and configuration post-provisioning to put together the proper cloud environment they need.

– The biggest obstacle is that they introduce a monolithic SaaS/PaaS/IaaS stack architecture where a one-size-fits-all mentality and vendor lock-in prevails. For instance, the SaaS cloud consumer is provided with a SaaS offering which resembles an indivisible block. The SaaS application is inseparable from the platform, which in its turn is inseparable from the infrastructure on which it runs. As a consequence developers cannot mix and match functionality from diverse cloud tiers and configure it dynamically to address their needs. Modularity incumbent with the advent of service-oriented (SOA) solutions is obviated.

– The consumer usually does not have knowledge of (or control over) the precise physical location, neighbouring workloads, hardware, hypervisor, and various other components that are provided by the cloud provider. The consumer has no freedom to manage the aggregate of all cloud services it needs to best optimize their environment. All the above deliberations lead to an inflexible and costly environment which adds serious complexity, demands serious programming efforts, requires multiple patches and perpetuates vendor lock-in. Many of the benefits of cloud, which are achieved through scale and consolidation, are less forthcoming when consumers cannot exercise any control over the cloud environment.

In a similar manner, *cloud management* – the ability to exercise administrative and supervisory actions to help providers manage operations, resource availability, and workload capacity effectively across a variety of distributed cloud infrastructures – is still not entirely automated even in a single cloud provider environment. To get the most value from the cloud, providers must manually resolve sub-optimal configurations, and maintain an on-going balance between capacity utilization, cost, and service quality [8].

To summarize the points raised above, integration and manageability problems are so intricate and serious that they should be addressed only by designing from basic principles (i.e., from scratch) a novel cloud computing integration and management reference architecture and delivery model to support and automate the integration and management of federated clouds. Moreover, this architecture must transform a silo-ed approach to one that is holistic and application aware.

3 Federated Clouds

Federated cloud frameworks allow for the deployment and integrated management of multiple external and internal cloud computing services. A cloud federation uses both external (under the control of a vendor) and internal (under the control of the enterprise) cloud capabilities that are bound together by standardized or proprietary technology that enables data and application portability.

3.1 Cloud Services

Cloud-delivered services (or simply *cloud services*) are fundamentally an emerging delivery/consumption model that is applied to all cloud offerings, e.g., SaaS, PaaS and IaaS. Cloud services can be constructed of many service-enabled component parts — operating systems, applications, middleware, databases, monitoring tools, and so on — to create a truly federated cloud environment [2]. These cloud services are placed into a secure, shared location (registry of cloud services) where they can be easily accessed as and when they are needed. Then a cloud system can be created by which each part can be independently selected by the user and then put together, on demand, by the cloud provisioning system.

Cloud services leverage the characteristics shown in Figure 1 and detailed below. These are:

1. Modular, Shared, Standard, and Easily Integratable: Cloud services are modular, shared, standard services, built for a market, not for any specific customer. These services are presented to clients as 'multitenant' offerings that allow service providers to use a variety of underlying deployment and architectural options. Cloud services are designed in such a way that can be easily combined (integrated) with similar cloud services.
2. Solution-packaged: One of the most obvious user benefits of the cloud service model is that it is 'turnkey'. This means that the client can seamlessly access underlying resources required to support the offering. The cloud service provider bears that burden, offloading it from the customer, making it much simpler and faster to adopt for customers.

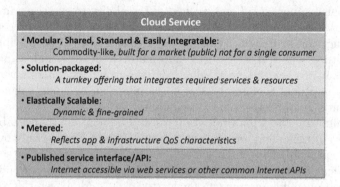

Fig. 1. Characteristics of cloud services

3. Elastically scalable: Cloud services can scale resources (CPUs, storage, bandwidth, etc.) both up and down as needed by client applications. Capabilities can be rapidly and elastically provisioned, in some cases automatically to quickly scale out and rapidly released to quickly scale in. To the client, the cloud appears to be infinite, and the client can purchase or lease capabilities available for provisioning in any quantity at any time.

4. Metered: Cloud services usually employ a metered, fee-for-service, or advertising based billing model. In a measured service, aspects of the cloud service (e.g., storage, processing, bandwidth, and active user accounts) are controlled and monitored and reported by the cloud provider ensuring transparency for both the provider and consumer of the utilized service. This is crucial for the process of billing, access control, resource optimization, capacity planning and other tasks.

5. Accessible via a published service interface: Cloud services are accessible over the Internet APIs that developers and customers use to manage and interact with cloud services. Provisioning, management, orchestration, and monitoring are all performed using these interfaces.

The above characteristics when taken together make consumer cloud services easier and more cost-effective to use. They help lower costs (for customers and suppliers), speed up and simplify access, accelerate and fine-tune provisioning (in line with true demand/usage), and improve the potential to integrate two or more such components.

3.2   Cloud Integration and Management

Cloud integration and management provides the means to integrate cloud services to ensure that a cloud application is both active and functioning properly, as well as to check the performance of an application (at any tier of the cloud stack) over time. Cloud integration and management address six necessary integration/management questions:

1. What cloud services need to be integrated or managed?
2. What are their properties?
3. How can we create composite cloud services when they are dependent on external cloud services and content that crosses organizational and geographic borders?
4. Can an aggregated cloud service that abstracts a resource support a specific workload or should this workload be partitioned between resources?
5. What are the relationships among the integrated and managed cloud resources?
6. How is the management information exchanged (operations, events, notifications, etc.)?

The functional parts for cloud integration and cloud manageability are depicted in Figure 2. The integration part in the center of this figure serves the purpose to guarantee architectural compatibility and inter-working of the planned cloud services and other critical applications. It comprises two integral functional parts: portability and interoperability.

- *Cloud portability* means that workloads can move around providers and clouds. It means the migration of full application configurations across clouds and the migration of live deployments across heterogeneous clouds (with bounded downtime).
- *Cloud interoperability* is the ability to use and seamlessly orchestrate cloud services from distinctly separate and independent cloud service providers and clouds [4,15]. Given that the various tiers in cloud stack pose different requirements with respect to interoperability, interoperability in Cloud-Sourcing is approached from the perspective of two dimensions:
  1. *Vertical cloud interoperability* is between adjacent tiers in the cloud delivery spectrum, e.g., SaaS-to-PaaS, and PaaS-to-IaaS, no matter if these are provided by diverse cloud providers.
  2. *Horizontal cloud interoperability* is between the same tiers in the cloud stack but between different cloud stack silos, i.e., cross-SaaS, cross-PaaS or cross-IaaS interoperation.

Cloud Service Management includes all of the service-related functions necessary for the management and operation of cloud services required by cloud developers. Cloud service management can be described from the perspective of the following technical dimensions [17]:

- Rapid resource provisioning: A cloud-based application must have the capacity to handle all kinds of demands being made upon it at run-time, such as the need for additional servers to be provisioned and configured dynamically by an automated provisioning engine.
- Configuration: carries out the actual configurations, it reshapes the cloud environment to meet the needs of the requested services (pull-model). This can include definitions of application stack and system configuration as well as runtime configuration and scaling rules management.

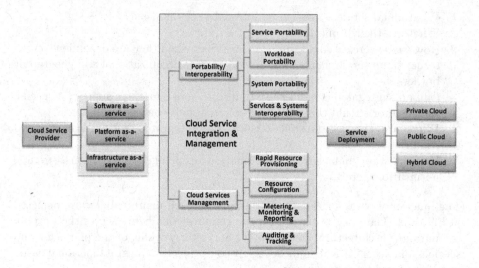

Fig. 2. Elements of cloud service integration and management

- Monitoring and troubleshooting: When a cloud-based application is running, cloud resources should be monitored for bottlenecks and for user-defined thresholds that exceed the prescribed limits to identify potential problems before they are manifested. This is cloud-sourcing for dynamic logging and testing.
- Auditing and Tracking: This provides the ability to observe aspects of a single unit of work or thread of execution across multiple inter-linked cloud resources. Cloud services should be audited and measurements can be used to compare against SLA stipulations. Tracking helps understand where the workload ran, if it completed, how long it took, and, if it did not complete, why. This provides an audit trail for use in operations management.

4   Efforts to Manage the Cloud

To represent and manage cloud resources, usually a meta-data or model-driven approach is pursued. Meta-data constructs, called templates, are used for providing an understanding of the features used to deliver reliable, and scalable cloud deployments, and achieving better interconnection between physical and digital infrastructures.

The Distributed Management Task Force (DMTF) uses templates that help manage cloud resources of various types and support the cloud service life-cycle by, for instance, describing the way in which a cloud offering is presented and consumed [5]. The service offering is abstracted from the specific type of cloud resources offered and service templates are used to describe in a general form what a cloud provider can offer. The cloud service template is then customized to reflect the fact that a service offering needs to be created for consumption by one or more specific consumers by including such information as which machines, Internet Protocol address ranges, and storage requirements.

One of the most prominent initiatives in DMTF, the Open Virtualization Format (OVF) [20] describes a specification of software packaging and distribution to be run in VMs. OVF is a platform independent, efficient, extensible, and open packaging and distribution format for VMs. OVF is virtualization platform neutral, while also enabling platform-specific enhancements to be captured.

There are several extensions of OVF to address low-level interoperability problems. Galán et al. consider configuration parameters (e.g., hostnames, IP and other application specific parameters) for software components included in the VMs as one of the capabilities that should be exposed by an IaaS provider [9]. Horizontal VM scalability by relying on non-infrastructure metrics is also briefly dealt with in this publication. In a continuation of this work the authors describe a system for a more complete application life-cycle management on top of an IaaS cloud [19]. However, all OVF-based approaches are very restrictive as they focus on specific points of the application life-cycle: definition and deployment time configuration. The fact that the application horizontally scales and load balances its VMs cannot be considered beyond the configuration step.

Finally, the OASIS Topology and Orchestration Specification for Cloud Applications (TOSCA) [14] builds on OVF efforts and plans to enable the interoperable description of application and infrastructure cloud services, the relationships between parts of the service, and the operational behavior of these services (e.g., deploy, patch, shutdown) – independent of the supplier creating the service, and any particular cloud provider or hosting technology.

Model-driven approaches are also employed for the purpose of automating the deployment of complex IaaS services on cloud infrastructure. For instance, [11] propose a virtual appliance model, which treats virtual images as building blocks for IaaS composite solutions. Virtual appliances are composed into a virtual solution model and deployment time requirements are then determined in a cloud-independent manner using a parameterized deployment plan. In a similar way, [3] describe a solution-based provisioning mechanism using composite appliances to automate the deployment of complex application services on a cloud infrastructure.

Model-driven approaches have been employed for automating the deployment on top of IaaS clouds. Goldsack et al. [10] propose a declarative configuration framework (SmartFrog) in which component descriptions were specified as ordered hash tables. The provided description is checked against a data model representing the life-cycle status of the component and inferences are made as to what changes are required to take the component from its current status into the one that matches the hash table declaration. Configurations and descriptions may contain data that comes from different stages of the processing of a description.

All the previous approaches concentrate mainly on the physical-level, i.e., predominantly IaaS cloud services. In addition, templates capture static information and cannot be combined easily with other templates to describe composite offerings.

5 The Cloud Blueprinting Approach: Simplifying and Accelerating Federated Cloud Development Efforts

Cloud Blueprinting is a novel approach that provides the ability to rapidly and easily deploy pre-built, pre-configured, pre-optimized application payloads on virtual resource pools on the cloud and helps configure a federated cloud environment to meet a broad range of application requirements and policies, (e.g., consistency, security or privacy requirements) by clearly separating service processing concerns.

The term Cloud Blueprinting refers to a detailed deployment plan and a high-order packaged integration solution that provides a description of everything necessary to integrate, and manage the interaction between cloud services provided by different providers [16,18]. The rationale of Cloud Blueprinting is about abstracting away the technical details of how one interacts with cloud services and instead providing a way to treat these interactions as part of the abstract description of an entire cloud-based solution.

Cloud Blueprinting is a coordinated effort to modularize and commoditize elements of the Cloud stack and make them available over the Internet for wider use. It provides both a reference architecture and an approach for integrating and managing cloud federations. This approach helps consumers and developers, alike to request, query, and aggregate cloud services into value-added offerings and manage integration flows connecting any combination of cloud-based services within individual, or across multiple, clouds. It consequently offers the foundation for delivering flexible and readily-integrated cloud services sourcing as utilities over the Internet.

Cloud blueprinting offers an innovative reference architecture, an enhanced cloud delivery model, which breaks down the rigidity of the cloud stack and transforms it into modular and easily combinable components that offer *integration-as-a-service* functionality. Cloud blueprinting targets cloud developers by striving to make their role simpler, more intuitive and more cost-productive. To this end it empowers an 'end-user centric view' which considers cloud consumer application needs and provides readily available standard but highly configurable building blocks (blueprints) that can be used to "assemble" the cloud application. This drastically increases the speed at which tailor-made applications can be developed.

Figure 3 shows that the activation of a new application or function is consumer-triggered and involves the use of a request language in which the consumer or developer poses requests without being inundated with the technical complexities of the underlying cloud infrastructure. Cloud resource allocation becomes just a matter of fitting together prefabricated building blocks (blueprint images aka service plug-ins), which are described using a simple definition language. Blueprint solutions are then configured for deployment by being transformed to API calls and then executed on the physical cloud. As a result, organizations can implement and configure federated cloud computing incrementally at the pace best suited to their needs and on-premise resources. The unimportant details are handled below the surface.

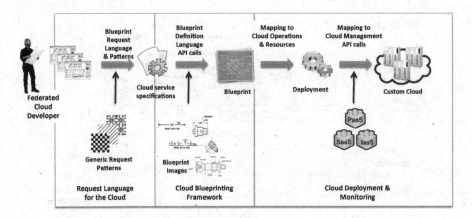

Fig. 3. Overview of the Cloud Blueprinting Approach

Cloud Blueprinting supports 'seed and grow' activities that lead to faster assembly of cloud services that span all the delivery tiers (IaaS, PaaS and SaaS) in the cloud stack. The traditional role of the system developer will become simpler, more intuitive and more cost-productive. Cloud system development will become a matter of assembling disparate prefabricated, customizable 'Lego' blocks and stack them together to make robust, flexible, scalable, and secure cloud environments. This enables all types of organizations to meet the integration challenges of cloud computing and benefit from new innovative cloud-centric business models.

5.1   Enhanced Model for Cloud Delivery and Integration

When we examine the three cloud delivery models (IaaS/PaaS/SaaS), we observe a recurrent theme. They are all constrained by the capabilities available via the provider at the respective delivery tier and do not allow for easy extensibility or aggregation options. This is due to the monolithic structure of the cloud stack that does not support modularity (see section 2).

The monolithic cloud-stack solutions that permeate the cloud today enforce one-way vertical deployment 'channels'. Seen from the perspective of a consumer who leases a SaaS application — for example, order management or tax and tariff administration — it means that the consumer receives a monolithic SaaS/PaaS/IaaS stack. This implies that if the consumer wishes to develop a new cross-SaaS (or business process as a service) application that combines this SaaS application with external billing and collection management services provided from another cloud stack, or wishes to run the SaaS application on a different type of PaaS middleware, the consumer cannot achieve this without the intervention of the original provider.

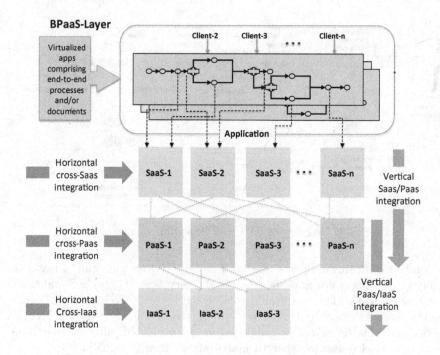

Fig. 4. Syndicated mixed-channel cloud delivery model

The only way to address the serious limitations highlighted above is by breaking the cloud monolith into its constituent (modular) parts and letting a consumer (or developer) who leases an SaaS application freely choose and intermix the lowest-cost and best quality PaaS/IaaS-layer offerings (which different providers might supply) to service it [16], [18]. This approach, which leads to the syndicated, multichannel cloud delivery model illustrated in Figure 4, promotes autonomous services (at all levels of the cloud stack). It supports consumers or developers combine or swap any service at any layer of the cloud stack with a service at the same layer without having to stop and modify components elsewhere in the stack.

The syndicated cloud delivery model converts all cloud-stack layer components into general-purpose cloud commodities to attract partners and build a true federated cloud ecosystem. As a result it naturally supports cloud developers (and providers) in the creation of end-to-end business processes as part of a business process as a service, or BPaaS, solution. BPaaS syndicates internal and other external services (possibly provided by diverse SaaS providers and clouds that run in the best possible combination of PaaS and IaaS resources. BPaaS requires effective integration and management of cloud resources.

As Figure 4 illustrates, the syndicated cloud delivery model promotes horizontal and vertical (upstream or downstream) integration by supporting mixed-channel combinations of cloud services along the horizontal and vertical cloud-stack axes. The syndicated, multi-channel cloud delivery model in Cloud-Sourcing is implemented by means of cloud blueprints as will discussed in the following section.

The syndicated cloud delivery model lowers the cost of ownership, reduces the risk of vendor lock-in, and ensures greater architectural enforcement and applied automation. Solutions based on the enhanced cloud delivery model described above are integrated and provide a high level of visibility, finer-grained control, and automation.

The cloud integration and management reference architecture promotes standardization and best practices by facilitating a shift from organic growth in business to prescriptive deployment of cloud applications with greater consistency among implementations, ease and reduced implementation effort. Central to this effort is the Cloud Blueprinting approach [16], which realizes the syndicated cloud delivery model illustrated in Figure 5.

Cloud Blueprinting empowers cloud developers to orchestrate and configure cloud applications by combining self-describing modular, reusable virtual cloud components (abstracting service application fragments, documents, or platform/infrastructure resources) at any layer of the cloud stack. The primary objective of this approach is to break the cloud stack monolith by creating a highly fluid, configurable cloud-computing environment that allows federating SaaS/Paas and IaaS cloud services on demand. Cloud Blueprinting declaratively maps pre-built, pre-configured points for abstract cloud service specifications to available cloud resources, and composes them into complete solution models (using simple aggregation and cross-configuration of virtual services). To achieve this, it uses blueprint images (or templates) that abstract specific applications, libraries, data, processes, documents, resources, and associated configuration settings and are hosted within the cloud. Blueprint images are minimally distilled in the following interrelated blueprint images (shown in Figure 5): blueprint images for operational service description, performance-oriented capabilities, resource utilization, and policies, each of which is defined in a packaged resource integration flow image configuration.

The combination of blueprinting and service virtualization at all tiers of the cloud stack grounds this new service-oriented delivery approach for cloud services.

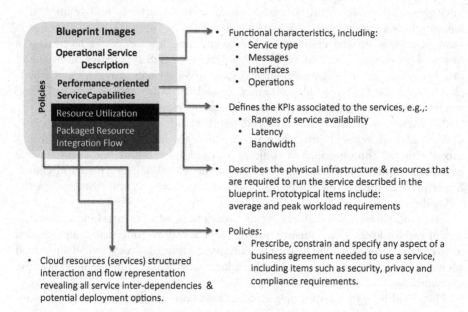

Fig. 5. Information contained in blueprint images

5.2   The Blueprint Framework

To achieve cloud service integration and management, the blueprinting approach relies on a blueprint framework. This is a lightweight framework that exemplifies the progressive state of cloud application development and the steady migration away from complex application methodologies. To fulfill its purpose, it provides a clear separation of service processing concerns by offering a family of four simple cloud service domain-specific languages created explicitly to solve blueprint-related problems, such as defining and manipulating the set of blueprint images described above (see Figure 5).

The attributes of blueprint images described in Figure 5 are specified in a simple Blueprint Description Language (BDL). The BDL uses a graphical Blueprint Constraint Language (BCL) to express constraints and associated compliance patterns applicable to blueprint images and their attributes. Finally, a simple Blueprint Manipulation Language (BML), which is based on handful of model-management algebraic operators, such as match, merge, compose, compare, extract, delete, etc., is used for manipulating, comparing, and redefining blueprint images, without compromising backward compatibility. These XML-based languages are part of the blueprint framework shown in Figure 6.

Blueprint descriptions of cloud services are available via a registry of cloud services and providers, an efficient online platform in which providers store their

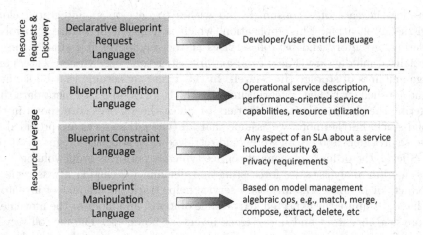

Fig. 6. The blueprint framework and its cloud service domain specific languages

offerings and clients can discover and deploy third-party cloud applications that they can integrate with their own. The blueprint approach lets consumers focus on their core application requirements and shields them from dealing with the technical complexity of integrative solutions. It provides a declarative graphical Blueprint Request Language (BRL) by means of which consumers provide fully formed resource requests (e.g., 'I need this many servers with this much CPU', or 'I need this VM capacity and storage') and higher-level application requests (e.g., 'I need enough capacity to perform this specific service') over standardized blueprint images stored in a registry of cloud services and providers. In this way, developers discover blueprint instances of a cloud service (possibly abstracting an entire application), locate its configuration details, extract configuration settings and determine dependencies and relationships between this and other services.

Due to the modularity of design, developers can use blueprint manipulation operators to bundle together several compatible blueprints, for instance, an order management service, with a cargo handling and distribution serviceman inventory service, and so on, to produce a value-adding turnkey application (e.g., an integrated logistics application in the cloud). This type of application essentially describes a resource model of inter-connected blueprint images via resource integration flow that is packaged as part of a blueprint (see Figure 5). It exposes a series of interconnected virtual cloud services, which become valuable communication rendezvous points that are actually deployed and executed by a cloud runtime environment.

5.3 Putting It All Together: Simplified Logistics Cloud Example

To provide better insight into how the concept of the syndicated cloud delivery model (in conjunction with blueprinting) can help with cloud solutions, we consider the case of a consumer who wishes to develop an integrated cloud logistics application. This application, which is depicted in Figure 7, involves ordering, inventory and payroll services at the SaaS-level and should run on specialized middleware (PaaS-level) and infrastructure, e.g., virtual servers and large amounts of storage (IaaS-level). In this figure we assume that all services come adorned with their blueprint images, which are cloud-based meta-data that describe the characteristics of the tiers to which the services correspond in the cloud-stack. Furthermore, we assume that all (virtual) services are provided by diverse providers and are all stored and retrieved from a logistics registry. At the SaaS-level, the order management service typically performs order volume analysis, margin analysis, sales forecasting and demand forecasting across regions, products or periods. The inventory service helps track the amount of inventory on hand, compute the expected arrival time of items, and monitor the movement of physical inventory and it can track inventory flows, etc. The payroll service allows for keeping constant track of such information as payroll costs, absence data or holiday entitlements. Logistics applications, such as the one presented above, need a cloud solution as they rely on masses of supplier, product, inventory and supply chain information that is typically shared by thousands of customers and supply chain partners.

At the PaaS level, we assume that the consumer wishes that the payroll management service be available for the Android smartphone operating platform so that small business owners can take advantage of this consumers payroll solution on a mobile device. Further, we assume that the consumer wishes to lease a specialized inventory management platform from the same PaaS provider (provider#4 in Figure 7). The PaaS provider requires large amounts of storage and a virtual server that installs directly on server hardware with x86 Intel processors that support PAE (Physical Address Extension). We assume that both storage and virtual server are provided by the same IaaS provider (provider#5 in Figure 7).

Figure 7 shows how the individual services can be combined to create a BPaaS-level integrated logistics application. To create the integrated logistics application, we rely on a distinctive feature of the Cloud-Sourcing approach, which is its ability to hide the technical complexity of solutions and their management from the user. Instead of requiring IT personnel, e.g., developers, to have low-level nuts-and-bolts expertise with systems, networks, and storage, Cloud-Sourcing removes most of those requirements. Instead, it provides a number of highly configurable cloud services (IaaS, PaaS or SaaS) described as blueprint images, which developers can treat as 'Lego' blocks and combine in such a way that they provide value by creating very powerful customized cloud computing environments on-demand – as is the case in Figure 7. For reasons of simplicity the above application assumes that the SaaS/PaaS/IaaS services are compatible and therefore easily composable. This may, of course, not be the case in reality.

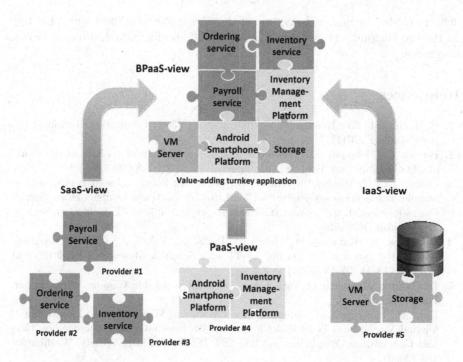

Fig. 7. An integrated logistics application combing a number of cloud services

6   Summary

One of the greatest challenges facing longer-term adoption of cloud computing is the ability to automatically provision services, effectively manage workload segmentation and portability (that is, the seamless movement of workloads across many platforms and clouds), and manage virtual service instances, all while optimizing the use of cloud resources and accelerating the deployment of new services. Within such a cloud environment, it is also important to equip developers with a unified approach that lets them develop cloud applications on top of existing applications at any layer of the cloud stack from multiple cloud providers.

The cloud blueprinting approach that we presented in this paper greatly helps cloud application developers deal with such challenges. It improves cloud service interoperability while alleviating the pains of vendor lock-in. The overarching goal of cloud blueprinting is to break the cloud stack monolith by creating a configurable cloud computing environment that syndicates services on demand across all layers of the cloud stack no matter whether they are supplied by diverse providers. Cloud blueprinting supports dynamic expansion or contraction of capabilities (virtual machines, application services, storage, and databases) for efficient workload segmentation and handling of variations in cloud service demands. This approach transforms the fabric of the current inflexible service delivery models by making heavy use of knowledge-intensive techniques that rely on the use of cloud service definition, constraint specification and manipulation languages.

References

1. Bittman, T.J.: The Road from Virtualization to Cloud Computing. Technical Report, Gartner (2011)
2. Breiter, G., Behrendt, M.: Life Cycle and Characteristics of Services in the World of Cloud Computing. IBM Systems Journal 53(4), 3:1–3:8 (2009)
3. Chieu, T.C., Mohindra, A., Karve, A., Segal, A.: Solution-based deployment of complex application services on a Cloud. In: International Conference on Service Operations and Logistics and Informatics, pp. 282–287. IEEE Computer Society, Washington DC (2010)
4. Dikaiakos, M., Katsaros, D., Mehra, P., Pallis, G., Vakali, A.: Cloud Computing: Distributed Internet Computing for IT and Scientific Research. IEEE Internet Comput. 13(5), 10–13 (2009)
5. Distributed Management Task Force (ed.): Interoperable Clouds. White Paper, DMTF (2009)
6. Elmroth, E., Larsson, L.: Interfaces for Placement, Migration, and Monitoring of Virtual Machines in Federated Clouds. In: 8th International Conference on Grid and Cooperative Computing, pp. 253–260. IEEE Computer Society, Washington DC (2009)
7. EMC (ed.): EMC's IT Journey to the Cloud. White Paper, EMC (2011)
8. Fehling, C., Mietzner, R.: Composite as a Service: Cloud Application Structures, Provisioning, and Management. IT - Information Technology 53(4), 188–194 (2011)
9. Galán, F., Sampaio, A., Rodero-Merino, L., Loy, I., Gil, V., Vaquero, L.M.: Service Specification in Cloud Environments Based on Extensions to Open Standards. In: 4th International Conference on Communication System Software and Middleware. ACM, New York (2009)
10. Goldsack, P., Guijarro, J., Loughran, S., Coles, A., Farrell, A., Lain, A., Murray, P., Toft, P.: The SmartFrog configuration management framework. SIGOPS Oper. Syst. Rev. 43(1), 16–25 (2009)
11. Konstantinou, A.V., Eilam, T., Kalantar, M., Totok, A.A., Arnold, W., Snible, E.: An Architecture for Virtual Solution Composition and Deployment in Infrastructure Clouds. In: 3rd International Workshop on Virtualization Technologies in Distributed Computing, pp. 9–18. ACM, New York (2009)
12. Kurze, T., Klems, M., Bermbach, D., Lenk, A., Tai, S., Kunze, M.: Cloud Federation. In: 2nd International Conference on Cloud Computing, GRIDs, and Virtualization, pp. 32–38. ThinkMind (2011)
13. MacVittie, L.: Fog of Definitions Hides Hybrid Cloud's Truth. ZDNet UK (2010), http://www.zdnet.co.uk/news/cloud/2010/08/20/fog-of-definitions-hides-hybrid-clouds-truth-40089810/
14. OASIS Topology and Orchestration Specification for Cloud Applications (TOSCA) TC, http://www.oasis-open.org/committees/tc_home.php?wg_abbrev=tosca
15. Parameswaran, A.V., Chaddha, A.: Cloud Interoperability and Standardization. SETLabs Briefings 7(7), 19–26 (2009)
16. Papazoglou, M.P., van den Heuvel, W.J.: Blueprinting the Cloud. IEEE Internet Comput. 15(6), 74–79 (2011)

17. Papazoglou, M.P.: Web Services and SOA: Principles and Technology, 2nd edn. Prentice-Hall, Upper Saddle River (2012)
18. Papazoglou, M.P., Vaquero, L.M.: Knowledge-Intensive Cloud Services: Transforming the Cloud Delivery Stack. In: Kantola, J., Karwowski, W. (eds.) Knowledge Service Engineering Handbook, pp. 449–494. CRC Press (2012)
19. Rodero-Merino, L., Vaquero-González, L.-M., Cáceres-Expósito, J.-A., Hierro-Sureda, J.-J.: SOA and Cloud Technologies. CEPIS Upgrade 11(4), 25–29 (2010)
20. Virtualization Management (VMAN),
http://www.dmtf.org/standards/mgmt/vman/

Dynamic Service Composition and Deployment with OpenRichServices

Ingolf Krüger, Barry Demchak, and Massimiliano Menarini

UC San Diego, La Jolla, CA, USA
{ikrueger,bdemchak,mmenarini}@ucsd.edu

Abstract. We present OpenRichServices (ORS) as an Architecture Definition Language (ADL) for the compositional specification, deployment, and reconfiguration of systems of services. Key distinguishing features of ORS are its treatment of services as first-class citizens of the language, a clean separation between application and infrastructure flows to address cross-cutting concerns at the architectural level, and dynamic service binding to facilitate service instantiation, distributed deployment and reconfiguration. ORS specifications are executable – they can be deployed together with an ORS runtime system, and then coordinate the interactions between subsystems. To evaluate ORS, we developed an implementation of our ADL as a Domain Specific Language (DSL) using the JVM-based *Clojure* programming language; this allows us to leverage Clojure's lock-free concurrency, high-performance immutable data structures, and dynamic binding capabilities. We compare the ORS ADL and its capabilities with Darwin, Wright, Rapide and SADL using a case study drawn from a mobile sensing platform.

Keywords: Service-oriented computing, system-of-system integration.

1   Introduction

Over the past two decades software has taken a significant leap from closed-box, monolithic components to open, highly distributed services. This has further increased the software developer's need to harness the ever-increasingly complex interplay of distributed software. In addition, today's deployment story is vastly different from the past – "data" centers and their arrays of computing, storage and networking resources together with the broad availability of high-bandwidth networking to the fringes of the Internet have become commodities that, collectively, can be utilized as a vast virtual computing platform (aka "the cloud.")

Architecture Definition Languages (ADLs) such as Wright, Rapide and AADL, architecture frameworks such as DoDAF [1], and the Unified Modeling Language (UML) and its cousins are challenged by this development in the following ways. First, architecture specifications in these approaches are removed from enforcing the specified architecture; this is because the architecture documents are treated as separate from the executable code. Second, they do not embrace service-orientation fully,

M. Heisel (Ed.): Krämer Festschrift, LNCS 7365, pp. 120–146, 2012.

if at all: services, dynamic binding, and runtime-reconfiguration are rarely conceptualized seamlessly from syntax to semantics in these languages. Third, the disentanglement of cross-cutting concerns – as popularized by aspect-oriented programming languages – is not supported seamlessly either. This leads to deeply entangled specifications of functional and non-functional requirements, diminishing the value of an architecture specification. In effect, every cross-cutting concern has to be architected (and intermingled with application concerns) explicitly in the architecture specification. This leads to singular specifications that are hard to reuse and maintain. Technologies that do come with support for cross-cutting concerns (such as AspectJ and its cousins) lack the abstraction mechanisms to qualify as ADLs – in particular, the expression of interaction protocols capturing the interplay of subsystems, is syntactically cumbersome and distracts from the core of the specification, or does not allow dynamic changes to support runtime-evolution of the system under consideration. Fourth, most ADLs provide only partial support for specifying deployment architectures, if at all. This leaves important architectural concerns, such as physical distribution, unaddressed. Where they do exist (such as in the case of AADL), they target very specific domains (such as automotive and avionics), and come with steep learning curves, high syntactic ceremony, and limited architecture enforcement support.

There are notable exceptions, including AADL, C2 SADL, DRADEL, xADL, Darwin, Executable UML, Orc, and Rapide to mention just a few. Each of these has powerful features for specifying the structure and behavior, some even for evolution of complex systems. However, neither addresses the above-mentioned concerns together seamlessly.

Contributions. This paper introduces OpenRichServices (ORS) as an ADL and runtime environment that (a) presents services as first-class units of composition, (b) cleanly separates application concerns from infrastructure concerns, and has an explicit language for expressing the interaction between such concerns, (c) has a deployment sub-language to indicate where services should be deployed, (d) allows for dynamic changes to the system's structure and behavior, and (e) is executable in the sense that the architecture specification is part of the code that is ultimately deployed, and governs the interactions among the services of which the system is composed. To demonstrate feasibility, we have implemented ORS as a DSL on top of the Clojure programming language, which allows us to leverage its capabilities for concurrency, dynamic binding, and interoperability with Java to enable using ADL specifications in realistic scenarios.

Outline. In Section 2, we introduce a case study as a running example and a basis for evaluation. In Section 3, we describe the ORS ADL using this case study. In Section 4, we describe the design of a prototype implementation of the ADL and its architecture. In Section 5, we compare our results in relationship to Darwin, Wright, Rapide and SADL. In Section 7, we describe the prior work in the context of related work. In Section 8, we present our conclusions and an outlook on further research opportunities.

2   Case Study

Consider a system ("CellSense") consisting of a cell phone with a display, a data store, and a processing capability – each internal to the cell phone. Attached to the cell phone is a sensor, say, for monitoring CO levels. Furthermore, there is a remote data store, and a remote processing capability. The basic behavior of the system shall be that sensor values are stored and, in parallel to storing the value, a derived value is computed and subsequently displayed. If we informally represent capabilities or "functions" by words, sequencing by juxtaposition, and parallel execution by a prefix "||", respectively, we can describe the basic behavior of the cell phone below (with parentheses to group elements of the specification). We label it and refer to it throughout as "(*)".

(*)   sense (|| store (process display))

Assume further that the system is supposed to fulfill a number of additional requirements, listed as rules in Fig. 1. These rules refer to the cell's and the sensor's power level as CPL and SPL, respectively.

---

1)   CPL high: store locally and remotely, compute locally.
      CPL low: store locally only, compute remotely.
      CPL very low: stop storing, computing, and displaying.

2)   SPL high: provide a value every second.
      SPL low: provide a value every minute.
      SPL very low: provide a value every hour.

3)   Encrypt messages before sending them to the global store and the global compute function. Decrypt the result returned from the global compute function before it is displayed.

4)   Once a day, if CPL is at least low, send the contents of the cell's local store to the global store.

5)   The location for the remote processing capability can be set at system startup and changed dynamically.

Fig. 1. CellSense Case Study Requirements

CellSense brings forward a number of concerns worth discussing in more detail.

First, requirements (1) and (2) refer only to the cell phone and the sensor, respectively. Yet, they constrain all behaviors of each. Solutions that entangle (*), (1) and (2) will become brittle if any one concern were to change.

What does entanglement mean in this context? Consider where and how you would implement the logic for (*), (1) and (2), respectively. At a high level, (*) describes the cell phone's behavior overall. (1) and (2) express that CPLs and SPLs need to be monitored, and depending on the monitored value, multiple modifications to (*) are necessary. For instance, the CPL has an influence on all of storing, computing and displaying. Clearly, we could implement this with conditionals in each of the implementations of store, process, and display. Similarly, the SPL could result in conditionals within the implementation of sense – which would be contained either within the sensor's or the cell phone's implementation, depending on whether sensor readings are pushed or pulled, respectively. Now, if either one of (*), (1), or (2) were to change, you would have to go back to all of the implementations separately to effect and validate the proper change. While this is manageable within this small-scale example, this effort becomes quickly intractable for any larger scale.

Second, (1) influences the behavior (*); it does not request a change in the general behavior pattern. Under the entangled implementation described above, the general behavior pattern is obscured by the conditional logic to support (1) – even in this small example this becomes distracting, due to the requirements' simultaneous impact on multiple steps of the behavior pattern.

Third, (2) and (4) both demand a "scheduling" capability, which signifies another common behavior pattern that repeats across system components, despite the obvious differences between eventual implementation and deployment environments.

Fourth, the behavioral influence of (3) is tied to the constraints imposed onto (*) via (1) and (4). Therefore, neither an entanglement with (*) nor with each of (1) or (4) is desirable.

Fifth, requirement (5) implies the ability to indicate, and modify at runtime, where a particular system capability is to be deployed.

Throughout this paper, CellSense requirements will be referred to solely by their number – "requirement (1)" and "(1)" are interchangeable.

CellSense, while defined and scoped specifically for this paper, is representative of a large class of distributed, reactive, and dynamic systems. This class includes, for instance, sensor/actuator networks, observatories, and other cyber-physical systems. The specifics of CellSense were extracted from CitiSense[1], a system for community-driven behavioral and environmental monitoring currently under development at UCSD. CitiSense presents many additional challenges, ranging from energy-management to observation of privacy policies, to fault-tolerance, to highly diverse resource capabilities of devices that participate in the infrastructure to the need for elasticity and scalability in the number of participants, sensors/actuators, computation, storage and networking capabilities. Most of these requirements fall under the categories introduced above; others, such as resource and deployment diversity deserve additional attention and are outside the scope of the current paper.

3   ORS as a DSL

We work with the following basic vocabulary: Services are functions in the sense of functional programming languages. Specifically, we understand services as functions that can be called and executed – but also reasoned about as functions in the mathematical sense. SOAs, then, are dynamic functional programs. Here, dynamic refers to the ability to discover and bind the name of a function to its behavior at runtime – in

---

[1] http://citisense.ucsd.edu

particular, this binding will include the location where the behavior is executed; this location can also change at runtime. In this definition, we abstract from the mechanism by which function calls are effected – this can occur in many different ways, including local function calls, remote procedure calls and messaging, to name but a few. In particular, Web Services then emerge as a SOA where particular standards and technologies combine to create an Internet-accessible dynamic functional program.

Based on our prior work on RichServices [2], we have developed the OpenRich-Services (ORS) architecture and associated ADL as a type of executable message-flow-based SOA with the following benefits:

1. Services are first-class units of composition; this is a consequence of identifying services and functions and using a functional programming language for implementation.
2. Clean separation between application concerns and infrastructure concerns. An application concern is an identifiable feature, or workflow, of the application domain. Infrastructure concerns are those features that support, or influence, multiple other application or infrastructure concerns. A typical example for an application concern is behavior pattern (*) from our CellSense example. It represents a workflow or business process of the application domain. A typical example for an infrastructure concern is encryption. In our CellSense example encryption is used in multiple places. Re-implementing it would result in waste; offering it as a service exposes an opportunity for reuse. ORS has an explicit language for expressing the interaction between such concerns.
3. Availability of a deployment sub-language to indicate where services should be deployed. Any such language within an ADL needs to strike a balance between abstraction from implementation details, and enough concreteness to still be of value in expressing locations at which deployment can occur. To that end, ORS introduces the concept of *node* as the target of a deployment, and *instances* of services as the deployed and addressable behaviors associated with a service.
4. Enabling dynamic changes to the system's structure and behavior via the use of a dynamic functional programming language as the runtime environment for the ADL.
5. Executability of the ADL in the sense that the architecture specification is part of the code that is ultimately deployed, and governs the interactions among the services of which the system is composed.

To make the ORS ADL executable, we have defined a corresponding DSL and embedded it into a host language, which affords us the base syntax for structure and computations. In Section 3.1, we briefly discuss Clojure as the host language. In Section 3.2, we introduce the DSL itself. We introduce the language by example, referring back to the base behavior (*) and requirements (1)-(5) introduced in Section 2.

3.1   Clojure

As the host language we have chosen Clojure [3] [4], a new LISP on the Java Virtual Machine (JVM) with immutable, highly performant data structures [5] (including lazy lists, key/value maps, vectors and sets). Clojure is a non-pure functional programming language with explicit in-process concurrency support via a software-transactional memory. This combination allows us to leverage Clojure's functional fragment to model services as functions, and service composition as the composition of functions. Furthermore, we can use Clojure to specify structure and behavior to any desired level of detail – we have the full power of a complete programming language at our disposal when necessary, while being able to articulate architecture specifications at a high level as well.

Clojure's code-as-data philosophy inherited from LISP provides significant flexibility in defining the DSL in anticipation of its use as a tool for model-driven engineering. Because Clojure embraces the JVM, the DSL inherits excellent interoperability features with Java libraries. The interoperability goes both ways: any Clojure module can be compiled such that it can be called from Java programs. Although we use Clojure syntax in the following paragraphs, we believe the notation to be accessible also for readers from other backgrounds.

3.2   DSL Elements for ORS

In the following paragraphs, we introduce the basic concepts and language elements of ORS. In ORS, we distinguish between logical and deployment architecture, which we explain next.

Logical Architecture. The main entity of the logical architecture is the notion of *Rich Service* (RS). An RS is either *basic* or *composite*. A basic RS is a function taking a message as input and producing a message as output. The following example shows a "basic-compute" RS – it simply returns the message it receives.

```
(defn basic-compute [rsm] rsm)
```

The syntax for specifying basic services is from Clojure: we use **(defn** f [args] bdy) to define function *f*, whose formal parameters are denoted by *args*, via the body *bdy*. In the example above, *basic-compute* is the function name, *rsm* is the name of the argument, and the body consists of returning the argument unchanged.

A composite RS also maps input messages to output messages. However, it does so by coordinating any number of its operand RSs (which are, in turn, either basic or composite). Coordination happens by routing messages from one service to another. Therefore, a composite service comes equipped with a specification of the message flow among its constituent services.

Fig. 2 shows an example of a composite RS. Here, we define *cell-phone* as a composite, which coordinates a number of basic services named *:compute*, *:store*, and *:display* (among others). The actual coordination is specified as the *:sense* service. This represents the function to be executed when a new sensor value is available. When *:sense* is called, in parallel, the :store function and the sequential composition of *:compute* and :display are executed. In ORS, parallel composition is denoted by a prefix "||" operator[2]; sequential composition is indicated by the **compose** function, whose argument is the sequence of function names to be applied in the given order. ORS specifies *bindings* between names and an implementation. For instance, in Fig. 2 we specify a binding between the name *:compute* and the implementation (the Clojure function from above) *basic-compute*. This binding can be specified and changed at a later time – even dynamically at runtime.

The services of a composite RS fall into two categories: *application* and *infrastructure services*. Application services define the application logic. Infrastructure services, on the other hand, *manipulate* application and data flow, or provide supporting tasks to that flow. The example in Fig. 2 introduces multiple infrastructure services including *:encrypt*, *:decrypt*, and *:transfer*. The first two infrastructure services are again modeled as basic services specified elsewhere. *:transfer* uses a predefined infrastructure service schedule, which takes a frequency as its first argument, and a service to be executed according to that frequency as its second argument. The meaning of this specification is that when the *cell-phone* RS is instantiated (see below under Deployment Architecture), the *:transfer-data* function is scheduled to execute once per day (at the discretion of the system's scheduler, see Section 4). This addresses requirement (4).

The final element to specifying a composite RS is to declare *how* the infrastructure services manipulate or support the application services. To that end, we introduce the notion of *transforms*. A transform takes a given service (application or infrastructure), and places it in relation with another infrastructure service.

ORS supports four types of transforms: *pre*, *post*, *pre-post* and *bind*. Recall that a service definition ":sn s" binds a service *s* to the name *:sn*. The name *:sn* can subsequently be used in place of the service itself. In this paragraph, we assume that *s* is initially bound to *:sn*. For a given name :sn, the *pre* transform ":sn **(pre** p)" routes messages originally intended for *s* first into *p*, then takes the output of *p*, and routes that into *s*. Effectively, this means replacing the binding of *:sn* by a fresh one that wraps *s* around *p*. Analogously, the *post* transform ":sn **(post** q)" replaces *:sn*'s original binding with one that takes *s*'s output and applies *q* to that. The *pre-post* transform ":sn **(pre-post** p q)" combines a *pre* and a *post* transform around *s*: the original binding of *:sn* is replaced by one that first applies *p*, then *s*, then *q*. The *bind* transform ":sn **(bind** r)" explicitly rebinds *:sn* to *r*.

In the example of Fig. 2, we use a *pre* and a *pre-post* transform to address requirement (3). We use two *bind* transforms to address requirement (1). In the *bind* transforms, we use two predefined infrastructure services: **cond-flow** and **:skip**. The **cond-flow** service has a sequence of condition/service pairs as its argument. If none of the conditions evaluate to **true**, the result is equivalent to **:skip**. Otherwise, the result is the first service whose condition evaluates to **true**. **:skip** is equivalent to the identity function.

---

[2] In LISPs, we denote a call to function *f* with argument list *a1* through *an* by prefix notation within parens as *(f a1 ... an)*.

```
(def cell-phone
   (rich-service
      (app-services
         :ls            local-store
         :lc            local-compute
         :display       display
         :transfer-data transfer-data
         :sense
         (|| :store
             (compose :compute :display))


      (infra-services
         :encrypt       encrypt
         :decrypt       decrypt
         :power-high high-power-test
         :power-low  low-power-test
         :power-vlow vlow-power-test
         :store         basic-store
         :compute       basic-compute
         :rs            remote-store
         :rc            remote-compute

      (transforms
         :rs (pre :encrypt)
         :rc (pre-post :encrypt :decrypt)
         :store (bind
                  (cond-flow
                   :power-high (|| :ls :rs)
                        :power-low  :ls
                        :power-vlow :skip))
         :compute (bind (cond-flow
                        :power-high :lc
                        :power-low  :rc
                        :power-vlow :skip)))))


      (schedules
         :transfer (every :Day
                     (cond-flow
                     (not :power-vlow)
                      :transfer-data))))
```

Fig. 2. The cell-phone Composite Rich Service

In Fig. 2, we *declare* the RS cell-phone as a prototype for creating *cell-phone* instances. Section 0 describes service instantiation and deployment. In our next example we show the partial declaration of the *sensor* RS.

```
(def sensor
  (rich-service
    (app-services
      :val (fn [rsm] ...))
    (schedules
      :delivery (every :Hour
        (compose :val :cell-phone/sense)))))
```

This example demonstrates how to "call" another RS: this call indicates the RS name (*:cell-phone*) before the "*/*" followed by the application service to be called (*sense*). Recall that ORS uses late binding: resolution of the call to *sense* will be attempted, at runtime, first on the node on which *sensor* is deployed (see the following paragraph); if an instance of *cell-phone* is deployed there, it will receive the call. Otherwise, the call will be forwarded to another node housing such an instance. If the call cannot be resolved, an exception occurs. This example can be refactored easily to comply with requirement (2) in the spirit of *cell-phone*'s conditional flow.

Deployment Architecture. The deployment architecture determines (a) how many separate *nodes* (locations of computation) exist in the system, (b) what instances of an RS will be created, and (c) on which *nodes* these instances will run. The following example shows two *cell-phone* and *sensor* services, each being deployed on two separate *nodes*.

```
(rs-start)
(let [[n1 n2] (launch-nodes 2)]
  (deploy-instance n1 :cell-phone1
    "examples.adl1/cell-phone")
  (deploy-instance n1 :sensor1
    "examples.adl1/sensor")
  (deploy-instance n2 :cell-phone2
    "examples.adl1/cell-phone")
  (deploy-instance n2 :sensor2
    "examples.adl1/sensor"))
```

The built-in **rs-start** command starts the ORS system on the node on which it is executed. We describe the details of this startup process in Section 4. The **launch-nodes** command starts additional nodes – two in this case, bound to the variables *n1* and *n2*, respectively. Finally, **deploy-instance** addresses requirement (5) by creating service instances and deploying them on a given node. To that end, we specify the node on which to deploy, the name of the new instance, and the service specification relative to the Clojure namespace in which it is defined.

4   The ORS System

We now describe the ORS system we have designed and implemented[3] as an execution platform for the ORS ADL introduced in Section 3. Clearly, this is only one specific instance of how the ORS concepts can be mapped to a concrete execution environment; we use it to demonstrate feasibility of these concepts. One of the benefits of this particular demonstrator is that it highlights the direct relationship between services and functions, and the use of dynamic binding to yield SOAs. Furthermore, the embedding of the DSL within Clojure makes the DSL specification part of the executing system, as an artifact that can be inspected and modified even at runtime.

4.1   Basic Deployment Concepts

The basic deployment environment for ORS is theJVM, with Clojure as the actual execution environment. We refer to the physical machine on which the JVM runs as the *host computer*, or *host* for short. We refer to an instance of the Clojure system running on a specific JVM as a *node*. The node from which the system is *launched* is referred to as the *root-node*. Launching the system consists of loading a file containing an ORS DSL specification.

Each DSL specification is executed in the context of a RunTime System (RTS) implemented in Clojure. This RTS provides implementations of all the built-in services, such as *schedule*, *cond-flow*, ||, and *bind*, as well as the other transforms. It also provides the facilities for registering/binding and rebinding services to names. Each node has its own *registrar*, which is a data structure and associated functionality to store bindings between service names and the Clojure functions to be executed when that service is called. The *root-node*, by default, houses the *master registrar*, which serves to resolve cross-node service calls. All service names within the RTS are represented as Universal Resource Identifiers (URIs). Furthermore, the RTS maintains data structures that keep track of the launched nodes so they can be safely shut down when no longer needed.

The "clean-slate" startup sequence for an ORS system is as follows: First, the Clojure system is brought up on the host as a Clojure Read-Eval-Print-Loop (REPL). Second, the DSL specification is loaded into the Clojure system. At this point, the RTS is instantiated, and it proceeds to parse the DSL specification, identifying all application and infrastructure services, transforms, and scheduled services. Each service definition is wrapped with a *service controller*, which performs pre-/post-processing of incoming and outgoing messages, and supplied hooks (plugin-points) for adding pre and post transforms (see Section 3.2). Then, the transforms are applied to the functions representing the application services and the resulting functions are registered with the node's registrar. Third, the deployment information in the ORS specification is parsed and executed. On the root node, all services contained in the specification are registered with the master registrar. If the ORS specification starts additional nodes, the same startup sequence is executed on these nodes, with the

---

[3] http://ors.ucsd.edu

exception that their registrars, in addition, register with the *master registrar* of the root-node. Each node is started with a JAR file containing the RTS, including the DSL specification. Fifth, scheduled tasks are launched on the respective nodes. At this point, all services defined by an ORS specification are accessible to the node's environment.

4.2   Communication and Service Controllers

Service Implementation. Every service is implemented as a Clojure function that accepts a message as input, and produces a message as output. An example for an "encryption" service looks as follows:

```
(defn encrypt [rsm]
  (let [input (get-param :in)]
    (if input
      {:response (interpose "~" input)}
      rsm)))
```

Service parameters and responses are Clojure maps, which are denoted by curly braces. Inside the body of a service function, we can access any specific parameter using the built-in (**get-param** name) function. A response map must have at least the following key/value pair: {**:response** return-value}. *encrypt* extracts the *:in* parameter, if it exists, from the input message, and binds it to the name *input*. It then interposes the twiddle character between all characters of the input, and constructs and returns a response map with the result. If there is no *:in* parameter in the input map, we simply return the input unaltered.

Service Presentation. Services are presented to their environment via *input-* and *output-adapters*, as illustrated in the top row of Fig. 3. We call the input/output adapter pair the *service presentation*. We have implemented an example input-adapter using an HTTP server accepting HTTP requests (*req* in Fig. 3) encoding the service name and parameter values. The input-adapter translates these HTTP requests into the

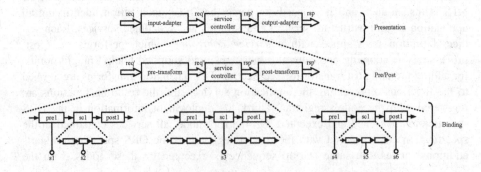

Fig. 3. ORS Service Controller Hierarchy

Clojure maps needed for the service implementation (*req'*). Analogously, we have implemented an output adapter that encodes the service function's result (*rsp'*) as an HTTP response (*rsp*).

Service Controllers: Implementing Transforms. A key element in the ORS ADL is the ability to transform a given service implementation with *pre-*, *post-* and *bind*-transforms.

Every service function, or *controlled service*, is wrapped into a *service controller*. The service controller provides two hooks, one each for a Clojure function to be executed prior to and after executing the controlled service, respectively. The *pre* and *post* transforms establish a binding to these hooks (see Fig. 3). The *bind* transform serves the purpose of associating a name with the service controller it represents. We are now in a position to clarify the role of the registrars in the ORS system: the registrar on each node maintains the binding between a service name and the service controller wrapping that service. Similarly, a service controller establishes a binding between the *pre* and *post* transforms and *their* service controllers. The *bind* transform allows us to establish and change both types of bindings by updating the corresponding registrar or service-controller-entries. These bindings are established as part of the instantiation of services on the respective node, and can be changed at runtime.

This design is compositional via the compositionality of Clojure functions. This allows us to arbitrarily chain and wrap given service implementations, as indicated in Fig. 3. As described in Section 3.2, basic services (without *pre/post* transforms) are the leaves of this binding chain; see services *s1* through *s6* in Fig. 3 as an example.

Note that in a given service controller tree, bindings need only be there for the functions that get called-upon during service execution – this supports the concept of *partial* service specification, where only some of an RS's service controllers and pre/post hooks have leaf bindings.

Runtime Service Lookup and Proxy Controllers. Whenever a service is selected for execution, the RTS looks up the corresponding binding in the registrar. This lookup yields either a service controller, or a basic Clojure function within the same node (called the *local node*). If the service to be executed is located on another node (i.e., a *remote node*), the registrar holds a binding to a *proxy controller*, which forwards the calls to the remote node. This requires preparing an external call using the desired output adapter. Then, service execution proceeds on the remote node as explained above. When the response comes back to the proxy it applies the appropriate input adapter to make the response available to the local node. Fig. 4 shows the corresponding flow.

4.3   Built-In Services

For the implementation of built-in services, we leverage the capabilities of Clojure. **:skip** is implemented as the identity function. **compose** utilizes function composition to chain service controllers sequentially. **||** relies on Clojure's built-in **pmap** function to invoke the argument service controllers in parallel on the same request map. (**if-then** :test :s1 :s2) runs the input through *:test*'s service controller. If the response evaluates to **true**, then the original request is routed to *:s1*'s service controller and to *:s2*'s otherwise. **cond** expands to a corresponding sequence of **if-then** applications, successively applying the service controllers associated with test until the first of them returns **true**; then the service controller corresponding to that test is returned. If none of the tests return true, then the returned controller is equivalent to a **:skip**. The RTS implements a basic scheduling function, allowing the scheduled execution of services at specific intervals: (**every** frequency sn) executes the service controller *sc* associated with *sn* at the specified frequency. The current implementation delegates the scheduling to Java's *ScheduledThreadPoolExecutor*. Currently, the **every** function supports predefined frequencies of **:Day**, **:Hour**, **:Minute**, and **:Second**. Others can be easily implemented.

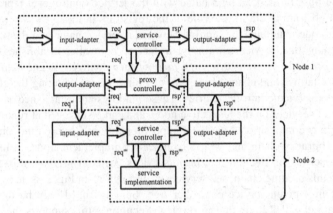

Fig. 4. Service Controller Request Flow

5   Compare Existing Approaches

In this section, we briefly discuss how existing approaches to architecture development address the concerns raised in Section 1, drawing upon the excellent comparison of ADLs by Taylor and Medvidovic [6]. Their comparison predates the emergence of service-oriented techniques – especially as it pertains to the dynamic binding of service consumers to service providers, aspect-oriented architecture, and programming capabilities, as well as the changing engineering landscape in terms of cloud deployment. However, our service notion rests on functions and dynamic functional programming, which are well-established concepts that can very well be juxtaposed to the comparison presented in [6]. To avoid redundancy, we explicitly focus on the differences between the different approaches. As noted in [6], and following the structuring of the core language elements in [7], most ADLs focus on the introduction of components (as the location of computation), connectors (the location of interaction), interfaces (to bound scope), as well as more or less constrain specifications to enable the software architect to limit the set of "allowable" structures or behaviors. Mindful of space, we present one example language (Wright) in more detail, and highlight the relevant differences for the others. Each candidate introduces novel capabilities to architecture specifications, and was chosen as representatives of the classes of ADLs discussed in [6]. We describe each ADL in terms of how it addresses CellSense requirements, and we summarize our findings in Table 1.

5.1   Wright

A key innovation of Wright-style ADLs is the appearance of explicit *connector types*, which localize interaction patterns among a set of components by defining *role* entities they service, and by using process logic (called *glue*) to specify interactions between the roles. Connectors can be instantiated multiple times across an architecture (by binding *roles* to *component* instances), thereby promoting reuse of interaction patterns. Wright incorporates an explicit process language, based on Hoare's Communicating Sequential Processes (CSP), to capture an interaction pattern, thereby enabling precise specification and formal architectural analysis.

Each role is a CSP process specifying the *expected* behavior of a component that participates in the interaction pattern defined by the connector. The behavior can include branches predicated on either *internal* or *external* choice – meaning the state of the connector or its environment. However, in both the *internal* and the *external* choice the condition governing what branch is taken is abstracted from the specification.

Using Wright, it is possible to define a *Mediator* connector type that implements the behavior required by (*), (3), and (4). The glue specifies an *internal* choice between the sense/store/process/ display behavior, and the daily transfer of the local store to the remote store. It can specify the parallel activities of storing locally and processing remotely, all followed by displaying the result.

Fig. 5 shows a *Mediator* connector specification for the cell phone example[4].

In this example, each role is a CSP process specifying the expected behavior of a component that participates in the interaction pattern defined by the connector. For instance, an RStore (remote store) must be prepared to handle either an rsin or a dump action, and then, in sequence (indicated by the "->" operator), behaves like an RStore again, i.e. an RStore is modeled as a potentially infinite sequence of rsin and dump actions. The "[]" operator signifies external choice, i.e. the decision whether the RStore engages in the rsin or the dump action is external to the RStore process itself. The roles presented in the *Mediator* connector specify expectations at their behavioral interface. The glue is a process specifying how the roles interact. In this case we have used the glue to implement the behavior required by (*) and (1)-(3): The glue specifies an internal choice (via the "∏" operator) between the sense/store/process/display behavior, and the daily dumping of the local store to the remote store. The glue uses the operator "||" to indicate parallel composition in multiple places. As an example, consider the case of local storage in parallel with remote processing followed by displaying the result.

---

[4] We have taken minimal syntactic liberty to simplify presentation of this example; furthermore, we bypass the specification of data transfer. We refer the reader to [20] for the details of the Wright language.

```
connector Mediator
    Role Encryptor = encin -> encout -> Encryptor [] §
    Role Decryptor = decin -> decout -> Decryptor [] §
    Role Display   = dispin -> Display [] §
    Role Sensor    = sout -> Sensor [] §
    Role LProc     = lpin -> lpout -> LProc [] §
    Role RProc     = rpin -> rpout -> RProc [] §
    Role LStore    = lsin -> LStore [] §
    Role RStore    = (rsin [] dump) -> RStore [] §


    Glue [] Sensor.out ->(∏ (   (  LStore.lpin
                             || (  Encryptor.encin
                                 -> Encryptor.encout
                                 -> RStore.rsin))
                         || (LProc.lpin -> Display.dispin))
                      ∏ (   LStore.lpin
                         || (  Encryptor.encin
                            -> Encryptor.encout
                            -> RProc.lpin
                            -> Decryptor.decin
                            -> Decryptor.decout
                            -> Display.dispin))
                   ∏ skip) -> Glue
        [] Encryptor.encin -> Encryptor.encout -> RStore.dump -> Glue
        [] §
```

Fig. 5. Mediator connector

Wright also defines a *component type*, which consists of an *interface* and a *computation*. An interface defines input and output *ports*. A computation, like the glue in the connector example, binds together the input/output processes.

In Wright, a component type specifies an interface and a computation. The interface is given in terms of input and output ports. A port is another CSP process indicating the expected behavior as this component type engages with its environment. The computation defines the input/ouput relationship between the ports. Below, we show an example using the Processor component type. The computation, like the glue in the connector example, binds together the input/output processes.

```
component Processor
  port
    request = in -> out -> request
  computation
    in -> process_data -> out -> computation
```

A Wright architecture specification defines a *configuration* comprising *component types*, *connector types*, instances of components and connectors, and *attachments*. Attachments bind component ports to corresponding roles in connectors. The next example shows a configuration specification. Here, we create an instance for each component and connector in the system; subsequently, we bind the processes defining the input/output behavior of the components to the corresponding roles in the connector.

```
configuration CellPhoneSystem
   instances
      enc : Encryptor
      dec : Decryptor
      d   : Display
      lp   : Processor
      rp   : Processor
      ls   : Store
      rs   : Store
      s   : Sensor
      m   : Mediator
   attachments
      lp.request as m.LProc
      rp.request as m.RProc
      enc.encrypt as m.Encryptor
      dec.decrypt as m.Decryptor
      ls.store    as m.LStore
      rs.store    as m.RStore
      s.sense    as m.Sensor
      d.display as m.Display
```

A fleshed out *CellSense* configuration is shown graphically in Fig. 6. It shows the *Mediator* connector defining eight roles. Each role is attached to an instance of a component, where the *Processor* and *Store* component definitions are reused. ① shows that a connector has glue code (g), and depends on expected behaviors (e) defined for the roles it references. ② shows an attachment between a role and a component instance containing a computation (c) that realizes (e). We use this graphical representation to more easily compare the otherwise syntactically very different ADL types we discuss in this Section.

The *Mediator* connector addresses (1)-(3) and behavior (*) to a significant degree, although the precise conditions expressed in (1)-(3) could not be expressed. Wright has no notion of scheduling; so (2) and (4) can be addressed only in abstract form using nondeterminism. Because the language addresses neither deployment nor dynamic binding, (5) could not be addressed.

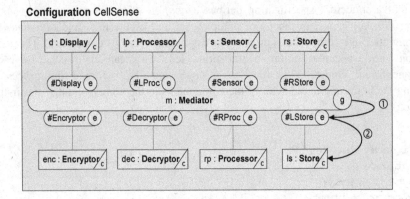

Fig. 6. CellSense in Wright ADL

5.2   Darwin

[8] introduces Darwin as "a notation for high-level organization of computational elements and the interactions between those elements." Darwin's major concepts are components, services, and bindings. A component consists of sub-compenents; each sub-component names service ports it provides, and service ports it requires. Darwin allows for component-level hierarchical decomposition by defining a sub-component in the same way as a component.

Darwin allows the specification of structural relationships between components by enabling components to bind service ports provided by one sub-component to service ports required by another sub-component. Bindings coordinate to realize services by forming a network of components that processes incoming requests into responses. Unlike Wright, it has no process language for specifying component behavior or interaction – these must be defined outside of the ADL.

As in Wright, a Darwin architecture realizes the cell phone requirements via the creation of *Encryptor*, *Decryptor*, and *Mediator* components. Because Darwin bindings are static and bear no process logic, Darwin implements (3) by specifying separate instances of *Encryptor* for each data path (i.e., to the remote processor and store). A central *Mediator* can be used to localize logic necessary to address (1) and (2) by encapsulating scheduling logic that periodically delivers sensor values and local store contents. While Darwin includes an operator specifying component deployment, (5) can be implemented only to the extent that corresponding bindings were defined at design time and are instantiated at load time.

5.3   Rapide

Rapide consists of multiple languages that, together, form a highly flexible and comprehensive notation for Complex Event Processing (CEP) systems, which are a combination of an executable architecture specification and a runtime system. The architecture defines the set of components and their involvement in a set of event sequences. The runtime system instantiates the components and ensures that their interactions conform to architectural specification. Rapide posits a universal "event cloud" into which new events are placed, and from which events can be observed. Besides an event pattern language it introduces classes and instances of event processing agents (EPA).

In Rapide, an *architecture* specifies an EPA network (EPAN), in which EPAs are modeled as *types* declaring input and output actions they accept and produce. The types can be connected statically by defining maps between the output of one type and the input of another. They can also be connected dynamically by executing expressions stimulated by the receipt of an event – this is Rapide's way of programming event-driven behavior. Such expressions can branch based on local state, and can execute sub-expressions serially or in parallel.

Fig. 7 shows a fleshed out Rapide model of CellSense.

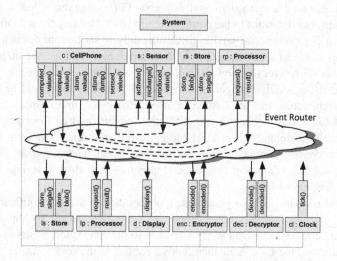

Fig. 7. CellSense in Rapide ADL

The *System* component is an architecture that contains *CellPhone*, *Sensor*, *Store*, and *Processor* sub-components, each of which defines input and output actions (represented by vertical rectangles either accepting or emitting arrows). The *System* architecture defines a number of static connections (shown as dashed lines) that link sub-component input and output actions. *CellPhone* is specified as an architecture itself, indicating a hierarchical decomposition, and implements the same linkages as in the Wright example. (The Clock sub-component is a pre-defined Rapide type.)

To implement (1), an appropriate event handler is supplied within *CellPhone* (*store_dump()*, as depicted). (2) can be implemented by a clock event handler within a *Sensor* (not depicted); and (4) is implemented by a clock event handler within *Cell-Phone*. (3) is implemented within *CellPhone* by sending an event to the *Encryptor* or

Decryptor and providing an event handler to receive the reply and forward the data to the appropriate component. Because Rapide has no high-level deployment operators[5], (5) could not be addressed.

5.4   C2 SADL

The SADL embraces the C2 architectural style [9]. In C2, *components* and *connectors* each have a defined top and bottom. *Connections* are allowed only as follows: the top of a component can attach to bottom of at most one connector; the bottom of a component can attach to at most one connector; no component-to-component connections are allowed; the bottom of one connector can attach to the top of at most one connector; there are no restrictions on the numbers of components and connectors attaching to a connector. Thus, connections induce structural and behavioral constraints on an architecture.

C2 also introduces two distinct types of messages that can flow between components and connectors: *notifications* and *requests*. Each component has a top and a bottom domain. Notifications to the component arrive exclusively from its top domain and, in turn, a component can send notifications only to its bottom domain. Furthermore, a component can send requests only to its top domain and receive them from its bottom domain. This forces *behavioral constraints* onto the architecture.

Topologically, a SADL configuration for the cell phone system could be similar to the Rapide architecture in Fig. 7 where a *Store*, *Processor*, and *Display* component connect to a *CellPhone* connector as notification targets, and an *Encryptor* and *Decryptor* component connect as request targets. Similarly, the *CellPhone* connector connects to a *System* connector as a notification target, and a *Sensor*, *Store*, and *Processor* component connect as request targets. This dual layering illustrates hierarchical decomposition.

In CellSense, when a *Sensor* generates an observation, it sends a notification to the *CellPhone* connector, which sends a request to the remote *Store*. To implement (3), the *CellPhone* connector instead sends a request to the *Encryptor*, which then returns encrypted data, and the *CellPhone* then sends a request to the remote *Store*.

Such message patterns match those described for Wright because once SADL's relationship rules are satisfied, the SADL components function just as Wright components would, and the aggregation of the SADL connectors functions as the Wright *Mediator* would – with similar restrictions, entanglements, and results. Similarly, SADL has no notion of scheduling.

Unlike Wright, SADL has no notion of conditional or process specification (other than the rules for its structure-based message flow). Additionally, SADL differs from Wright because of its ability to use runtime libraries to attach and detach components and connectors at runtime, thereby fulfilling (5).

---

[5] At least as documented in [23], though in prior versions there was a dedicated deployment sublanguage.

Table 1. Comparison of ADLs in Meeting Requirements

Req#	Issue	Darwin	Wright and SADL	Rapide	ORS
1	Cell phone state drives data routing	☒ Central mediator shim encapsulates logic, but has no conditional or flow expressions	■ Wright central mediator shim has flow expressions but no explicit conditionals. SADL has no flow expressions	☑ Event handler in cell phone w/explicit conditional and flow expressions	☑ **bind** transform replaces basic flow w/conditional flow
2	Sensor state drives scheduling of data	☒ Same as (1), and no scheduler/timer	☒ Same as (1), and no scheduler/timer	☑ Clock event handler in sensor w/explicit conditional and flow expressions	☑ Same as (1), based on **schedule** service
3	Insertion of filters along data paths	☑ Wire in 2 Encryptors and 1 Decryptor	☑ Central mediator shim orchestrates Encryptors/ Decryptor	☑ Same as (1)	☑ **pre** and **pre-post** transforms orchestrate Encryptors/ Decryptor
4	Cell phone state drives data routing on a schedule	☒ Same as (1), and no scheduler/timer	☒ Same as (1), and no scheduler/timer	☑ Same as (2), but in cell phone	☑ **schedule** service invokes conditional flow
5	Static/dynamic placement of components	■ Deployable components, but wiring not changeable at runtime	■ Wright cannot specify deployment. SADL runtime library attaches/ detaches components/ connectors.	☒ Cannot specify deployment	☑ **deploy-instance** creates/deploys service instances
	Entanglement	☒ Mediator shims for (1) and (2) share similar, non-reusable functionality	☒ Mediator shims for (1)-(2) share similar, non-reusable code. Mediator shim for (1) overloaded with (3)-(4).	☒ Cell phone overloaded with (1), (3)-(4)	☑ Avoided/ alleviated by service composition and service transforms

☑ = present, ☒ = not present, ■ = partially present

6   Conclusions

In the preceding sections, we have shown how existing ADLs cope with requirements (*) and (1)-(5), as summarized in Table 1. The requirements specification has proven a challenge for existing ADLs, largely because of the following points:

In the case of Darwin, Wright and SADL, there is no language for explicitly specifying conditions on the interaction patterns among components.

None of the ADLs explicitly distinguishes between application- and infrastructure-level interaction patterns. In the specification, this leads to the entanglement of the interactions to implement (*), as well as to make sure that consistent policies are followed, as for encryption and decryption. None of the ADLs offers AOP-style separation of concern capabilities.

There is varying support for avoiding repetitive specifications when defining interaction patterns (be it as connectors or event patterns) across hierarchical structures in the architecture. An example is the similarity between the behaviors of the sensor and the cell phone when addressing power-level-dependent behaviors, which are explicitly repetitive patterns under each ADL except Rapide.

With the exception of Rapide, none of the ADLs offers a significant scheduling feature. Architecture-level language features support reasoning about an architecture's quality of service properties.

Except for Darwin and earlier versions of Rapide, none of the ADLs has an explicit deployment sublanguage articulating the deployment system in terms of nodes and their network connections.

With the exception of basic elements in Darwin, Rapide, and SADL, there is no effective support to address dynamic binding (at load time or runtime) or the runtime reconfiguration of an architecture (e.g., via a component rewiring the system to address an emergent requirement).

None of the ADLs have a runtime system that embeds the architecture as a "reflectable" element at runtime. This precludes, or at least complicates, runtime-monitoring and verification. In Section 7 we discuss extensions specifically of the SADL line of work that address runtime adaptation and evolution of architecture models; however, these focus primarily again on the component/connector dichotomy without establishing a full embedding of the architecture specification into the executable code, as we attempt in this paper.

Each ADL faces challenges in avoiding entanglement and promoting reuse while representing component interaction patterns. These issues often arise out of the inability of the ADL to express the composition of simple concerns into complex ones. Consequently, the architect resorts to manual composition, which results in the duplication of effort and the distribution of partial solutions throughout an architecture, which ultimately results in higher maintenance costs, lower reliability, and less scalability. The ORS **transform** facility (described in Section 0) and the associated service controller system (described in Section 0) combine to avoid this issue by allowing an architect to express simpler concerns, then composing them at runtime.

Having an executable ADL is a significant leap from the traditional use of architecture models that represent structural aspects of systems, wherefrom the workflow and algorithmic implementations are largely separate. While this has served well in the context of hierarchically structured component systems, the requirements in a service-oriented, networked context demand flexible (re-)composition and deployment of functions at the expense of static structures or behavior patterns. Attempts at maintaining a significant distance between the architecture model and the more fine-grained behavioral aspects of the system under consideration require heavy-handed approaches for keeping the two in sync at runtime [10] [11]. Our approach, on the other hand treats architecture models as executable code, thus removing this distance entirely – whether this yields enough benefit to justify the inherent loss of abstraction is to be seen in future research. For instance, ORS with its Clojure implementation supports dynamic function (re-)binding with little ceremony. On the other hand, this flexibility comes at the price of reduced potential for reasoning about the specification and its evolution at runtime.

That said, there are multiple aspects to the software development process, and any one ADL represents only one of them. There is the process that takes requirements to structural and sequential modeling at various levels of abstractions, and there is the deployment mapping, too. Changing an ADL, even an executable one, does not immediately address the coordination of changes in other aspects of the software development process. This is a limitation ORS shares with its more traditional ancestors, including the ones discussed above; we intend to address and overcome this limitation in future research.

While ORS has strengths in the areas of service composition, directly executable specification, and dynamic deployment, it has much room for further improvement. It lacks a formal interface notion and a formal semantics definition. Therefore, there are no formal analysis tools available for it, whereas ADLs such as Wright and Darwin have very powerful analysis tools. These are areas for future work.

7   Related Work

Our work builds on and is influenced by a broad range of approaches across ADLs [12] [13] [14], modeling notations [15], aspect-oriented programming techniques [16], and Enterprise Service Bus (ESB) technologies [17]. It also draws upon our earlier work on Message Sequence Charts [18], services [19], and related process-oriented languages. In the interest of brevity, we now discuss a selection of this related work in more detail.

ADLs and Tools. Our work builds upon prior ADLs such as Darwin [8], Wright [20], UniCon [12] [13], MetaH [21], AADL [22], and Rapide [23]. Each of these introduces innovations, including connectors, process and interactions specifications, and complex event processing. Moreover, the idea of leveraging architectural styles (introduced in SADL [24], which leverages the C2 [9] style) has inspired the development of ORS, which supports ESB style architectures. We note that there are approaches that leverage and expand SADL's capabilities, especially in the areas of reuse, implementation inference from architecture specifications, and dynamic reflection upon and modification of running systems. DRADEL [10], for instance, introduces novel capabilities for deriving implementation skeletons from SADL-style architecture specifications, enriched by a component type-system affording consistency checking prior to code generation. xADL [25], on the other hand introduces architecture specifications as XML artifacts that can be parsed and manipulated at both design- and run-time, especially with a view towards configuration management and product families. However, both focus primarily on components rather than services as the unit of composition, and are similarly restricted in their support for the modeling of both cross-cutting concerns and dynamic re-binding of behaviors. The latter concern is addressed in [11] where the same authors present an ambitious approach to runtime reconfiguration of components and connectors of event-based systems – this uses xADL specifications at runtime to determine differences between current- and target-architecture to manipulate the architecture specification at runtime. This does make the architecture specification reflectively available at runtime; however, it maintains the difference between architecture specification and the code for its execution – our philosophy, on the other hand, is to reduce the distance between the two types of specification via Clojure/LISP's "code = data" approach. In [26], the authors present a set of architectural styles for software adaptation at runtime – to our knowledge, this work is not yet accessible in the form of an ADL; a combination between these architectural styles and the ORS DL, however, seems promising.

Our work also builds upon research in the field of frameworks and execution tools for ADL specifications [7], leveraging, for example, the Java runtime [27]. It differs in providing executable specifications for dynamically-adaptive systems of services, with clear disentanglement of infrastructure from application concerns. ORS specifications are directly executable: we provide a runtime engine based on Clojure [4], which executes on standard Java JVMs.

Modeling Notations. Many successful modeling approaches use graphical notations. For example, the UML [15] is a generic language that can be tailored to different domains. Other similar languages such as ROOM [28], MARTE [29], and UML-RT [30] have been proposed, together with a more specific semantic model, to target particular system classes such as telecommunication, automotive, and avionics. As noted in [6], they are not ADLs proper. However, they provide modeling capabilities useful in constructing architectures.

In ORS, we deliberately opted for a textual notation. Among others, this was motivated by the authors' long and mixed experience with graphical modeling tools. Often, the amount of work required to construct a graphical model that is equivalent to a simple textual specification is extraordinary. Moreover, many graphical modeling techniques focus on rather simple box- and line-diagrams, and simple behavior specifications (if any). Constructing graphical editors well is an expensive proposition both in academia and industry; this results in various gaps, such as inconsistencies between graphical notations, or a lack of integration between them (say, between data modeling and behavior modeling). These gaps are then hard to bridge for non-trivial specifications. Finally, large graphical models require stringent version control to be effectively useful in team-settings. Version-control of graphical models remains a challenge for most tool vendors; the result is a conversion of the graphical model into textual exchange formats, which can then be version controlled. Unfortunately, these exchange formats often are unable to restore models faithfully when read back into another (or even the same!) tool.

However, many parts of our language could be represented using UML-like graphical notations. For example, interactions can be mapped to UML Sequence or Activity Diagrams. Because different languages are supported by tools with different capabilities, an important factor in choosing a modeling notation is evaluating how models can be leveraged. Solutions such as ACME [31] were introduced to support interchange between different ADLs and their tools. ORS models are directly executable. Thus they can be leveraged as source code. Translating ORS specifications to leverage analysis tools developed for other ADLs is a topic of future research.

Aspect-Oriented Techniques. The ORS language supports separation of concerns – infrastructure services are injected into application services. A similar capability is available in AspectJ [16]. While both ORS and AspectJ target Java virtual machines, ORS has an architecture view and injects behavior at the interaction level while AspectJ injects functionality at the Java method level.

Enterprise Service Bus Technologies. Several frameworks and APIs have the ability to load, remove, and rewire services during runtime (such as OSGi [32] Java-based frameworks). In addition, ORS has the ability to deploy services across JVMs and comes with a dedicated DSL for modeling interaction patterns. Existing ESB implementations, such as Mule [17] and ServiceMix [33], come with DSLs to specify service interaction and deployment. ORS advances the state of the art by providing an interaction language. Furthermore, ORS can specify the topology of distributed systems in a single model. Finally, ORS comes with a Java based runtime system that can reuse connectors and components implemented in previous Java-based ESBs.

Process-Oriented Languages. Several approaches have been proposed to orchestrate services. One example is WS-BPEL [34]. Another one is the Orc [35] orchestration language, which compared to WS-BPEL is inspiring in its concise expression of a broad range of workflow patterns. Similarly, ORS provides a terse language for orchestrating services. Other approaches, such as Live Sequence Charts [36] and Executable UML [37], support specifying interactions and workflows using graphical notations. The use of a graphical version of the interaction specification language for ORS is an area of future work. ORS also provides an ADL, the ability to specify system deployment models, and operations for composing cross-cutting concerns.

Services and Feature Composition. The complex issue of composing services or features has been addressed in the seminal Distributed Feature Composition (DFC) [38] and Feature Oriented Model Driven Development (FOMDD) [39]. ORS extends the functional feature composition approach of DFC and FOMDD by addressing both dynamic service binding and explicit treatment of crosscutting concerns.

8   Summary and Outlook

We have introduced OpenRichServices (ORS) as an Architecture Definition Language (ADL) for the compositional specification, deployment, and dynamic reconfiguration of systems of services. The foundation of our approach is to view services as (mathematical) functions and SOAs as dynamic functional programs. The ADL and its prototypic implementation enable executable SOA specifications that constrain the behavior of deployed services; both draw inspiration from existing Architecture Definition Languages, Patterns and Styles, and Aspect-Oriented Programming, as well as Enterprise Service Bus technologies. To validate the language's feature set we have modeled the architecture of a simplified mobile sensor platform as it occurs in an emerging Citizen Sensing infrastructure. In comparison to established ADLs, such as Darwin, Wright, Rapide and SADL, ORS innovates by cleanly separating application from infrastructure concerns, as well as by supporting late binding to facilitate incremental service specification, deployment, and dynamic system reconfiguration. ORS is embedded into the JVM-based Clojure as its host language – this results in flexibility in specifying base services, interoperability with Java, and built-in support for concurrent programming at the architectural level. Being an ADL under active development, ORS is intended to be flexibly adapted and evolve with the tasks for which it is chosen. Future research directions include semantic foundations, the formulation of explicit interface definitions and corresponding refinement notions with runtime monitoring support, simplified instantiation, and deployment across distributed network nodes, as well as tool support for model-driven engineering.

Acknowledgments. The first author is grateful to Bernd Krämer for insightful comments and suggestions that have shaped my views on services and service-oriented architectures, as well as for his calm and persistent work in building a scientific community around these topics. This is fundamentally important to any field of science, but specifically so in one that draws both foundations and applications from so many diverse disciplines. All authors are grateful to Eric Dashofy, David Garlan, Jeff Kramer, David Luckham, and Nenad Medvidovic for generously answering our questions about their respective ADLs and styles. We are also grateful to Bill Griswold, Tajana Simunic-Rosing, and all members of the CitiSense project for their help in forming our CellSense case study. We thank David Liebke for his help with the implementation. This research was supported in part by NSF Grant CNS-0932403, as well as by the California Institute for Telecommunications and Information Technology (Calit2).

References

1. Department of Defense, DoD Architecture Framework (DoDAF) v2.0, May 28 (2009), http://cio-nii.defense.gov/sites/dodaf20/archives.html (accessed August 19 2010)
2. Demchak, B., Ermagan, V., Farcas, E., Huang, T.-J., Krüger, I., Menarini, M.: A Rich Services Approach to CoCoME. In: Rausch, A., Reussner, R., Mirandola, R., Plášil, F. (eds.) Common Component Modeling Example. LNCS, vol. 5153, pp. 85–115. Springer, Heidelberg (2008)
3. Hickey, R.: Clojure, http://clojure.org/ (accessed August 18, 2010)
4. Halloway, S.: Programming Clojure, Pragmatic Bookshelf, p. 304 (2009)
5. Noël, C.: Extensible software transactional memory. In: Proceedings of the Third C* Conference on Computer Science and Software Engineering, Montréal, Quebec, Canada (2010)
6. Medvidovic, N., Taylor, R.N.: A Classification and Comparison Framework for Software Architecture Description Languages. IEEE Transactions on Software Engeneering 26(1), 70–93 (2000)
7. Dashofy, E.M., van der Hoek, A., Taylor, R.N.: A comprehensive approach for the development of modular software architecture description languages. ACM Transactions on Software Engineering and Methodology (TOSEM) 14(2), 199–245 (2005)
8. Magee, J., Dulay, N., Kramer, J.: Structuring parallel and distributed programs. IEEE Software Engineering Journal 8(2), 73–82 (1993)

9. Taylor, R.N., Medvidovic, N., Anderson, K.M., Whitehead Jr., E.J., Robbins, J.E., Nies, K.A., Oreizy, P., Dubrow, D.L.: A Component- and Message-Based Architectural Style for GUI Software. IEEE Transactions on Software Engineering 22, 390–406 (1996)

10. Medvidovic, N., Rosenblum, D.S., Taylor, R.N.: A language and environment for architecture-based software development and evolution. In: Proceedings of the 21st International Conference on Software Engineering, Los Angeles, CA (1999)

11. Dashofy, E.M., van der Hoek, A., Taylor, R.N.: Towards Architecture-Based Self-Healing Systems. In: Proceedings of the First Workshop on Self-Healing Systems, WOSS 2002, New York, NY (2002)

12. Shaw, M., DeLine, R., Klein, D.V., Ross, T.L., Young, D.M., Zelesnik, G.: Abstractions for software architecture and tools to support them. IEEE Transactions on Software Engineering 21(4), 314–335 (1995)

13. Shaw, M., DeLine, R., Zelesnik, G.: Abstractions and implementations for architectural connections. In: Proceedings of the Third International Conference on Configurable Distributed Systems, Annapolis, MD, USA (1996)

14. Tajalli, H., Garcia, J., Edwards, G., Medvidovic, N.: PLASMA: A Plan-based Layered Architecture for Software Model-driven Adaptation. In: Proceedings of the 25th IEEE/ACM International Conference on Automated Software Engineering (ASE 2010), Antwerp, Belgium (2010)

15. OMG, UML Version 2.3 (May 2010), http://www.omg.org/spec/UML/2.3/ (accessed August 19, 2010)

16. Kiczales, G., Hilsdale, E., Hugunin, J., Kersten, M., Palm, J., Griswold, W.G.: Getting started with ASPECTJ. Communications of the ACM 44(10), 59–65 (2001)

17. Mule ESB, http://www.mulesoft.org/ (accessed August 20, 2010)

18. Krüger, I.H.: Distributed System Design with Message Sequence Charts, Technische Universität München. Ph.D. Thesis, p. 386 (2000)

19. Broy, M., Krüger, I.H., Meisinger, M.: A Formal Model of Service. ACM Transactions on Software Engineering and Methodology (TOSEM) 16(1), 5 (2007)

20. Allen, R.J.: A Formal Approach to Software Architecture (May 1997)

21. Vestal, S.: MetaH support for real-time multi-processor avionics. In: Proceedings of the Joint Workshop on Parallel and Distributed Real-Time Systems, Geneva, Switzerland (1997)

22. SAE International, Architecture Analysis & Design Language (AADL) (January 20, 2009), http://standards.sae.org/as5506a/ (accessed August 18, 2010)

23. Luckham, D.C.: The Power of Events: An Introduction to Complex Event Processing in Distributed Enterprise Systems. Addison-Wesley Longman Publishing Co., Inc., Boston (2001)

24. Taylor, R.N., Medvidovic, N., Dashofy, E.M.: Software Architecture: Foundations, Theory, and Practice. John Wiley and Sons (2009)

25. Dashofy, E.M., van der Hoek, A., Taylor, R.N.: An Infrastructure for the Rapid Development of XML-based Architecture Description Languages. In: Proceedings of the 24th International Conference on Software Engineering (ICSE 2002), Orlando, Florida (2002)

26. Taylor, R.N., Medvidovic, N., Oreizy, P.: Architectural Styles for Runtime Software Adaptation. In: Joint Working IEEE/IFIP Conference on Software Architecture 2009 and European Conference on Software Architecture 2009, Cambridge, UK (2009)

27. Aldrich, J., Chambers, C., Notkin, D.: ArchJava: connecting software architecture to implementation. In: Proceedings of the 24th International Conference on Software Engineering (ICSE 2002), Orlando, Florida (2002)

28. Selic, B., Gullekson, G., Ward, P.T.: Real-Time Object-Oriented Modeling. John Wiley & Sons (1994)
29. Faugere, M., Bourbeau, T., De Simone, R., Gerard, S.: MARTE: Also an UML Profile for Modeling AADL Applications. In: IEEE International Conference on Engineering of Complex Computer Systems (ICECCS 2007), Auckland, New Zealand (2007)
30. Krüger, I.H.: Specifying Services with UML and UML-RT: Foundation, Challenges and Limitations. In: Validation and Implementation of Scenario-based Specifications, VISS 2002 (Satellite Event of ETAPS 2002), Grenoble, France (2002)
31. Garlan, D., Monroe, R.T., Wile, D.: Acme: An Architecture Description Interchange Language. In: CASCON 1997, Toronto, Ontario (1997)
32. OSGi Alliance, OSGi Service Platform Core Specification (June 2009), http://www.osgi.org/download/r4v42/r4.core.pdf (accessed August 18, 2010)
33. ServiceMix 4, http://servicemix.apache.org/ (accessed August 20, 2010)
34. OASIS Web Services Business Process Execution Lang, Web Services Business Process Execution Language Version 2.0 (April 11, 2007), http://docs.oasis-open.org/wsbpel/2.0/OS/wsbpel-v2.0-OS.html (accessed August 20, 2010)
35. Kitchin, D., Quark, A., Cook, W., Misra, J.: The Orc Programming Language. In: Lee, D., Lopes, A., Poetzsch-Heffter, A. (eds.) FMOODS/FORTE 2009. LNCS, vol. 5522, pp. 1–25. Springer, Heidelberg (2009)
36. Harel, D., Marell, R.: Come, Let's Play: Scenario-Based Programming Using LSCs and the Play-Engine, p. 382. Springer, Berlin (2003)
37. Mellor, S.J., Balcer, M.J.: Executable UML, p. 423. Addison-Wesley Pearson Education, Indianapolis (2002)
38. Jackson, M., Zave, P.: Distributed feature composition: A virtual architecture for telecommunications services. IEEE Transactions on Software Engineering 24(10), 831–847 (1998)
39. Trujillo, S., Batory, D., Diaz, O.: Feature Oriented Model Driven Development: A Case Study for Portlets. In: Proceedings of the 29th International Conference on Software Engineering (ICSE 2007), Minneapolis, MN (2007)

An Architecture for Dynamic Service-Oriented Computing in Networked Embedded Systems

Kirill Mechitov and Gul Agha

Department of Computer Science
University of Illinois at Urbana-Champaign
201 North Goodwin Avenue Urbana, IL, USA 61801
{mechitov,agha}@illinois.edu

Abstract. Software development in real-time and embedded systems has traditionally focused on stand-alone applications with static models for scheduling and resource allocation. Our goal is to facilitate the development of embedded applications in an open system, where tasks and resources arrive and leave dynamically, and their execution is concurrent. We model such applications as a dynamic composition of network services. This paper presents an enabling framework for dynamic service orchestration in cyber-physical systems, based on a modular, reusable, and extensible service-oriented architecture. By taking advantage of a network-wide programming model, adaptive global resource management, and late binding of tasks to resources, the architecture enables execution of dynamic embedded application workloads in a resource-efficient manner.

Keywords: networked embedded systems, open systems, service-oriented architecture.

1 Introduction

The typical cyber-physical system (CPS) environment is a large-scale distributed system comprising a mix of low-power embedded computing devices, sensing and actuation elements, networked mobile devices, and traditional computing and network platforms. One of the principal challenges of computer science research in networked embedded systems is to find ways of creating scalable, robust, and efficient software capable of operating in this environment.

Current practice considers CPS in the context of a single application, e.g., a system for target tracking, environment monitoring, or structural control. This model of application development, together with the small scale of most experimental networked embedded system deployments, has led to the design of middleware services that are highly efficient but often tightly coupled or customized to a particular application. This practice hampers service portability and reusability, such as when a data aggregation service is designed to work only with a specific routing protocol.

M. Heisel (Ed.): Krämer Festschrift, LNCS 7365, pp. 147–164, 2012.
© Springer-Verlag Berlin Heidelberg 2012

Application development is particularly challenging due to the lack of software engineering tools and programming languages commonly used in modern large-scale software development. Due to resource constraints and efficiency requirements, low-level C programming remains the dominant application development method in this domain [5]. Even small modifications to existing codebases require significant programming skill and embedded systems experience.

Some recent work has proposed supporting several concurrent applications in a sensor network [19]. As CPS deployments become more numerous and their scale increases, we envision these networked embedded systems becoming an *open computing platform* used concurrently by multiple users and multiple applications for different and uncoordinated activities. For instance, as illustrated in Fig. 1, middleware services should be shared among unrelated applications. In this context, efficient customized middleware services specific to each application are a poor solution, as common functionality is needlessly replicated.

In our view, these requirements imply the need for a software architecture that provides a looser coupling between services and applications, and among the services themselves, in a resource-efficient and context-aware manner. We consider applications that make use of a number of general network-wide middleware services, such as routing, localization, and time synchronization. In order to accommodate the vast collection of services and protocols already developed by the embedded and cyber-physical systems communities, we adopt a very broad definition of a middleware service, concerning ourselves only with their interfaces to applications and other services, and not their internal semantics or implementation method. Specifically, we propose a dynamic service composition-based architecture for networked embedded systems, based on the principle of *self-mediated execution*, with the dual goals of facilitating large-scale application development and enabling global, network-wide optimization, rather than application-focused local optimization of the constituent middleware services. Our approach is based on postponing the binding of applications to specific network resources and implementations of middleware services from design- or compile-time to the runtime. Appropriate service implementations are chosen at runtime and deployed on demand.

By dissociating middleware services from the application context and from each other, we give up some possible performance advantages due to explicit customization and tight coupling. In return, we provide a more scalable software development process, support for multiple concurrent applications, and the possibility of global resource management across applications.

The remainder of the paper is organized as follows. First, we review related work on service-oriented architecture in Section 2. Section 3 states our overall design principles. Sections 4 and 5 then describe a dynamic service composition-based architecture implementing these principles and Section 7 illustrates its use in the context of a target tracking application, and Section 8 discusses the properties of our architecture.

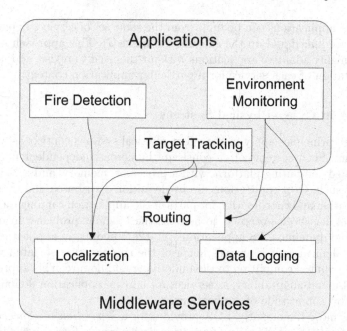

Fig. 1. Middleware services are shared among concurrently executing applications, resulting in a many-to-many relationship between applications and services

2   Service-Oriented Architecture

With the exponential growth in available computing power over the last 50 years, the complexity of computer software has likewise increased dramatically. Advances in the fields of programming language design and software engineering allow application developers to deal with this complexity by dividing the software system into smaller, manageable parts. Notably, *object-oriented programming*, which encapsulates data together with the methods used to operate on it, and *component-based software engineering*, which proposes building applications as a composition of self-contained computing components, have been instrumental to the design and development of large-scale software systems. Expanding on this idea, *service-oriented architecture* (SOA) has recently been proposed as a way to bring this design philosophy to building dynamic, heterogeneous distributed applications spanning the Internet [13, 16, 18].

Services, in SOA terminology, are self-describing software components with well-defined interfaces in an open distributed system. The description of a service, called an interface or a contract, lists its inputs and outputs, explains the provided functionality, and describes non-functional aspects of execution. Service interfaces, unlike those of components, are generally location- and implementation-agnostic. Krämer has proposed a merger of component- and service-oriented software development as a *service component architecture* (SCA) [8]. We follow a similar approach in our work, defining applications as a composition of service components.

Different applications can be built from the same set of services depending on how they are linked and on the execution context [7]. This approach makes for dynamic, highly adaptive applications without the need to revisit and adapt the implementation of each service for a particular application context.

2.1   SOA in Cyber-Physical Systems

SOA design principles apply in the cyber-physical systems context as well as on the Internet. Such systems often consist of numerous independent nodes, each an embedded computing platform with a processor, memory, and a radio transmitter. As such, CPS applications are by definition distributed and thus require communication and coordination for parts of the application running on different nodes. SOA has been proposed to address the inherent problems in designing complex and dynamic CPS applications [11,12]. Building an application from a set of well-defined services moves much of the complexity associated with embedded distributed computing to the underlying middleware. This approach also fosters reuse and adaptability, as services for a given application domain can be employed by a multitude of applications.

Perhaps more importantly, SOA provides for a *separation of concerns* in application development. That is, application designers can focus on the high-level logic of their application, service programmers can concentrate on the implementation of the services in their application domain, and systems programmers can provide middleware services (reliable communication, time synchronization, data aggregation, etc.) that enable the services to interact. In cyber- physical systems, which are often tailored to application- and context-specific requirements, it especially important for the high-level design of the application and the domain-specific algorithms used by the services to be separated from the low-level infrastructure necessary to make the system work.

2.2   Dynamic Execution in Cyber-Physical Systems

Implementing service-oriented architecture requires as a basis the ability to dynamically reconfigure and adjust the behavior of a running system. A dynamic code execution framework is thus necessary to accomplish this. Traditionally, real-time and embedded systems favored static, compiled models due to their deterministic properties. In recent years, however, several platforms for dynamic execution in networked embedded systems have been proposed.

The Melete system provides a method for concurrently executing uncoordinated applications in a wireless sensor network (WSN) [19]. Melete applications are written in the TinyScript language and executed by a virtual machine on an arbitrary subset of nodes in the network. In contrast to this approach, we propose a more comprehensive method of executing concurrent applications, which allows global resource management and a higher level of optimization. In fact, Melete may be used as part of our architecture, acting as the code deployment method for service instances.

The Tenet architecture enables service composition for multi-tiered applications incorporating WSNs [6]. Most of the coordination and processing functionality is relegated to more powerful tiers, while the WSN nodes are used primarily to retrieve sensor data. Our approach differs in that we treat the system as a collaborative distributed computing platform. By associating asynchronously interacting, autonomous actors to service instances on sensor nodes we make possible *in situ* collaborative problem solving.

The SONGS architecture and programming model considers sensor network applications as a composition of semantic services [11]. Semantic services are a type of semantic data transformation functions, and do not correspond to what we call services in this paper. We are interested in facilitating composition of less structured infrastructure and middleware services, a vast quantity of which has already been developed for cyber-physical systems.

ActorNet [9] is a mobile agent platform for sensor networks, designed to support multiagent applications on these resource-limited, real-time systems. ActorNet agents, are called actors, and are based on the actor model of computation [1]: concurrent active objects communicating via asynchronous message passing. They are specified in a relatively high-level interpreted language based on Scheme, which allows highly dynamic, mobile code to be executed across multiple sensor nodes. The ActorNet runtime environment provides all the underlying functionality necessary to support the interpreter for mobile code on sensor network platforms: memory management, scheduling, communication and migration. These features enable the execution of complex, highly dynamic mobile agent applications in the severely resource-constrained environment of wireless sensor networks. We employ ActorNet as the code deployment framework for dynamic macroprogramming, since Scheme-like code is very easy to generate automatically based on a behavior template.

Agilla [4] is another WSN mobile agent platform, and is in many respects similar to ActorNet. The principal difference is in the trade-off between power and expressiveness of the actor language versus efficiency. Agilla agents are based on virtual machine code, which is considerably more compact than ActorNet's Scheme representation. For the same reason, however, Agilla agents are not as flexible or capable as their ActorNet counterparts.

3   Design Principles

Service- and component-based architectures are widely used, providing greater ease and scalability to the software design and implementation process. We aim to apply the same approach to the cyber-physical systems domain, adapting to its unique limitations and requirements. We identify the following key principles for the design of scalable, resource-efficient WSN applications as a composition of middleware services:

1. *Network-wide Programming Model.* The networked embedded system is treated as a collaborative distributed computing platform. Applications are specified as a collection of network-wide tasks and not as a unique program image per embedded node.
2. *Sharing and Reuse.* Multiple uncoordinated applications and middleware services need to coexist in the network without prior knowledge of each other. Therefore, both network resources requiring exclusive access (sensors, actuators, etc.) and middleware services are shared among several applications. Resource management cannot be relegated to each application individually, it must be performed globally.
3. *Late Binding.* Application specification is sufficiently flexible to allow runtime adaptivity in selecting the services and resources to be used. We do not know in advance which services or resources will be used by which application, or when. Postponing the choice of which service or resource best fits the application opens up more opportunities for optimization.

In the following section we present a service composition-based software architecture that follows from these design principles.

4   Architecture Overview

Our architecture leverages the concept of dynamic service composition to support application development for open WSN systems. We adopt a two-level architecture, separating the two major concerns: that of controlling the execution process, including strategic decision making and adaptation, and that of the execution itself. First, we restate our assumptions about the problem more formally.

We consider applications specified in terms of a composition of calls to middleware service interfaces, and we refer to the service interface specification as a *contract* and each call to a service a *service request*. A repository of available services for a given CPS or application domain is provided.

To facilitate the use of a large number of pre-existing middleware services within our architecture, we choose not to constrain the model of a service's behavior, e.g., whether it is distributed, centralized, single-threaded, etc. Since services and applications need to interact and coordinate, however, we fix a model for their interaction. We use the Actor model of computation [1] to represent service interfaces connecting services to each other and to the application. Thus, services are used by our system as if they were implemented as *actors*: concurrent active objects interacting via asynchronous messaging. We distinguish between the actors representing the service itself from *meta-actors*, which are control threads supervising deployment and execution of the services.

Responsibilities of the meta-actor include controlling the lifecycle of a service (deploying, starting, stopping and disposing of the service) and interaction with other services. Note that once the appropriate services are deployed, they may choose to interact directly, rather than through their corresponding meta-actors. Interaction then occurs through the actor interface specified in the service contract. Only interactions through actor interfaces are mediated by our architecture; any side effects are not captured by this model.

We further assume the existence of a functional service composition language, where service requests are *self-sufficient* and *minimally constrained*. The service composition language is functional in that (1) the control flow between service requests is partially ordered and driven by data dependencies, and (2) it allows for a recursive graph traversal to autonomously process each service request in the specification. Self-sufficiency refers to the fact that each individual service request is provided with the required knowledge about the arguments, resources, context and method required for its execution. Minimally constrained refers to delaying as long as possible placing constraints necessary to execute a specific instance of the service, in other words, the service instance does not refer to information that can be computed or supplied to it at run-time.

The last requirement is a fine-grained dynamic code execution method, such as a mobile agent system like ActorNet [9] or Agilla [4].

Consider how a typical localization service request is represented in our architecture. To be self-sufficient, the contract includes a reference its execution method, e.g., a compiled library implementation of a localization algorithm, the type of sensors used, such as distance measuring or angle of arrival, and data types for the output (locations and error intervals). To be minimally constrained, it must not specify a deployment location (node addresses or coordinates) or method (a specific range measurement service), referring instead to the contracts in the repository. Execution-specific information is filled in at run-time based on the specified constraints.

5   Architecture Components

Given an application comprising a composition of middleware service requests represented in such manner, its execution consists of a self-decomposition and self-deployment process. This results in a system of distributed interacting meta-actors responsible for handling the interaction among the services. Execution proceeds concurrently and asynchronously as the preconditions for the deployment of each service request are satisfied. We call this process *self-mediated execution*.

Let us now focus on the role of the meta-actors in this process. Fig. 2 highlights the governing behavior of a meta-actor in processing service requests. These meta-objects are dynamic, they have the capability to observe the application objects and the environment (*introspection*), and to customize their own behavior by analyzing these observations (*intercession*), as seen in Figure 3.

Due to service request self-sufficiency, each meta-actor can decide *how*, *where* and *when* to execute its associated service. We now explain the function of each component of this architecture and their interactions.

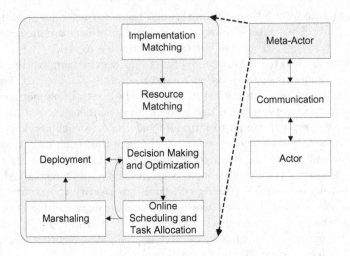

Fig. 2. Self-mediated execution architecture for middleware services

5.1   Choice of Implementation

Deciding *how* to execute the service request involves matching a particular service implementation to an interface from the service contract repository, and then finding the network resources required by that implementation.

Implementation Matching. This component finds all implementations that match the constraints of a given service request. For example, we might search for implementations of a ranging service with a MeasureDistance method that also satisfy a maximum distance constraint. This is done by querying the contract repository and filtering the results according to the constraints specified in the service request. Pattern matching or a linear constraint solver may be used to filter the available service implementations.

Resource Matching. Likewise, the resource matching component finds all suitable resources for a given service implementation. Matching algorithms used by this service depend on the resource description language employed by the system. Several methods are available for indexing a dynamic set of geographically distributed resources, including a yellow pages service, tuple spaces and actor spaces. For instance, if tuple spaces are used, sensor nodes entering the system can publish their resource descriptions in the tuple space, and the resource matching component performs a search in the form of pattern matching [2]. Caching and prefetching techniques can make the process more efficient, eliminating the need to scour the network for each query. Due to the location-dependent nature of most WSN computations, we expect most queries to be limited geographically, avoiding the need to flood the network even in cases when cached information is unavailable.

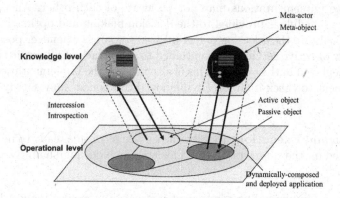

Fig. 3. Two-level architecture for controlling active objects

Location and Deployment. Second, the meta-actor needs to decide *where* to execute the service request. For the sake of efficiency, deployment and invocation are treated separately. As such, code deployment starts as soon as possible, while the invocation is delayed by the scheduling component until the necessary resources become available.

Decision Making and Optimization. Given a list of possible resources and implementations, this component chooses which implementation/resource combination best fits the application requirements or system performance considerations. The output of this service is a platform-specific executable code segment, along with a list of its required resources, which dictate where in the WSN the service must be located. This component comprises the core of the self-mediated execution approach. Choosing an appropriate option from a list of resources and service implementations is critical to efficiently executing composite service-based applications.

Deployment. This component is responsible for transporting the executable code segment to the destination platform, thereby making the service available to other services and applications. If an implementation of the service is already available at the destination platform, the code deployment step is skipped entirely, and the service request is sent to the deployed service.

Scheduling. Third, the meta-actor decides *when* to execute the service request. This is accomplished by the scheduling and task allocation component.

Online Scheduling and Task Allocation. The goal of this component is to decide when the service instance can be deployed and executed. If the resources required by the service instance are not immediately available, its execution is postponed, along with all services that depend on it. Shared resources requiring exclusive access, *e.g.*, certain types of sensors and actuators, must be scheduled globally, since service implementations may not be aware of each other. An up-to-date resource use schedule is provided to the decision making and optimization component to facilitate the selection of less-utilized resources whenever possible, and a repository of active services is maintained to keep track of all service instances currently deployed in the system. This is also used by the implementation matching component to check if an already-deployed component may satisfy a service request.

Invocation and Execution. Finally, the service request is ready to be deployed and executed on the target platform. This step includes marshaling and remote invocation.

Marshaling. The marshaling component packages the service request for transport and deployment on the destination platform, using the deployment component. The method is platform-dependent. In our system, this involves wrapping the service invocation code in a mobile agent, which can move to the destination node without relying on an external routing service.

The service request is then handed off directly to the run-time environment to launch or query the selected implementation of the service. From this point onward, the service instance interfaces via its actor interface with its meta-actor and with other services in the CPS by means of asynchronous message passing, implemented by the communication component (Figure 4). Asynchronous messaging is used both to deliver computation results and error notifications from the executing services and to deliver control messages from the meta-actor.

6   Mobile Code Deployment

Finally, we consider the operational level of the architecture, where the actual interaction with the cyber-physical system takes place. We employ ActorNet [9], a mobile agent platform for wireless sensor networks, as the mobile code deployment platform. There are several reasons why ActorNet fits well into this role.

Cyber-physical systems are well-suited to the multiagent approach: agent autonomy reduces the need for communication, saving precious energy. Mobile agents are also an intuitive technique for remotely reprogramming sensors deployed in the field. However, implementing agent programs directly on a CPS is complicated by the many limitations of sensor nodes, including limited memory, slow processors, low bandwidth and finite energy. ActorNet eases development by providing an abstract environment for lightweight concurrent object-oriented mobile code on WSNs. As such, it enables a wide range of dynamic applications, including fully customizable queries and aggregation functions, in-network interactive debugging and high-level concurrent programming on the inherently parallel sensor network platform. Moreover, ActorNet cleanly integrates all of these features into a fine-tuned, multi-threaded embedded Scheme interpreter that supports compact, maintainable programs—a significant advantage over primitive stack-based virtual machines.

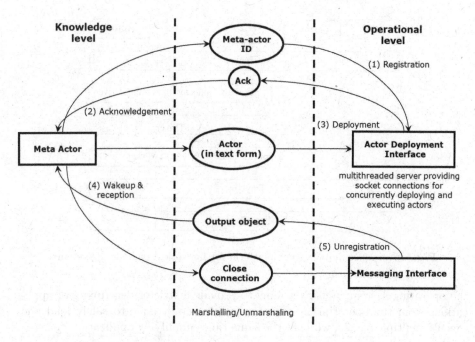

Fig. 4. Communication protocol between actors and meta-actors

6.1   ActorNet Platform

ActorNet is a distributed actor platform targeted primarily at resource-constrained wireless sensor networks. Each ActorNet node is a multi-threaded interpreter for a high-level actor language (Figure 5).

An ActorNet network can span several Internet-connected sensor networks, as well as PCs. It consists of three types of nodes: sensor nodes, which directly execute actor code; repeaters, which distribute actor messages in local sensor networks; and forwarders, which bridge ActorNet systems across the Internet and provide an external access point to the actor system. It currently executes on TinyOS, a popular operating system for embedded sensors, as well as Windows- and Linux-based PCs. Like other virtual machines, the ActorNet platform provides a uniform computing environment for all actors, regardless of hardware or operating system differences; actors can seamlessly migrate between all these hardware platforms.

Figure 5 depicts the layered architecture of an ambient node ActorNet platform. Actors only use the interpreter module directly; thus implementation details are hidden from actor programs. Lower-level services are necessary to reconcile the desired properties of simplicity and platform-independence in the high-level language with the specifics of the wireless sensor network environment. The layered architecture alleviates some of the complexity of application development for sensor networks, which currently involves a significant amount of low-level programming due to the tight coupling between the application and

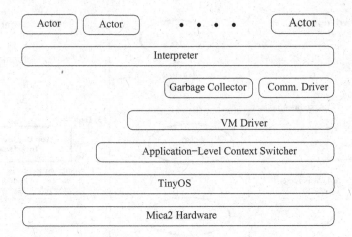

Fig. 5. ActorNet mobile agent platform for networked embedded systems

the operating system. ActorNet aims to provide a stricter decoupling of applications from the operating system, enabling a sensor node to safely load and execute multiple agents, while at the same time simplifying application development.

The ActorNet virtual machine features several services necessary to meet the challenges presented by the CPS environment. These platform services allow efficient memory management and blocking I/O operations for the actor language.

1. *Virtual Memory.* Since the small amounts of RAM available on most embedded devices is insufficient for many applications, ActorNet provides a virtual memory subsystem. It builds a page structure on the permanent storage (e.g., serial data flash) and uses an inverted page table to access pages stored in an LRU cache in RAM.

2. *Application-Level Context Switching.* ActorNet provides an application-level context switching mechanism that allows efficient blocking I/O on top of the strict non-blocking model of TinyOS. This mechanism eases development of maintainable applications. To preserve portability and modularity, the context switching mechanism is implemented purely as an application-level service; it does not modify the underlying OS scheduler.

3. *Multi-phase Garbage Collector.* The ActorNet platform provides a mark-and-sweep garbage collection mechanism. System-level support for garbage collection has many benefits: it eases application development, eliminates the chance of memory leaks, protects other applications from misbehaving actors, and reduces the actor code size. In order to prevent long-running garbage collection tasks from blocking other applications, we divide the sweep step into many short phases. Combined with the context switching functionality, this greatly reduces the impact of garbage collection on application performance.

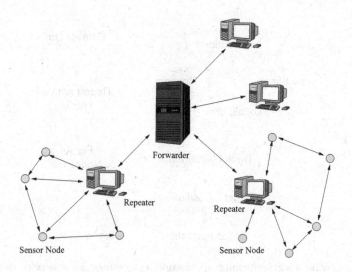

Fig. 6. The network structure of ActorNet

7 Illustration

We now demonstrate how a sensor network application can be executed by our self-mediated execution architecture. As an example, we consider a distributed target tracking service similar to one proposed by Liu *et al.* [10].

Distributed target tracking is one of the canonical problems in sensor networks. Target tracking algorithms typically consist of detecting a signal emitted by the target, identifying or classifying the target by its type or signature, and once detected and classified, keeping track of its position as it changes over time. We assume that the tracking application is provided to us as a composition of Signal Detection, Target Classification and Track Maintenance application-level services, along with Localization, Time Synchronization, Routing and Group Formation middleware services, whose dependency graph is shown in Fig. 7. In this figure, Forever Do and For All Nodes Do are special control constructs, which are executed entirely by meta-actors.

Let us look at how this composite service is deployed and executed. In response to a request, the self-mediated execution architecture creates a meta-actor for the composite service, and recursively for its individual subcomponents, made possible due to the functional nature of the service composition (see Section 4).

Consider a request to the Signal Detection service, which is the first service instance ready to execute, due to having no dependencies. The target tracking service meta-actor requests to deploy a Signal Detection service on all nodes in the network. The Signal Detection service contract specifies that it needs a certain type of sensor, say a magnetometer, to detect the target. The resource and implementation matching components will locate a suitable implementation by pattern matching the request with service and resource descriptions.

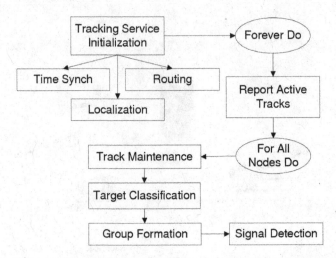

Fig. 7. Composite target tracking application represented as a service dependency graph

At this point we have an executable code segment that is ready to be transported to the destination node. After the scheduling process is completed, the service request is also marshaled and transported. This in effect creates a platform-specific relocatable executable.

The only resource used by the Signal Detector service is the magnetometer; however, since multiple uncoordinated applications may be concurrently executing on the WSN, the magnetometer at the target node may currently be in use by another service. It is the responsibility of the scheduling component of the architecture to control its invocation time, such that the required resource is available prior to request deployment. This means that the Signal Detector service request may be blocked from deployment until the magnetometer at its destination node becomes available.

Now consider a scenario where after the target tracking service starts executing, an intrusion detection application enters the system, ready to be executed. It is also represented as a composition of services, and happens to rely on the same target tracking service in its computation. However, its specification contains additional constraints on the Target Classification service, e.g., requiring a higher confidence threshold before a target is positively identified.

Due to our design choices (dynamicity and late binding), we have an opportunity for run-time optimization. When this new application starts the self-mediated execution process, the implementation matching service lists the instances of the already-deployed services as matching the requested service contracts. This is suitable for Signal Detection and Track Management services, but the Target Classification service will fail a constraint check. With negligible incremental deployment cost, the former two service instances will be reused by the system and linked to a newly instantiated Target Classification service instance meeting the more stringent requirements of the new application.

8   Discussion

To summarize our approach, applications represented as a functional composition of services with well-defined interfaces are executed in a concurrent and distributed manner by the self-mediated execution architecture. Service implementations fitting application requirements are found and deployed on demand, sharing or reusing already-deployed implementations whenever possible. Invocation requests to these services are also generated on demand. Let us first address the benefits of taking this approach to building WSN applications.

8.1   Benefits

Late binding of service implementations and network resources is a key distinguishing feature of our architecture. By postponing the explicit identification of methods and resources until the point when they are actually used, we avoid the problem of *overspecification*. Overspecification occurs when the programmer implicitly or explicitly supplies constraints on execution beyond what is strictly necessary to specify the desired behavior. Sampling a sensor at a *given* node within a region of interest, where sampling a sensor at *any* node within that region would have been sufficient is an example of overspecification. This leads to inefficient use of limited shared resources within the networked embedded system, since the scheduler or optimizer is subjected to unnecessary constraints imposed by the programmer. With late binding, we postpone the decision-making process as to which method or resource to employ from design-time to run-time, thus allowing the scheduler or optimizer components more freedom.

We also argue that service abstraction, a reusable service composition machinery, and fine-grained code deployment and execution allow creating more dynamic, maintainable and customizable applications for WSNs. Code mobility also enables predictive behavior or system-directed load balancing: a service may decide to move from one node to another to better achieve its goal, or to do so more efficiently.

8.2   Requirements

Our self-mediated execution architecture requires the application specification to be provided in the form of a composition of service descriptions. This specification may or may not be immediately executable, as not all elements are fully specified. For example, the composition may not contain a reference to a specific Target Classification service implementation, but rather to a Target Classification service contract. It is up to the mediated execution architecture to identify an appropriate implementation or resources matching the contract.

We require all composable services to conform to such a contract specification. This translates to a substantial amount of work on the service designer's part to supply a sufficiently rich service contract to turn an existing middleware service into a composable service usable by our architecture. Fortunately, the transition process can be facilitated by starting with a very rigid constraint on the interface (e.g., it is only usable by the service it was originally designed for) and gradually relaxing it as a more comprehensive service contract is constructed.

The dynamic service deployment and execution process relies on the availability of a fine-grained code deployment method for the WSN, meaning that it should be possible to deploy a service to a single node or to a subset of nodes in the network at runtime.

8.3 Implementation Issues

We have a prototype implementation of an architecture supporting a subset of the described functionality in the context of dynamic application deployment for Ambient Intelligence applications, called *Ambiance* [14]. This system reuses Dart [15] at its knowledge level, which is an example of a service composition framework in alignment with our design principles, for both representing applications and supporting the self-mediated execution process. Additionally, Dart supports creating intuitive Web interfaces for interactive specification of applications by multiple uncoordinated end-users at run-time. At the operational level, Ambiance deploys the ActorNet mobile agent platform. The interactions between these two levels conform to the logical architecture described in prior sections.

Our architecture makes use of a service composition framework, online resource scheduling and task allocation algorithms, fine-grained runtime code deployment, and implementation- and resource-matching methods. Several approaches to these tasks have been proposed:

An extensive body of distributed resource scheduling and task allocation research is available from the real-time and parallel processing communities, and may be applied to the WSN domain given allowances for limited bandwidth, memory and processing capabilities and high likelihood of failures of typical sensor nodes.

Mobile agent platforms such as ActorNet and Agilla [4,9] or virtual machine-based code migration systems such as Melete [19] satisfy our requirement for a fine-grained run-time code deployment method.

We consider the Decision Making and Optimization component to be one of the most challenging aspects in the implementation of our architecture. While a simple heuristic-based approach is sufficient for a prototype implementation, achieving efficient resource utilization is vital to making WSNs a suitable platform for deploying large, concurrent applications. Developing novel algorithms for this task is an important direction for future research. We believe that the clean separation of request processing and execution aspects in our architecture facilitates the integration of these components.

8.4 Potential Applications

We see a number of application opportunities for this architecture. In [14], we have described a possible application to a query processing engine for end-user defined concurrent queries integrating with sensor networks.

Another promising possibility is sensor-rich business processes, where sensors are attached to "smart items," and the interactions between these items is modeled within the business process. The goal then consists of enabling the execution on the sensor nodes of that part of the business logic. For example, in a safety process, smart chemical containers collaboratively ensure continuous compliance with certain storage regulations. Any violation of these rules results in local alerts, as well as reporting to the back-end systems [3].

Such processes are considered to increase visibility, enable real-time decision making and business process adjustment, and thus allow responding to situations more efficiently, with a higher degree of quality and end-user satisfaction. They also allow for management by exception, where the relocated processes only notify the back-end system of extraordinary situations, increasing scalability and speed of detecting situations that require action (avoiding latency of control loop), and does not require a constant connection to the back-end [17].

9 Conclusion

Our research aims to improve programmability of complex cyber-physical systems by separating context-independent application logic, known at design-time, from the low-level execution context considerations that are often unavailable until run-time, by means of a dynamic service-oriented architecture. An expanded version of the current architecture prototype, taking advantage of real-time operating system features for scheduling, control and synchronization, is under development. The primary focus is on incorporating the high-level decision making and optimization components into the existing scheduling model of an embedded RTOS. This includes a study of which aspects of low-level service optimization and control decision can be externalized.

We believe that the design principles and architecture defined in this paper have wider implications beyond the adaptive execution of composite middleware services in cyber-physical systems. We are specifically interested in coordination behaviors within the CPS as well as their relation to outside platforms and applications. We are thus investigating the scalability of our architecture in the context of complex hierarchical processes running in a pervasive computing environment, which also includes cyber-physical components. We consider system-wide optimization of independent concurrent applications in a shared CPS environment to be a major open research topic.

Acknowledgments. The authors gratefully acknowledge the support of this research by the National Science Foundation, under grants CMS 06-00433 and CNS 10-35773.

References

1. Agha, G.: Actors: A Model of Concurrent Computation in Distributed Systems. MIT Press (1986)
2. Carriero, N., Gelernter, D.: Linda in context. Communications of the ACM 32(4), 444–458 (1989)

3. Decker, C., Spiess, P., sa de Souza, L.M., Beigl, M., Nochta., Z.: Coupling enterprise systems with wireless sensor nodes: Analysis, implementation, experiences and guidelines. In: Pervasive Technology Applied @ PERVASIVE (May 2006)
4. Fok, C.L., Roman, G.-C., Lu, C.: Mobile agent middleware for sensor networks: An application case study. In: 4th International Conference on Information Processing in Sensor Networks, pp. 382–387 (April 2005)
5. Gay, D., Levis, P., von Behren, R., Welsh, M., Brewer, E., Culler, D.: The nesC language: A holistic approach to networked embedded systems. ACM SIGPLAN Notices 38(5), 1–11 (2003)
6. Gnawali, O., Greenstein, B., Jang, K.Y., Joki, A., Paek, J., Vieira, M., Estrin, D., Govindan, R., Kohler, E.: The TENET architecture for tiered sensor networks. In: ACM Conference on Embedded Networked Sensor Systems (November 2006)
7. Gu, T., Pung, H., Zhang, D.: A service-oriented middleware for building context-aware services. J. Network and Computer Applications 28(1), 1–18 (2005)
8. Krämer, B.J.: Component meets service: what does the mongrel look like? ISSE 4(4), 385–394 (2008)
9. Kwon, Y., Sundresh, S., Mechitov, K., Agha, G.: ActorNet: An actor platform for wireless sensor networks. In: International Conference on Agents and Multiagent Systems (2006)
10. Liu, J., Liu, J., Reich, J., Cheung, P., Zhao, F.: Distributed Group Management for Track Initiation and Maintenance in Target Localization Applications. In: Zhao, F., Guibas, L.J. (eds.) IPSN 2003. LNCS, vol. 2634, pp. 113–128. Springer, Heidelberg (2003)
11. Liu, J., Zhao, F.: Towards semantic services for sensor-rich information systems. In: International Workshop on Broadband Advanced Sensor Networks (October 2005)
12. Mechitov, K., Razavi, R., Agha, G.: Architecture design principles to support adaptive service orchestration in WSN applications. ACM SIGBED Review 4(3) (2007)
13. Papazoglou, M.P., Traverso, P., Dustdar, S., Leymann, F., Krämer, B.J.: Service-oriented computing: A research roadmap. In: Cubera, F., Krämer, B.J., Papazoglou, M.P. (eds.) Service Oriented Computing (2006)
14. Razavi, R., Mechitov, K., Agha, G., Perrot, J.-F.: Dynamic macroprogramming of wireless sensor networks with mobile agents. In: 2nd Workshop on Artificial Intelligence Techniques for Ambient Intelligence (January 2007)
15. Razavi, R., Perrot, J.F., Johnson, R.: Dart: A meta-level object-oriented framework for task-specific, artifact-driven behavior modeling. In: Proceedings of DSM 2006, pp. 43–55 (2006)
16. Singh, M.P., Huhns, M.N.: Service-Oriented Computing: Semantics, Processes, Agents. John Wiley and Sons (2005)
17. Spiess, P., Vogt, H., Jutting, H.: Integrating sensor networks with business processes. In: Real-World Sensor Networks Workshop at ACM MobiSys (June 2006)
18. Tsai, W.T.: Service-oriented system engineering: A new paradigm. In: Proc. IEEE International Workshop on Service-Oriented Systems Engineering, pp. 3–8 (2005)
19. Yu, Y., Rittle, L.J., Bhandari, V., LeBrun, J.B.: Supporting concurrent applications in wireless sensor networks. In: 4th International Conference on Embedded Networked Sensor Systems, pp. 139–152 (2006)

Location-Based Services for Technology Enhanced Learning and Teaching

Christoph Rensing[1], Stephan Tittel[2], and Ralf Steinmetz[1]

[1] Multimedia Communications Lab, Technische Universität Darmstadt,
Darmstadt, Germany
{christoph.rensing,ralf.steinmetz}@kom.tu-darmstadt.de
[2] Hessian Telemedia Technology Competence-Center,
Darmstadt, Germany
stephan.tittel@httc.de

Abstract. Learning does not only take place in a conventional classroom setting but also during everyday activities such as field trips. The increasing availability of mobile devices and network access opens up new possibilities for providing location-based services which support for such learning scenarios. In this paper, we argue the need for providing context aware services for authors of learning content as well as for learners. We present two scenarios and new services which fit to these scenarios. The first is an extension of docendo, an open learning content authoring and management platform, to support teachers while creating location-based learning material for field trips. Second service is a mobile application which allows learners to participate in the creation of learning resources by writing a wiki article and retrieve learning modules from a semantic MediaWiki using a facetted search. Learner location is one search parameter within the search.

Keywords: location-based learning, technology enhanced learning, mobile learning.

1   Introduction

Due to the increasing popularity of mobile devices like smartphones or tablet PCs, and the extensive and increasingly cost-effective availability of wireless Internet connections, mobile learning will become more important. The outstanding importance of mobile learning is reflected in the Horizon Report [1]. An expert survey in [2] shows that mobile technologies offer many opportunities, especially in terms of access to learning and contextual learning.

An important benefit, which can be achieved by mobile technologies, is contextual learning, in which learning content is made available and learning activities are selected depending from the learner's context. The current location or an object, like a building, exhibit or instrument, which is located near the learner are important characteristics of the context. With this kind of contextual learning the authenticity of the learning process can be increased, by learning at the learning object, for example the

M. Heisel (Ed.): Krämer Festschrift, LNCS 7365, pp. 165–179, 2012.
© Springer-Verlag Berlin Heidelberg 2012

building. Beyond this, learning can be realized based on learner's needs, if for example the challenge is to repair an instrument like a ticket machine. To support location-based learning and teaching as type of contextual learning is the goal of our efforts.

In this paper we introduce two different scenarios of location-based learning and teaching and describe our technical solutions as well as our experiences in these two different scenarios. The first scenario is a so-called field trip. We extend existing approaches for support of field trips by assisting the teacher in his/her role as the author of learning material, especially during the process of content authoring for a field trip scenario. In the second scenario we place the emphasis on active participation of the learners as authors of learning material which is related to a location or to a stationary object by using a wiki system. Furthermore we consider a semantic description of the location or the stationary objects which are content of the learning task.

This paper is organized as follows. Section 2 introduces the two scenarios, their benefits and resulting challenges in depth. Section 3 summarizes different existing approaches and projects in location-based learning and teaching and in social learning. Social learning means learning where learners participate actively in the learning process especially by using Web 2.0 tools. Section 4 emphasizes our solution to support the first scenario based on an extension of our open learning content authoring and management platform *docendo*. In Section 5, we look at our solution for the second scenario. The paper ends with a summary of the experiences made during the use of our new services at our university in Section 6 and a summary and an outlook.

2   Scenarios

2.1   Field Trip, a Basic Scenario of Location-Based Learning

In location-based learning, like in field trips, the mediation of learning content shall be illustrative and will be held outside the classroom, in order to increase the motivation of the learners. In addition, each learner shall make his or her own individual experiences and deepen his or her knowledge him- or herself by interacting with the learning material which is assigned to a location for example by answering and reflecting on test questions. Therefore, the learner has to determine in what order and at what pace learners wish to learn, which means that he has to select the stations of a field trip.

To access the stations of a field trip usually the learners either use a map created by the teacher or search for physical labels which mark the stations. Physical labels are not viable in public space where it is not allowed to put them. In mobile learning using mobile devices the learner usually gets a map on his mobile devices where the locations of the stations as well as her own location are indicated, like shown in Figure 1. This figure is taken from our solution for the first scenario, which is described in Section 4. If the learner has arrived at a station he or she selects the learning resources provided by the teacher for the station on the mobile device.

Fig. 1. Map View of field trip stations

Stations presented to the learner in the map have to be filtered if the clarity is compromised by a multitude of stations in the range of a learner or if stations are not equally suitable to reach the individual learning goal. Therefore we want to allow the filtering of stations presented to the learner, like shown in Figure 2 which is taken from the realization of our second scenario. The definition of features differs for different scenarios. Therefore it shall be adaptable by the authors. In our example the learner can filter the stations, which are bridges, in the basis of different criteria like Bearing, form of construction or period of construction.

Fig. 2. Filtering of different features for selection of stations

2.2   Authoring of Learning Content for Field Trips

Preparing a field trip is a challenging task for teachers. They have to determine specific learning stations to be visited by the learners and have to document the location of the station, for example by highlighting them on a map, so that they will be able to locate the learning material correctly. The teachers also have to collect relevant information about the stations which will be presented in processed form as learning material to the learners at the various stations later on. Information collection can be done by taking photographs or films of the stations and by writing down instructions or questions for the learner.

In a second step, back in the classroom or office, the teachers have to prepare the information collected to provide learning material to the learners. First they have to retrieve the resources they collected, such as the pictures they took on their camera or instructions they wrote down and assign these to the respective stations. The various stations will also need to be located electronically on a map for the learners to be easily accessible.

As shown in this scenario, the preparation of the resources for each station without technical support is very time-consuming and tedious. The teachers have to associate every resource to a station and have to document the location of the station manually.

We therefore want to support this scenario in the following manner: The teachers create resources using their mobile devices by making photos and noting down questions using a mobile authoring application. They can do this initially in form of a draft, and revise it at a later stage. When a resource is created, the location is automatically determined and assigned to the resource. The allocation of resources to a station is done by matching the location information of the resource to the location of the station. The resources collected are automatically transferred and stored in a repository. These resources can thus be easily retrieved later by the authoring system when the teachers do the final authoring of the learning material back in the classroom or office.

2.3   Learner Participation in Authoring of Content for Location-Based Learning

The scenario described above is characterized by the activation of the learners at the different stations. The creation of learning content is solely done by the teacher. Greater participation of learners offers further potential. This potential is demonstrated by different experiences made in the use of so-called Web 2.0 applications in learning [3]. Learners actively take part in the learning process and become content producers sometimes. Our goal is to combine the advantages of mobile learning with the advantages of activation which can be achieved by participation of learners in the content preparation process.

Due to very good motivational experiences in creation of wiki articles by learners [4], we also want to use a wiki system. In the wiki learners can create the learning resource which belongs to a station as wiki page. At the same time we want to motivate the learners in using their mobile devices to collect and localize information and pictures for the wiki pages like the teachers in the preceding scenario of authors support.

3   Related Work

There is a huge amount of projects in which mobile learning scenarios and technologies have been developed and have been evaluated. The museum and tourism sectors have been active early on in developing material and systems for contextualized location-based learning. In examples from these sectors quite often specialized devices are needed, for example in a museum environment, or physical markers are used to detect the location, for example in guided city tours. In recent years, there are several approaches to use everyday devices like smart phones in location-based learning. These approaches focus on supporting the learner by detecting his context, especially her location, and thereby delivering learning content that fits to the location of the learner, meaning the base scenario introduced in Section 2.1.

Examples which address the mobility of the learner in this base scenario are manifold. In ARLearn [5] learners, as they move within a city, get information about learning resources which are related to objects like buildings or monuments in the nearby environment of the learners. Not only textual content but also audio and video documents are presented.

As example for the integration of playful elements in location-based learning [6] has to be mentioned. The authors realize a game in which students explore the university campus and city. They have to visit different stations within the site and solve tasks at the different stations. Sensor technology is acquired, to prove that they are at the correct station.

Activation of the learners at different stations or objects is also done in MyArtSpace [7], which supports mobile learning during school trips to museums or art galleries. Students take pictures, make voice recordings and take notes on a smartphone and send the collected material to a personal weblog. The collected material can be worked on later in the classroom. A similar approach is used in [8], where learning activities both outside the school and in the classroom are supported. Learners use PDAs to record observations in an ecosystem in a park and to localize them by using GPS coordinates. Tasks, which have to be fulfilled, are presented to the learners in form of cards. Due to the lack of an Internet connection of the PDAs, cards and observations are exchanged locally by using a laptop as server. Ambient Wood [9], MOBIlearn [10] or Math4Mobile [11] are other examples for mobile learning projects.

Apart from these projects in the area of mobile learning there are many activities to use Web 2.0 applications for learning and teaching, which are also important to highlight in the context of this paper, pursuing the goals of our second scenario. The term Web 2.0 was originally used in 2003 and has been given broad notice since 2006, when it has been used in [12]. It refers to technologies and applications that facilitate creativity, information and knowledge sharing, and collaboration. These attributes are assumed to be useful in learning processes too [13]. By now, different experiences have been made, especially in using wikis [14] [15] [16] and blogs [17] [18] [19] in learning scenarios.

Building on these general experiences and the excellent experience gained by our project partners in the application of wikis we decided to combine location based learning and participative learning as presented in Section 2.3. Besides MyArtSpace [7], to the best of our knowledge, none of the existing approaches supports Web 2.0 content creation by the learner in a mobile scenario. Our approach to collect information and photos by the learner for preparation of a wiki page will be described in Section 5 in detail.

Also there exist no tools which actually support the mobility of the author during the creation of learning material for a field trip in the sense of collection of information and material in a repository and description of the information by geo-coordinates. In order to meet these needs of the author, we extended our existing learning content authoring and management platform docendo. This approach will be presented in the next section.

4   Location-Based Learning Content Authoring

As we have explicated before, there exist no tools which support authors in creating learning resources for location-based learning regarding the requirements we collected in Section 2.2. Hence we developed a new tool, which is an extension to our own authoring platform docendo. Below we will first introduce docendo, followed by a description of the extensions for location-based content authoring.

4.1   The Open Learning Content Authoring and Management Platform docendo

docendo is an open source web-based platform for the authoring of web-based trainings (WBT), which can be complex trainings but small modules also. In addition it has functions for management and exchange of resources to support collaborative authoring.

The different functions of docendo are shown in Figure 3. The authoring component of docendo is composed of different editors (the Course Structure Editor, the Section Editor, the Testitem Editor, and the Reference and Glossary Editor). By using these editors the author creates resources of different granularity and type. Only the creation of assets, like images, videos or animations, takes place outside the docendo platform using external tools. A course using the edited resources is structured using the Course Structure Editor, which is shown in Figure 4. Complete courses are exported using an XSL-transformation to generate a content package which is compliant with SCORM (Sharable Content Object Reference Model) [20]. These are offered to the learner generally by using a separate learning management system. docendo provides in addition to the SCORM-export the facility to generate small modules in form of HTML pages. We assume that for location-based learning small modules are used most of the times.

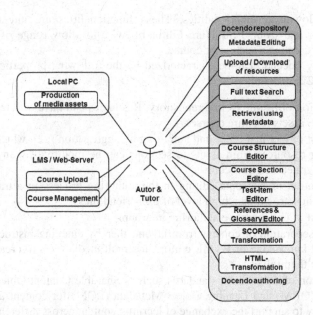

Fig. 3. docendo Use Cases

Course editor

	Edit metadata
Title:	**docendo - Concepts and Features**
Description:	This course presents the different scientific concepts of docendo as well as its features.
Keywords:	docendo	concepts	features

Title used within this course	Differing title in metadata	
○ 1 ☐ About this course	Information page for course "docendo - Concep	✏ ✕
○ 2 ☐ Introduction		✏ ✕
○ 3 ☐ Platforms for Technology Enhanced Learning		✏ ✕
○ 3.1 ☐ WBT Authoring Tools		✏ ✕
○ 3.2 ☐ Repositories		✏ ✕
○ 3.3 ☐ Learning Management Systems		✏ ✕
○ 3.4 ☐ Learning Content Management Systems		✏ ✕
○ 3.5 ☐ Functions of LMS and LCMS		✏ ✕

Fig. 4. Course Structure Editor

All resources, which are edited using the different editors mentioned before, are stored in the docendo repository. Same applies to multimedia assets, which are integrated in a section of a course. Resources and assets are described by metadata using the LOM (Learning Object Metadata) set [21]. The resource repository offers search, upload and download functionalities. These functionalities are integrated in the Section Editor and Course Structure Editor likewise to allow usage of existing resources while creating a section or course.

In summary docendo can be characterized by the following properties, which are described in [22] in detail:

- The provision of resources in a repository. Resources can have different aggregate levels, from assets to entire courses.
- The support of modular reuse and authoring by aggregation [22], which means that all existing resources from assets to sections can be modified by any author and can be integrated in a new course.
- The integration of metadata editing in the authoring process in a transparent fashion and thus providing a high level of user friendliness.
- The support of collaborative authoring in groups.
- The strict separation of content from layout, thereby enabling instructors without specialized knowledge of HTML editors and multimedia tools to create self-study material by themselves.
- The adoption of data format standards such as Sharable Content Object Reference Model (SCORM) and Leaning Object Metadata (LOM) for content and metadata respectively to support the exchange of learning content across different platforms.

4.2   Location-Based Content Authoring in docendo

After introducing docendo we want to explain how we support authors in creation of learning resources for location-based learning as required in Section 2.2. For that we have to extend the docendo use case by the support of mobile devices, as shown in Figure 5. Authors need functionalities which allow the editing of notes, which are stored as drafts of docendo sections in the docendo repository, and the creation and upload of assets, photos and videos in particular. Learners need location-based access to courses or sections of a course to realize the advantages of contextual learning which have been explained in the motivation.

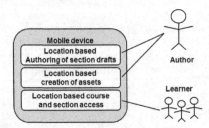

Fig. 5. Extension of docendo Use Cases for mobile devices

To realize the use cases supporting the author we developed a mobile docendo editor for authoring on the Android operating system. The author can use this editor for writing descriptive texts, work orders or questions for test-items using his or her mobile device, see Figure 6. These drafts of sections are stored in the docendo repository.

The stored section can be revised and complemented at a later date using the existing docendo editors. In addition teachers can assign one or more assets, which they created with his mobile device, particularly photos or videos, to the section. Assets are uploaded to the repository also.

All sections and the resources are described by the location. To detect the location we usually use the GPS coordinates. If these are not available, we use the coordinates of a query with HTML 5.0. Since this can be inaccurate, it is possible to adjust the position in docendo later, like shown in Figure 6. The location information is stored in the LOM metadata set using the field General/Coverage, which is also shown in Figure 6.

To realize the use case "Location-based course and section access" we do not need a new application. The existing browser on the mobile device can be used to access courses and sections. Hence the sections are presented on a map, based on Google maps. The current position of the user and all sections are displayed, as shown in Figure 1 (where the current position of the user is panned out of view and the shortest route to the selected learning object is highlighted in blue). The sections in either view can directly be opened by the learner with a single click or tap.

Fig. 6. Upload of notes and later editing of their geo-location in docendo

5   Semantic MediaWiki for Location-Based Learning

As we said before, to the best of our knowledge there exist no approaches which support wiki content creation in a learning scenario in which the content is created by the learner in a mobile scenario. To support the requirements described in Section 2.3 we developed a mobile app for the Android operating system which is used by the learner to collect notes and photos in a wiki page. To allow the filtering of learning resources regarding different aspects in addition to the current location we use Semantic MediaWiki. Next we describe how we use Semantic MediaWiki to realize a flexible domain model and how the filtering of resources can be done by using this domain model. We explain the domain model using our evaluation scenario from civil engineering as example. In this scenario the objects used for contextual learning are bridges. The app for mobile content collection in wiki pages is shown at the end of this section.

5.1   Realization of a Flexible Domain Model Using Semantic MediaWiki

Semantic MediaWiki [23] is an open source extension to the MediaWiki software, providing means for semantic labeling of wiki content using explicit mark-up, so-called semantic properties. Semantic properties allow further characterization of links and data by semantically annotating the relationship between two wiki pages or between wiki page and data. Thus, content that has been annotated by semantic properties can by interpreted by a computer [24].

The application-specific domain model, which is used for filtering relevant learning material, is realized using semantic properties within Semantic MediaWiki. For that, it is only necessary to label concepts of the domain model within the running text of the wiki page with the extended wiki mark-up of corresponding semantic properties. Thus, the sentence

```
The Main-Bridge, the so-called Eiserner Steg, was built
in 1868 from a blueprint of J.P.W. Schmick.
```

becomes the semantically annotated sentence:

```
The Main-Bridge, the so-called Eiserner Steg, was built
in [[Construction period::1868]] from a blueprint of
[[Architect::J.P.W. Schmick]].
```

Effectively, this creates two semantic properties Construction period and Architect with values 1868 and J.P.W. Schmick, respectively. The data type of these properties is Page by default, which means that these properties are being rendered as links to wiki pages. Semantic MediaWiki however supports further data types, most notably Number, Date and Geographic coordinate, which can be set on the corresponding property page using the instruction [[Has type::<data type>]]. In this manner, all features of the domain model get mapped to specific semantic properties within the wiki.

5.2   Using the Domain Model for Location-Based, Facetted Content Provision

For realization of location-based learning and filtering of learning material as claimed in the base scenario described in Section 2.1 the domain model is exploited. The Android application, used by the learner during the field trip, communicates with a Semantic MediaWiki server as shown in Figure 7.

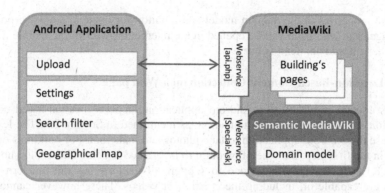

Fig. 7. Architectural overview of the software components involved

As soon as the the Android application is started it retrieves all semantic properties and their existing values as JavaScript Object Notation (JSON) formatted data from a web service, i.e. the page `Special:Ask`, which is provided by Semantic MediaWiki. These properties are then presented to the learner as filter facets, as shown in Figure 2 in Section 2.1. The active facet values, together with the learner's current location, are being used to define the parameters for searching for learning materials, buildings in our case, to match the learner's current information need.

Retrieving the filter facets is a two-step process. First, all semantic properties are requested from the wiki, that have the label `[[filter::true]]` defined on their property page. This way, it is possible to use semantic properties on wiki pages that do not necessarily serve as filter properties for the Android application. Second, all currently used values of the properties gained in the first step are retrieved. Hence the user interface for configuring search facets is domain independent and dynamically acts in accordance with the properties currently being employed in the wiki. Another advantage of this method is that changes in the content of the wiki are immediately reflected in the filter facets of the Android application.

The filter properties are being used to confine the search results to match the current information need of the user. To also embrace the current location of the user, all wiki articles are annotated with the geo-coordinates of the corresponding buildings. For that, we define a special property `[[Has coordinates]]` with data type `Geographic coordinate`. This data type allows defining latitude and longitude both in decimal and degree/minutes/seconds formats. The web service provided by Semantic MediaWiki, that is being used for semantic search, already contains an algorithm supporting perimeter search around a geographic coordinate. The radius being employed for this perimeter search can be configured in the settings of the Android application. The current location of the user is determined via GPS or, if not available, via Wifi- or GPRS-based localization. In summary, the request to the web service is comprised of the active filter properties, the current location of the user and the search radius.

The results of the location-based, facetted search are displayed as markers in the environment of the user on a Google Maps view, as shown in Figure 1. Tapping on one of these building markers opens a dialog containing the name of the building, its semantic properties of the domain model and a button for opening the corresponding wiki page. The wiki page will be opened in the internet browser of the mobile device, not in the Android application itself.

5.3   Location-Based Content Collection on a Wiki page

Besides content provision, the Android application supports location-based content collection as kind of learners participation, as mentioned in Section 2.3. The learners are to use the Android application to take photos and make notes of buildings on site. Hence in the first step, the type of medium to be created is being chosen, as shown in Figure 8. At this point we decided to support all media types that modern smart phones are capable of, including the creation of videos. These however cannot reasonably be embedded on wiki pages without format conversion and further adaptations of the wiki itself. For creating photos and videos, existing Android applications specialized for this are being used and the result is then further processed, as is common practice with the Android operating system.

Fig. 8. Selection of photo and Wiki page

After selecting the medium to upload, the user then chooses on which wiki page the medium and the additional text is to be inserted (Figure 8). In case this wiki page does not yet exist, it will be created. Otherwise the new content is appended at the end of the existing page. The text is meant to be in the form of a short note and due to the often tedious text entry interfaces of mobile phones, it intentionally does not support wiki mark-up. The final editing and formatting of the text is intended to be done by the students using conventional PCs. The current location is automatically appended to the text in the form of the semantic property [[Has coordinates]] when being transmitted to the wiki. This causes the corresponding wiki page to get extended by that property with the given location.

The entire communication between application and wiki uses, as shown in Figure 7, MediaWiki's web service „api.php". This service provides means for authentication, upload of media and modification of wiki pages. This way, the version history feature of MediaWiki can be used to inspect who did when what changes to a specific wiki page. All information needed for using the web service, namely the web address of the wiki and user account information, can be configured by the students in the settings of the application.

6   Experiences

We have proved the second scenario within two classes in civil engineering at Darmstadt University. In both classes each student has two select an existing building which is physical available to him or her. The student has to visit the building, has to make photos and has to write a wiki page about this building. In this wiki page he or she has to explain details about the construction of the building. Therefore a structure of the page was predefined. Photos have to be general views and have to show details.

In one class, which is about steel construction, the same task has been given to the students in previous semesters also. Then it was accepted from the students and they have been highly motivated [4]. In the last semester the use of smart phones and the app, described in Section 5 have been offered to the students to fulfill the task. The demand to use a smart phone, which was lent to the students for free, was low. Apparently the benefit to use a smart phone seems to be low for the students. They do not see an incentive to use it.

The second class is about history of constructive civil engineering. Students had to select a road bridge in the Rhein-Main region as building which has to be described. In this class more participants used our app even though the number of students in the class has been less. In this class collaborative authoring was a new method. Maybe students hence did not see an alternative to using the app.

In both classes students who use our app mentioned that the app works well in general but they are impatient of the quality of the pictures. They also said that they had to redact the page at home using a browser on a PC. The app has been used for collection of notices only.

7   Summary and Outlook

In this paper, we have presented two approaches to enhance location based learning and teaching. In the first scenario the focus is on the support of teachers which prepare resources for a field trip, which are used by the learners at a later time. The main novelty is the continuous support of the authoring process in docendo. Resources created by the teacher are stored at the docendo repository with assigned geo location automatically. Although a comprehensive evaluation has yet to be made, individual feedback received from teachers using docendo has been positive thus far. Teachers like the facility to create notices at the stations of the field trip, but they are restricted in editing these notices by the possibilities of the smart phones used.

In the second scenario a combination of participative content creation using a wiki system and location based content creation is realized. From technical point of view the software works well but it is not accepted by the learners. Compared to location based content access location based content creation lacks on incentives. Learners prefer to create high quality content, esp. making photos by using a digital camera and editing images before integrating them in a wiki page. They want to customize their wiki pages which can't be done on a smart phone. Maybe these hitches can be avoided using smartbooks as end device in both scenarios. Hence we want to do a study by using smartbooks in the near future.

References

1. Johnson, L., Smith, R., Willis, H., Levine, A., Haywood, K.: The 2011 Horizon Report. The New Media Consortium, Austin (2011)
2. Börner, D., Glahn, C., Stoyanov, S., Kalz, M., Specht, M.: Expert concept mapping study on mobile learning. Campus-Wide Information Systems 27(4), S.240–S.253 (2010)
3. Kerres, M.: Potenziale von Web 2.0 nutzen. In: Hohenstein, A., Wilbers (Hg.), K. (eds.) Handbuch E-Learning. DWD-Verlag, München (2006)
4. Lernen und Arbeiten im Stahlbau-Wiki: Einsatz Neuer Medien im Ingenieurstudium, H. Merle, J. Lange, Neues Handbuch Hochschullehre 12/2011. Raabe-Verlag, Berlin
5. Ternier, S., Börner, D.: ARLearn – interaktive Unterstützung ortsbasierter,mobiler Lernaktivitäten (2011), Online verfügbar unter http://www.httc.de/ws-mobile-learn ing/boerner.pdf (abgerufen January 31, 2012)
6. Lucke, U.: Design eines pervasiven Lernspiels für Studienanfänger. In: Die 9. e-Learning Fachtagung Informatik (DeLFI), pp. S.103–S.114. Köllen, Bonn (2011)
7. Sharples, M., Sánchez, I.A., Milrad, M., Vavoula, G.: Mobile Learning: Small devices, big Issues. In: Technology-Enhanced Learning, Part IV, pp. 233–249 (2009), doi:10.1007/978-1-4020-9827-7_14
8. Verdejo, M.F., Celorrio, C., Lorenzo, E., Sastre-Toral, T.: An Educational Networking Infrastructure Supporting Ubiquitous Learning for School Students. In: Proc. Sixth IEEE Int'l Conf. Advanced Learning Technologies, pp. 174–178 (2006)
9. Rogers, Y., Price, S., Harris, E., Phelps, T., Underwood, M., Wilde, D., Smith, H., Muller, H., Randell, C., Stanton, D., Neale, H., Thompson, M., Weal, M., Michaelides, D.: Learning through digitally-augmented physical experiences: reflections on the Ambient Wood project. Equator Technical Report (2002), Available online at: http://machen.mrl.nott.ac.uk/PublicationStore/ 2002-rogers-2.pdf
10. Lonsdale, P., Baber, C., Sharples, M., Arvanitis, T.N.: A context-awareness architecture for facilitating mobile learning. In: Proc. Learning with Mobile Devices (MLEARN), pp. 79–85. Learning and Skills Development Agency, London (2003)
11. Botzer, G., Yerushalmy, M.: Mobile Applications for Mobile Learning. In: Proc. Cognition & Exploratory Learning in Digital Age (CELDA), Algrave, Portugal (2007)
12. O'Reilly, T.: What is Web 2.0. Design Patterns and Business Models for the Next Generation of Software (2005), http://www.oreilly.de/artikel/web20.html
13. Anderson, P.: What is Web 2.0? Ideas, Technologies and Implications for Education. In: Proc. JISC Technology and StandardsWatch (February 2007)
14. Cole, M.: Using Wiki Technology to Support Student Engagement: Lessons from the Trenches. Computers & Education 52, 141–146 (2009)
15. Peterson, E.: Using a Wiki to Enhance Cooperative Learning in a Real Analysis Course. PRIMUS 19, 18–28 (2009)
16. Wheeler, S., Yeomans, P., Wheeler, D.: The Good, the Bad and the Wiki: Evaluating Student-Generated Content for Collaborative Learning. British J. Educational Technology 39, 987–995 (2008)
17. Williams, J.B., Jacobs, J.: Exploring the use of blogs as learning spaces in the higher education sector. Australasian Journal of Educational Technology 20, 232–247 (2004)
18. Chang, Y.-J., Chen, C.-H.: Experiences of Adopting In-class Blogs in the Teaching of Hands-on Computer Laboratory Courses. In: Proc. Seventh IEEE International Conference on Advanced Learning Technologies (ICALT 2007), Niigata, Japan, pp. 447–448 (2007)

19. Armstrong, K., Retterer, O.: Blogging as L2 Writing: A Case Study. AACE Journal 16, 233–251 (2008)
20. Advanced Distributed Learning Initiative: Sharable Content Object Reference Model (SCORM) 2004, 2nd edn. (2004)
21. IEEE Learning Technology Standards Committee: IEEE Standard for Learning Object Metadata 1484.12.1 (2002)
22. Hoermann, S., Hildebrandt, T., Rensing, C., Steinmetz, R.: Resource Center - A Digital Learning Object Repository with an Integrated Authoring Tool Set. In: Kommers, P., Richards, G. (eds.) Proceedings of World Conference on Educational Multimedia, Hypermedia and Telecommunications ED-MEDIA, pp. 3453–3460 (June 2005)
23. Semantic-Mediawiki.org, http://semantic-mediawiki.org/
24. Krötzsch, M., Vrandecic, D., Völkel, M., Haller, H., Studer, R.: Semantic Wikipedia. Journal of Web Semantics (2007)

Author Index